On anonymity 42-3,

                    povecoram — Pubsher 113

Ventriloquism (87)

Interesting tension in some how to representative institution (42)

---

criteria for evaluating systems of representations (political +
                                                     Imपरातिस)

    1. public debate on potentially "unsafe"   (see other
                                                  notes)
because it introduces private interests into "public" (45)

    2. notes shift in nature of rep body (from ruled to rulers) — 58

The Letters of the Republic

1. authority and time (99)

2. paradox of popular sovereignty (100-101)

3. Rousseau --keeping subjects "scattered" (103)

④ ambiguity of consent (110)
   A. authorization -- give consent to something
   B. compliance -- consent to something &

5. "we the people" an constraint (112)

6. "republican faith in the transparency of print" (114-15) →
   accurate?? JMi~ PP #37

THE LETTERS
of the
REPUBLIC

. . .

Publication and the Public Sphere
in Eighteenth-Century America

MICHAEL WARNER

HARVARD UNIVERSITY PRESS
CAMBRIDGE, MASSACHUSETTS
LONDON, ENGLAND
1990

Copyright © 1990 by the President and Fellows of Harvard College
All rights reserved
Printed in the United States of America
10 9 8 7 6 5 4 3 2 1

This book is printed on acid-free paper, and its binding materials
have been chosen for strength and durability.

Library of Congress Cataloging-in-Publication Data

Warner, Michael, 1958–
The letters of the Republic : publication and the public sphere in
eighteenth-century America / Michael Warner.
p. cm.
Includes bibliographical references.
ISBN 0-674-52785-2 (alk. paper)
1. Publishers and publishing—United States—History—18th
century. 2. Literature and society—United States—History—18th
century. 3. Literature publishing—United States—History—18th
century. 4. Books and reading—United States—History—18th
century. 5. American Literature—18th century—Political aspects.
6. United States—Popular culture—History—18th century.
7. Printing—United States—History—18th century. I. Title.
Z473.W36   1990   89-48644
070.5'0973—dc20   CIP

For
M. P. R.

CONTENTS

PREFACE

THE WEST treasures few moments in its history the way it treasures the story of the democratization of print. In the century preceding the American and French revolutions, men of letters commonly linked the spread of letters to the growth of knowledge. From an early date they linked it to the democratization of power as well. In their eyes the citizen's reading took on a mythic significance that it has never lost, even to the present. In this respect if in no other, we still regard the actors in the Enlightenment roughly as they thought of themselves: as members of a republic of letters. Few still have unqualified faith in the period's claims to reason and progress. But almost all consider it to have been a period that brought about the styles of rationalization and progressive thinking that we call modernity. And almost all would consider the letters of the republic to have played a role in the emergence of that modernity.

But this idea of a revolution in the reading of citizens raises some of the deepest problems in the self-image of Western modernity. Are we to think of the spread of print discourse as ensuring the triumph of the individual and the empowerment of the people? If so, one problem is that "individual" and "people" emerge from a historical change that they themselves could not have brought about. If printing helped give these entities their distinctively modern nature—citizen-individual and national people—then the change in print cannot be explained as the expression of the individual and the people. Instead it would signal a broad change in social and cultural systems, in which individual and people would be local outcomes rather than origins. Nor can we take for granted the timeless *value* of peoples and individualisms that have such a specific and recent history. Shall we, on the other hand, attribute the power of print discourse to the intrinsic logic of print technology? If so, nothing necessarily warrants the implication of progress, reason, and freedom. Modern uses of print might illustrate either a systemic sociocultural change or the determining force of technology; but neither of these need be very reassuring ways of telling our own history. Either way the narrative poses a problem for such uncontested terms of value as "individual," "people," "reason," and "democracy."

In *The Structural Transformation of the Public Sphere* (1962) Jürgen Habermas made one of the most powerful arguments that printing led to a change in the political life of the West. He describes a set of institutions that he calls the bourgeois public sphere, developed in the West beginning late in the seventeenth century. In this new public sphere political discourse could be separated both from the state and from civil society, the realm of private life (including economic life). It could therefore regulate or criticize both. Because of this autonomy, this space that allowed critical regulation, the bourgeois public sphere played a key role in bringing about both the democratic revolutions of the eighteenth century and the modern nation-states that followed. Habermas argues that the independence of the public sphere has since eroded; the media of publicity, in his view, have become increasingly colonized and have lost their critical relation to both the state and civil society. From the beginning, however, reading holds the key place in his narrative. Habermas tells the story of an increasing differentiation of a public sphere from state and civil society as primarily a story about new uses of texts. Newspapers, literary salons, coffeehouses, novels, art criticism, and magazines all play an important role in his account of how the fundamental structure of politics changed.

How did reading come to be so important? One of the great virtues of *Structural Transformation* is that it treats the reading practices of the late seventeenth and early eighteenth centuries not just as more reading, but as a new kind of institution. Reading was relevant in a new way because print discourse was now systematically differentiated from the activities of the state and from civil society. That is why the transformation Habermas describes is fundamentally structural, as his title implies. This perceptive analysis raises the question of how the citizen's reading acquired its new structurally relevant difference from other institutions. And on this score Habermas follows the traditional premises of the story: he describes a growing tendency of individuals to assert autonomy and citizenship by virtue of their reading and publishing. He sees the dissemination of print quite simply as creating new opportunities for individuals to make public use of their reason. This capacity of individuals to make public use of their reason is supposed as a constant potential. It may be brought into play by historical contingencies, but it does not itself vary locally and historically.

How can we describe the history of the transformation without holding constant the value-terms of modernity? There is no doubt that an important transformation took place. And there is no doubt that the transformation was fundamentally one of social structure, linked to the dominant institutions of our world: bureaucratic states, regulated economies, representational democracy, public media, and the like. This book can be read as an analysis of the bourgeois public sphere as it developed in colonial America; it too sees the political structures of modernity as generated in new uses of print discourse. Its major task, however, is to analyze the historical transformation in print discourse as (fully) histori- ← cal—to analyze it without attributing its significance to an ahistorical point of reference, such as the intrinsic nature of individuals, reason, or technology.

One of the theses of my book is that print discourse was a cultural matrix in which the definitions of "individual," "print," "public," and "reason" were readjusted in a new set of ground rules for discourse. The politics of printed texts in republican America lay as much in the cultural meaning of their printedness as in their objectified nature or the content of their arguments. The force of the technology and the act of reading performed by the individual citizen were redetermined in the course of this social transformation.

What I am calling the cultural meaning of printedness can easily remain Key invisible. Yet printed objects—which we would commonsensically call "publications"—are intelligible only under very special conditions. To think of them as publications, we must make certain assumptions about texts, speakers, addressees, and the "public." This book analyzes those special conditions as they obtain for print in North America in the eighteenth century. In one respect, therefore, the analysis is directed toward literary scholars, for it inquires into the conditions of meaning that inform the bulk of American writing in the period. In another respect, the analysis is directed toward scholars of cultural and political history, since the assumptions that make printed works intelligible as publications also help determine how the political arena operates. They are the basis for deciding who speaks, to whom, with what constraints, and with what legitimacy. Such power-laden but silent decisions could be called the Foucault metapolitics of speech. They are always linked to whatever passes for common sense about the medium in use. I shall examine the connections between the cultural matrix of the medium and the metapolitics of the speech within it, showing how those connections reshaped power.

The argument and its method might raise problems both for literary scholars and for historians. For literary scholars, because the textuality of printed works will be considered primarily as a feature of specific historical contexts rather than as what makes them "literature." The result will be a realization that the works of the period remain alien to us in fundamental ways. For historians, because the expected kinds of causal explanation may not operate here. This book does not explain changes in political culture by pointing to some noncultural version of reality; it tries to show that changes in political culture (republicanism, the Enlightenment, nationalism) in important ways refashioned the textuality of print.

It may seem circular to say this. I am, after all, also claiming that the textuality of print determined the character of political culture. But to my mind the material studied in this book derives much of its interest from the *reciprocal* determination it shows between a medium and its politics. This is a historical relation of causation that remains relatively untheorized and resists the ways we usually narrate the past. The writing of history usually requires us to ask which came first: printing or democratization? capitalism or individualism? modernity or the state? Protestant self or republican citizen? If I do not pose the questions in this form, it is because I do not wish to block from view the way a connection between, say, printing and republicanism changes the identity of each. Certain assumptions about print and certain assumptions about politics were coarticulated; neither is a fixed reference point against which to tell the story of the other. In the chapters that follow I will approach the material from different perspectives, sometimes foregrounding the effect of a political context on the medium, sometimes vice versa, but always with an eye to their changing mutual determination.

To make this kind of historical narrative implies a strong view about the determining force of culture. I explain that view in Chapter I, "The Cultural Mediation of the Print Medium," arguing that the nature of print varies in different historical and cultural contexts. Such a view challenges some of our commonsense assumptions about what print is, but makes it possible—indeed, necessary—to write a history of the ways we think about and perceive print. More particularly, this chapter argues against the premises of technological determinism that operate so powerfully, both in the specialist literature on print history and in our commonsense thinking about the nature of the medium. In different contexts of colonial America, print was linked to very different symbolic values and could be identified in very different ways.

Chapters II, III, and IV, the core of my argument, trace large-scale changes in the relation between print and political culture that happen at the microlevel of what printedness means. "The *Res Publica* of Letters" describes the transformation of the public sphere as it began in the early-eighteenth-century colonies. It argues that an emerging political language—republicanism—and a new set of ground rules for discourse—the public sphere—jointly made each other intelligible. Both were grounded in a new way of perceiving printedness. It was not self-evidently true that the routine use of print was valuable; the Anglo-American strand of republicanism in this period made it so. Within this cultural vocabulary, print discourse made it possible to imagine a people that could act as a people and in distinction from the state.

The most salient difference between the traditional culture of print and the republican one is a set of assumptions developed in the late seventeenth and early eighteenth centuries, on the basis of which print could be taken as normally impersonal. By "normally impersonal," I mean that the reader does not simply imagine him- or herself receiving a direct communication or hearing the voice of the author. He or she now also incorporates *into the meaning of the printed object* an awareness of the potentially limitless others who may also be reading. For that reason, it becomes possible to imagine oneself, in the act of reading, becoming part of an arena of the national people that cannot be realized except through such mediating imaginings.

When an individual reads in a manner that implicitly relates him- or herself to the indefinite others of a print public, certain consequences follow for the nature of the individual who reads or speaks. What did it mean to inhabit the new discourse? If the discourse of publicity allows individuals to make public use of their reason, what will individuals be like, and what will count as reason? The subjective dimension, or the private point of insertion into the public sphere, is what I turn to in "The Representational Politics of the Man of Letters." My example—Benjamin Franklin—is admittedly an extreme one. More than anyone else on either side of the Atlantic, he was involved in every phase of the transformations described in this book. Because the norms of print govern his rhetoric throughout his career, and even the shape of his career as a whole, he shows how certain ways of representing individuals could produce new kinds of individuals.

Franklin was not acting in a vacuum, and his style of being an individual was made possible only in a certain structure of power. "Textuality and Legitimacy in the Printed Constitution" analyzes the kind of power that developed from the print discourse of the public sphere. The example is the invention of written—and more particularly printed—constitutionalism, a key moment in the transition from bourgeois public sphere to national state. I argue that the national state grounded its legitimacy not just in the people or the rule of law, as we usually suppose, but in the very special cultural formation of print discourse described in Chapters II and III. It required special assumptions about the relation between persons and publics, between individual subjects and general sovereignty. These assumptions derived not just from any popular group, but from a model of a reading public. Through the new constitutionalism, the metapolitics of print discourse became entrenched as an ideology of legitimate power. If this is a way of saying that the modern state commits a kind of fraud in claiming to represent the people and the law, it is no simple fraud. For the fraud is only the pretense that representational democracy derives its legitimacy from the people and their law, when in fact it performs what it claims to describe. A way of representing the people constructs the people.

This distinctively modern structure of power is still with us. But many of the assumptions that made it possible did not survive after the erosion of republican print culture around the beginning of the nineteenth century. That becomes clearest when we examine the history of "literature" in the period, as I do in "Nationalism and the Problem of Republican Literature." This chapter examines key essays and the premises of a widespread discourse in magazines and newspapers to see how late-eighteenth-century Americans describe the values of literature and nationality. The culture of republican America gave extraordinary importance to ideas of the reading citizen, but these ideas did not translate into national literature. It was not sluggishness or incapacity that kept eighteenth-century Americans from developing a national literature in the modern sense; it was their way of valuing print. The same way of perceiving print that made the citizen's reading desirable also made something like a national literature undesirable, since the act of reading was linked closely to the performative values of civic virtue.

Republican print discourse was not monolithic, and by the 1790s republican notions of the nature of publication were becoming mixed with more recognizably literary strands. The more liberal values of literary textuality, which we so easily take for granted, were beginning to be registered by writers in the period—largely as a source of anxiety. In

"The Novel: Fantasies of Publicity" I examine the ways in which the old republican understanding of publication was now in tension with other strands in the novel. In order to treat the complexities of such a problem, this chapter, unlike those that precede it, includes an extended reading of a single text, Charles Brown's *Arthur Mervyn*. Like all other early American novels, *Arthur Mervyn* resists being a novel, striving instead to supply for itself the more public values of publication in general. With the early American novel I bring to a close my history of the politics of the medium and the mediation of politics, since this body of writing functions dramatically as a hinge between all that is alien to us in the print culture of republican America and all that is still with us in the environment of modernity.

Chapters II, III, and IV reuse some material that was published in different versions in the following: "The *Res Publica* of Letters," *boundary* 2 (November 1989); "Franklin and the Letters of the Republic," *Representations* 16 (1986):110–130; and "Textuality and Legitimacy in the Printed Constitution," *Proceedings of the American Antiquarian Society* 97 (April 1987):59–84 (Reprinted by permission).

Material assistance for writing this book came from the American Antiquarian Society, with its legendarily helpful staff, and from the National Endowment for the Humanities. If I were to name everybody who helped with advice, it would be hard to take any credit for myself. Luckily I can claim indirect credit in that these people all thought I was worthy of their help: Larzer Ziff and Sharon Cameron gave generous and invaluable help at an early stage of the work. Sacvan Bercovitch, Tim Breen, John Brenkman, Jerry Christensen, Jerry Graff, Jules Law, Michael Moon, and Tom McCarthy provided environments of interest and problems, at various stages. I took special inspiration from Jonathan Goldberg, whose own work bears on the framing of so many of the issues here. Mitchell Breitweiser, Jay Fliegelman, and David D. Hall gave me extensive and useful criticisms. Ben Lee proved to be the book's ideal reader. Lauren Berlant gave me the same kind of insightful criticism; I also counted on her friendship whenever I needed a new skin. And Mark Ring provided the light at the end of the tunnel.

M. W.

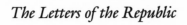

The Letters of the Republic

· I ·

The Cultural Mediation
of the Print Medium

Thy life to mend
This Book attend.
—*The New England Primer*

The eighteenth century was remarkable for its
literature and revolutions.
—*Arthur Walter,* 1805

IN 1765, in the early stages of an imperial crisis and of his career as a lawyer, John Adams wrote a brief retrospect of the political and legal history of the West. Appearing unsigned and untitled in four installments in the *Boston Gazette,* the essay depicts the history of power as a history of knowledge. It tells modern history as a story of human self-determination rising through reflection. Much of the power of such a narrative for Adams, as later for D'Alembert and other Enlightenment intellectuals, was that it offered him a political self-understanding. But Adams' history offers a more particular self-understanding in two main respects: its history of self-determination yields a protonationalist consciousness of America; its history of reflection takes the form of a history of letters. Writing at the very moment when America was emerging as a symbolic entity, Adams perfects a story of America's history. It is a history of literature, and its telos is emancipation.[1]

This is how it works. According to Adams, the papal and feudal political systems of Europe rested in the last analysis on what might be called a hegemony of letters: "All these opinions, they [the clergy and the feudal lords] were enabled to spread and rivet among the people, by reducing their minds to a state of sordid ignorance and staring timidity; and by infusing into them a *religious* horror of letters and knowledge" (1:112). Because the entire political system of feudal Europe depends on such a relation of populace and letters, a history of letters can be a history of emancipation. For the same reason, the emancipation for which the world has longed can be realized in America. "From the time of the reformation, to the first settlement of *America*," Adams writes, "knowledge gradually spread in Europe, but especially in *England;* and in proportion as *that* increased and spread among the people, *ecclesiastical* and *civil* tyranny, which I use as synonimous expressions, for the *cannon* and *feudal* laws, seem to have lost their strength and weight. The people grew more and more sensible of the wrong that was done them, by these systems; more and more impatient under it; and determined at all hazards to rid themselves of it . . . IT was this great struggle, that peopled America" (1:113). The Puritan colonists emerge as the heroes in a political history of enlightenment.

Adams is aware that the civic humanist terms of such a history conflict with the terms of American Protestantism's self-understanding. Yet he presses his point by arguing that the reason for the Puritans' emigration "was not religion *alone,* as is commonly supposed." Rather, he claims, it was that they "had become intelligent in general, and many of them learned"; "to many of them, the historians, orators, poets and philosophers of *Greece* and *Rome* were quite familiar: and some of them have left libraries that are still in being, consisting chiefly of volumes, in which the wisdom of the most enlightened ages and nations is deposited" (1:113–114). We are perhaps unaccustomed to seeing the Puritans described as republican classicists in this way. And the history of racial and sectarian conflict in New England has taught us to be skeptical of Adams' claim that they committed "no other crime than their knowledge, and their freedom of enquiry and examination" (1:114). But the story is a powerful one. Treating enlightenment republicanism as the latent meaning of Puritan history, and employing terms that are simultaneously world-historical and national, Adams' revisionist history became a pillar of American nationalism, and has remained so to the present.

The success of Adams' narrative depends on his ability to revise the meaning of the Puritans' relation to letters. Rather than simply arguing that they developed a critique of the canon and feudal laws, he argues that they bought libraries. With respect to the Bible, Adams' history is not far from the Puritans' self-understanding. John Foxe, for example, had famously claimed that "The Lord began to work for his Church not with sword and target to subdue His exalted adversary, but with printing, writing and reading . . . How many printing presses there be in the world, so many blockhouses there be against the high castle of St Angelo, so that either the pope must abolish knowledge and printing or printing at length will root him out."[2] Adams obviously draws on this rhetorical tradition in Protestantism. But there is a crucial difference between his version and Foxe's. Foxe was able to claim world-historical importance for printing only because of a very determinate assumption about *what* would be printed against the pope. As Stephen Greenblatt has argued in a chapter titled "The Word of God in the Age of Mechanical Reproduction," Prot- *Benjamin* estant reading reinforces the authority of the sacred text even as it trans- lates authority to the private register. "When Tyndale writes of arming oneself with the syllables of Scripture," Greenblatt writes, "or Bainham speaks of his fear that this word of God—pointing to the book in his hand—would damn him, we must take them at very close to the literal meaning: the printed English New Testament is, above all, *a form of power*. It is invested with the ability to control, guide, discipline, console, exalt, and punish that the Church had arrogated to itself for centuries."[3] Prot- estant printing did not take self-reflection as an independent goal; its absolute goal was divine truth, which could provide a basis for social organization because it was assumed to be fixed and knowable indepen- dently from, and as a limit to, the rational pursuit of self-interest. Ignoring this organizing and disciplinary force of sacred exegesis, Adams must see the Puritans' literacy as self-reflection for its own sake, and thus as eman- cipatory in character, if he is to regard their westward migration as the beginning of a national history of enlightenment.[4]

Between Puritanism and Adams' history of Puritanism, the cultural meaning of letters has begun to change, as has their relation to power. No longer a technology of privacy underwritten by divine authority, let- ters have become a technology of publicity whose meaning in the last analysis is civic and emancipatory. It will be recalled that the struggles leading to the colonial revolution were largely undertaken by writers. At the same time that colonists were engaging in violent crowd actions, organized law-breaking, and boycotts, they also engineered a newspaper and pamphlet war in a way that was arguably more integral to the Amer- ican resistance than to any other revolution. Those who organized the revolutionary struggle and were placed in power by it were men of letters. Their paper war articulated and helped to mobilize an intercolonial and protonational public—a public that remained a public of readers. And it was through the texts of that paper war that the democratic revolution in the colonies had such far-reaching impact both on the continent and in the New World. The transformation of letters that lies behind Adams' history was no mean affair.[5]

For Adams too the republican destiny of letters takes on a national importance in the context of a global revolution. And indeed, the rising

3

sense in the colonies of letters' importance had important transatlantic parallels. After 1695 printers had rapidly moved out into English towns such as Manchester, Birmingham, Liverpool, Bristol, and Canterbury. Just at the moment when colonists were setting up shop and establishing weekly newspapers, their counterparts in the English provinces were doing the same, and London printers were beginning to produce dailies. The appearance of the press in places like Annapolis, New York, and Charleston, therefore, figures in narratives that involve the British empire as well as Europe and its empires. The growth of the trade, for one thing, was clearly supported by the financial revolution of the 1690s, with its new methods of capitalization. And the new forms of print discourse sutured emergent forms of political and social organization. Printers were simultaneously products of the transformation of the West and agents in the creation of the West's self-identification, producing the universalizing discourses of the Enlightenment and of the democratic revolutions. American colonists such as Adams made major contributions to those discourses, so the historical horizon of modernity must be made visible in any account of the printing activities of the North American English creoles.[6]

What, then, was the relation between republican enlightenment and printing? Adams implicitly poses the question by arguing that they are identical. In this sense his history is also a theory of print: insofar as his narrative has a plot, the unity and progress of that plot stem from the nature of print. For while he argues that learning and the press bring about changes in the political world, Adams assumes that printing's purposes, uses, and meaning do not themselves undergo change. The press is a powerful instrument for enlightenment precisely because its nature is *not* contingent. If it were variable in its nature, it might in some circumstances support despotism rather than liberty, and the history of enlightenment would lack a propulsive logic. It would have been hard, for example, for Adams to argue for the democratically enlightening character of print and yet account for the ancient use of printing among the Chinese and the Uighur Turks—who represent, for eighteenth-century thinkers such as himself, the very types of Oriental despotism.

In order to pose our question with regard to Adams' rhetoric—to ask, in other words, what was the relation between printing and the Enlightenment, or between printing and republicanism—we have to assume that the purposes, uses, and meaning of print do change. The rhetoric of Adams' history would thus be seen as a part of a transformation in the character of print, though his history presupposes the contrary. The

4

establishment of newspapers, the rise of empiricism, capitalism, the Enlightenment, the novel, the democratic revolutions, the rise of a bureaucratic state—all these bear important relations to print; but they might entail transformations *of* print, not just social changes affected by a medium with its own unchanging logic.

The point is worth stressing. Most of the historians who work in the burgeoning field of the history of the book, and most people who speculate on the place of print in history, assume quite the opposite. At some level they suppose printing to be a nonsymbolic form of material reality. Printing, in this view, is naturally distinct both from rhetoric, such as the rhetoric of republicanism, and from forms of subjectivity, such as the enlightenment of citizens. It is mere technology, a medium itself unmediated. There are two main advantages to this set of premises: first, it guarantees that there will be a single object of study, despite vast and frequent changes in the world of culture; and second, it allows one to trace the effects of print within culture by bracketing cultural history itself, since it guarantees that the effects of printing will have a progressive teleology.

The history of print, conceptualized by means of these assumptions, was formed by Harold Innis and others in the years after World War II. It has often taken a McLuhanite cast, especially in the work of Elizabeth Eisenstein, Walter Ong, and those who are influenced by them. Print technology is seen as having a logic internal to itself, a logic which then exerts causative force in human affairs. The invention of printing, for example, is said to have encouraged rationalization and democratization.[7] And on this model of print history both the right and the left agree. It provides the basis for Ong's nostalgic and rather theological speculations as well as the critical Marxism of his colleague Alvin Gouldner. Gouldner summarizes baldly: "What the revolution in printing technology did was to democratize the culture of writing. It was consequential, though scarcely alone in this, for a quantitative increase in public discourse and, also, for qualitative changes in its character. Like writing, printing and printed objects *de*contextualized speech and tended to reduce the modalities of communication."[8] This kind of assertion has gone so unchallenged that it is now common even in the popular histories offered by the mass media. And it cannot go without remark that such a statement bears a striking resemblance to Adams' Whig history.

The assumptions behind the Whig-McLuhanite model of print history operate on a very deep level. Many of those who rely on the model would concede the argument that printing's force depends on its context. Eisenstein in particular regards her work as studying the character of print within the religious and scientific cultures of early modern Europe. Yet the appeal to the agency of print upon culture tends to reintroduce a privilege for technology, for the model of causation presupposes that printing and culture are discrete entities. At the very moment when historians draw their conclusions about the historical effects of printing, they bracket the political and symbolic constitution of print. Just after Eisenstein acknowledges that the consequences of early printing depended on its institutional context, for instance, she goes on to say:

> Yet the fact remains that once presses were established in numerous European towns, the transforming powers of print did begin to take effect . . . Intellectual and spiritual life, far from remaining unaffected, were profoundly transformed by the multiplication of new tools for duplicating books in fifteenth-century Europe. The communications shift altered the way Western Christians viewed their sacred book and the natural world. It made the words of God appear more multiform and His handiwork more uniform. The printing press laid the basis for both literal fundamentalism and for modern science.[9]

Politics and human agency disappear from this narrative, whether the agency be individual or collective, and culture receives an impact generated outside itself. Religion, science, capitalism, republicanism, and the like appear insofar as they are affected by printing, not for the way they have entered into the constitution and meaning of print in the first place. The result is that enlightenment and democratization, instead of being seen as politically contested aspects of social organization, now appear as the exfoliation of material technology. Despite the best intentions, print history tends toward Jack Goody's technodeterminism, which sees literate elites as rising with writing and falling with printing—an exchange that appears to have taken place independent of contingent social relations, actions, and representations. In some cases the model of analysis behind this picture is actually less sophisticated than John Adams', for while he saw printing as having the same progressive effects, he did not fantasize a history of those effects that would bypass the domain of politics and rhetoric.[10]

By attributing social changes of great scale partly to printing, the McLuhanite historians follow a model in which the logic of the technology is seen to "press on and impress both on social activity and human consciousness."[11] This kind of technological determinism must suppose, therefore, that a technology could come about, already equipped with its "logic," *before* it impinged on human consciousness and *before* it became a symbolic action. Otherwise the object of inquiry would not lie outside the field of collective action and the symbolic order, but would be a contingent part of that field. The technology would no longer appear to have determining power of its own, independent from the collective purposes, social organization, symbolic structure, and practical labor in which it would be constituted.

This fundamental premise—that technology has an ontological status prior to culture—must be rejected at the outset if we are to pose the question of printing's relation to republican enlightenment, or to anything else. To begin with, there is a logical problem for those who wish to see printing as a hard technology outside of the political-symbolic order, since it is not clear how print could even be identified on the basis of that assumption. Not all printing is done with a press, nor with ink, nor on paper, nor with movable types, nor even by the method of impression. No hard fact of technology dictates what counts as printing. We know what we mean when we talk about printing, but we know that because we are in a tradition; we have a historical vocabulary of purposes and concepts that gives identity to printing, and meaningfully distinguishes for us between books that have been impressed with types and those that have been impressed with pens.

That tradition has undergone some important changes. In Western culture a growing number of things have come to count as printing as the technique of impression has become less determinant in its definition: laser printing, jet printing, xerography, and so on. In recognizing such practices as forms of printing, we use the unspoken but increasingly important criterion of a negative relation to the hand. That is why we do not count some other tools of duplication as examples of printing, even though some of them *do* make use of impression. We exclude them from the category of printing because their metonymic link to the hand is too strong. Thomas Jefferson invented a machine for duplicating letters; a pen guided by the hand could by a series of levers be made to guide a second pen in an identical fashion. In Eisenstein's phrase, it was a tool for duplicating. But it would not therefore be regarded as printing, primarily because it is designed to record its metonymy with the hand. The typewriter is another good example; copies duplicated on a typewriter, perhaps even carbon copies, we do not recognize as printed. But the same copies run through a mimeograph machine could be counted as a kind of printing. They would have been relieved of the pressure of the hand. In some important ways, this cultural meaning for the hand, which by contrast

7

defines what counts as printing, has developed since the establishment of the printing trade.[12] Early printers, for instance, in no way distinguished their work from hand-produced documents. From a modern perspective, that seems to show how little they understood the latent "logic" of their medium. But that interpretation of the meaning of print is governed from the outset by a presupposed modern ideological definition of print.

Along a related line, although printing was initially another way of reproducing in quantity books that were already being reproduced in quantity, at a certain point printing came to be specially defined as publication, now *in opposition* to manuscript circulation. Later, as I shall argue in this book, publication in the new sense would take on a special political meaning involving a new way of defining the public. These changes were not dictated by any feature of the technology, but they did change our fundamental perceptions of the technology. It is because publication is a political condition of utterance that we meaningfully distinguish between books impressed by types and those impressed by pens, where we do not make the same kind of distinction between those impressed by plates and those sprayed by lasers. The history of printing, in short, cannot even define its subject properly without asking about the history of the public and other political conditions of discourse. What did it mean to publish, and what did it mean to identify printing *as* publishing? These are not questions about the empirical effects of printing; they are questions about the historical constitution of printing.

In addition to the logical difficulty of saying what will count as printing, a second and more serious problem results from the assumption that printing has an ontological status prior to culture. When media and technologies receive this kind of transcendental status, their social investments and rhetorical meaning disappear from the field of analysis, only to return in mystified form, disguised as the previously latent logic of the technology. Let us take the example, already cited, of the uniform mass production that was a feature of late medieval scriptoria before the invention of printing. Persons who already occupied the role of wholesale bookseller were sometimes able to place orders with the scriptoria for two hundred or even four hundred copies of a single work at once.[13] For several decades after the development of the press, editions were not typically larger than this, and were often much smaller. Moreover, because scriptoria had elaborate procedures designed to eliminate variants, and because printers often made changes in the middle of press runs, printed books were not necessarily distinguished for uniformity any more than they were for numbers. This is not to deny that uniformity and quantity came to be the distinctive characteristics of printing, but to reframe the question of how and why that happened.

A practice of specialized duplication had been in place from the outset to motivate the Mainz entrepreneurs in their experiments with printing, so the effects of regularization and multiplication represent not so much the consequences of printing as the tasks, desiderata, and perceptual categories by which printing was defined and made possible. From its first appearance in the West, printing was already organized by purposes that can be described as early capitalism. That is one reason why it was developed by goldsmiths, who by casting type were using not only their metallurgical skill but also their unique ability to deploy capital. In cultures where the practices of capitalism did not organize the emergence of printing, as among the Chinese or the Uighur Turks, printing took on different defining features and had different "consequences." Yet the implication of print historians—as well as of foundationalist Marxists such as Walter Benjamin—is that the technology of printing, once "discovered," yielded the result of standardized mass production, with its cultural symptoms.[14]

The assumption that technology is prior to culture results in a kind of retrodetermination whereby the political history of a technology is converted into the unfolding nature of that technology. Everything that has been ascribed to the agency of printing—from formal characteristics such as abstraction, uniformity, and visualization to broad social changes such as rationalization and democratization—has been retrodetermined in this way. What have historically become the characteristics of printing have been projected backward as its natural, essential logic. Meanwhile, its historical determinations have not been analyzed, for historians have learned to consider the realm of politics and culture only as the secondary field of technology's presumed effects.

In contrast, this book intends to analyze the immanent meanings of writing and print in the culture of republican America and the imperial context of enlightenment. How was printing defined as a technology of publicity, having an essentially civic and emancipatory character? How was the relation between subject and letters altered? What was the relation between the socially determined character of the medium and the texts produced in it? These questions, which together outline my subject, are united by the premise that the cultural constitution of a medium (in this case printing) is a set of political conditions of discourse. Those conditions include the practices and structured labors that we call technology. But I shall suppose that the latter have no ontological privilege over and at no point can be distinguished from their political meaning; that the practices of technology, in other words, are always structured, and that their meaningful structure is the dimension of culture.

Although this way of organizing a study in print history runs counter to the prevailing model, it is not unprecedented. Max Weber, for one, noted a close relation between printing and a systemic social rationalization of the West. Yet unlike those who have followed, he did not think of these in any way as cause and effect. Rather, he took the observed relation as the occasion to ask why printing had a rationalizing character in the modern West, when elsewhere it did not. In particular, he noted that only in the West did printing result in works planned for markets and publics. He concluded that the rationalizing results of printing, like those of the market and bureaucratic law, presuppose a transformation in subjective orientation. Hence Weber's culturally oriented study of capitalism.[15]

Despite the long and illustrious controversies that have followed, two features of Weber's project should be preserved: first, the insight that the nature of modernity can only be derived from a history of subjectivity and practice, rather than from a realm (such as "society" or technology) assumed to be extraneous to culture; second, that, however much culture might be irreducibly local, it has in the case of the West produced a systemic rationalization, the horizon of which is transcultural. It remains difficult to explain the second of these ideas without abandoning the first. Attempts to account for societal transformation—whether expressly functionalist or not—typically reduce culture, politics, and rhetoric to epiphenomena. And hermeneutic attempts to account for culture, politics, and rhetoric typically obliterate societal rationalization from view or presuppose it as background. Without attempting a full-scale theorization of such problems, I wish to keep the complex relation between the two subjects in view.

Any analysis of printing, even were it to begin with the Mainz goldsmiths, would have to begin in the middle. In early-eighteenth-century American society a wide range of uses for and perceptions of print were already established. Some were regional, others typical of the imperial periphery, and still others belonged to the tradition of writing in the West. What was printing for, and what was it like? What did it mean to buy a book, to read a newspaper, or to nail up a broadside in the American colonies? The answers to such questions will vary from context to context.

Imagine a career for what could only provisionally be called "a" book. Printed in Philadelphia, let us say, from materials mostly imported, it would likely consist of a text composed by various hands both in and out of the printer's shop. It might be copied largely from a text printed elsewhere, obtained by a publisher who saw an opportunity for a local edition.

cf Fliegel — or
"authorship"

The composition of the type and printing of the sheets would be done by one or more crews, not all of whose members would even be literate. So the text, before it has even attained the minimally objectified identity that would allow it to be sent to booksellers, customers, and binders, would already have a very different existence and meaning for those who would be said to be producing it. We can further imagine both a customer who, by chance perhaps, is familiar with the title, and a customer whose only familiarity with such titles comes from the local booksellers. We can imagine another life for the object among the carters or mariners who transport a small quantity of the printer's commodities along with other goods to another town. We can imagine yet other meanings for it as it is encountered variously by the printer's wife, his neighbor's slave, the purchaser's child, an Indian trader in the market, or a schoolmaster. Which of these objectifications do we have in mind when speaking of "print"? For it is only by a convention that we could group these different instances as having an identical object, while we exclude other instances, such as the sale of another edition (or state) of a text that is, as it were, more or less the same. More to the point, what are the salient differences among these different possible relations to printed goods—differences that are glossed over when we speak of the "logic" of "the" technology?

Even in its local discourse, print did not and could not have had a universal character or an undifferentiated audience. Both print and writing could only be alien to the entirely or even partially illiterate, including almost all Native Americans and the enslaved blacks. And saying that letters were "alien" to the illiterate is more than a tautology, since it is to these groups that writing and print may have appeared most clearly as technologies of power. For obvious reasons, historians know little about what colonial blacks thought about print. The texts of Jupiter Hammon and Phyllis Wheatley are the exceptions that prove the rule, since they define their public voices as white, even if only proleptically. They understand their literacy to prefigure their celestial assimilation.[16] The slave narrative of Olaudah Equiano, however, gives a vivid record of a nonliterate black's perception of books as a technology of power. Equiano, who was brought to America and the Western world of letters in the late 1750s, writes: "I had often seen my master and Dick employed in reading; and I had a great curiosity to talk to the books, as I thought they did; and so to learn how all things had a beginning: for that purpose I have often taken up a book, and have talked to it, and then put my ears to it, when alone, in hopes it would answer me; and I have been very much concerned when I found it remained silent."[17]

the representation or assumption of a future act or development as if presently existing or accomplished — anticipation

This account can be a useful piece of defamiliarization for us in several ways. First, because Equiano's master and his white companion, Dick, clearly have been reading aloud, and because Equiano has from the first been engaged in reading the visible world before him, in perceiving the technology of the book he does not initially attach importance to a distinction between reading and speaking. His early perception of writing is that of a mode of practical knowledge and authority—like English, or horseback riding. Second, his account belies the Enlightenment claim that print allows any person to communicate his thoughts to the public. Reading, he saw, was one of the distinguishing marks of white society; like horseback riding or sailing, it was one of the ways that society made itself different, singular. What Equiano registered, in other words, was the way in which writing had a meaning precisely in the limits of its communication. This does not imply that any other form of communication lacks such a meaningful limit, only that one of the meaningful limits of legibility was race.

The two whites in Equiano's story recognize the book primarily as communication rather than power. Today we may find it difficult to see the medium simultaneously as communication and as a structure of power, partly because our idea of communication contains a norm of universality.[18] It is also because we are accustomed to a negative perspective on socially structured illiteracy; we regard illiteracy as the exclusion of some groups from an otherwise emancipatory discourse. Yet we can take a different perspective on the problem by seeing that the boundaries of any communicative context have a positive social character.[19] This means not only that participation in a medium constitutes membership in a community—since to say that would leave a false impression that a medium could actually define a universal community—but also that the positive features of the medium implicitly differentiate the assumed collectivity.

Equiano encounters letters from the outside in a context where to encounter letters from the inside would require socialization into white Western colonial capitalism. Race in particular was made one of the social meanings of the difference between writing and speech by racial division in the reproduction of literacy, and by the consequent overlap between determinate features of the medium and traits of race. Black illiteracy was more than a negation of literacy for blacks; it was the condition of a positive character of written discourse for whites. By extension, printing constituted and distinguished a specifically white community; in this sense it was more than a neutral medium that whites simply managed to monopolize.

Printing was allowed to fill this function by the way its material conditions were arranged. These included the system of ownership that made printed artifacts available in the form of property and thus inappropriate to blacks and Indians; its coidentity with educational institutions that socialized whites into the community of learning whereby their status as civilized Christians was defined; and its content, which referred of course to issues in the white world. Just as important, the use of print was understood to entail the authoritative disposition of character that was the personal value of letters, a disposition that was understood as a racial trait and could find expression in a wide range of preferences and abilities under such headings as perspicuity, equanimity, temperance, and judg-ment. Just as the white community would not have been the same community without its opposition to other groups and its constitution through writing and printing, so also written media would not have entailed the same dispositions of character—and would not have had the same identity—had participation in them not entailed membership in that community.[20]

White colonists early learned to think of themselves as inhabiting the pure language of writing and to think of blacks as inhabiting a dialect, a particularized speech, that expressed their racial nature. In the early 1740s the Maryland doctor Alexander Hamilton, arriving near New York City with his black slave, Dromo, recorded in his journal an encounter between Dromo and a Dutch-speaking black woman: "Dromo, being about 20 paces before me, stoped att a house where, when I came up, I found him discoursing a negroe girl who spoke Dutch to him. 'Dis de way to York?' says Dromo. 'Yaw, dat is Yarikee,' said the wench, pointing to the steeples. 'What devil you say?' replys Dromo. 'Yaw, mynheer,' said the wench. 'Damme, you, what you say?' said Dromo again. 'Yaw, yaw,' said the girl. 'You a damn black bitch,' said Dromo and so rid on."[21]

In this drama of unregistered violence the one principle of intelligibility is Hamilton's external relation to the scene. That distance establishes his registration of the scene and produces his pleasure in it. Part of Hamilton's pleasure is that the slaves' difficulty with each other's language dramatizes what he doubtless perceives as their lack of mastery in their own languages (or what he would no doubt consider "their own" languages). Lack of mastery in both senses: dialect is perceived by Hamilton as a natural sign of the condition of servitude. Equally important is that his position of recorder, from which he produces simulacra of multiple incomplete dialects within a seamless narrative, matches mastery and writing against inferiority and illiterate speech.

The meaning of the scene for Hamilton was already established by his ability to scribble an account of it in his room at the New York inn. His comic perception of the two blacks' speech as dialects depends on a norm of written language, and this distinction between written language and the racialized particularities of dialect is clearly an invidious one. Yet what is invidious about it is not mere personal prejudice on Hamilton's part—a lapse from liberal tolerance—for he had only to record the scene for the valence of the linguistic media to appear. In that cultural context a difference between inclusive universality and blind particularity was immanent to the difference between the (non)dialect of writing and the spoken dialect. Dromo, speaking, identifies himself; Hamilton, transcribing Dromo's phonemic particularity, transcends the racialized identity of Dromo's speech. At the same time, Hamilton's pleasure in transcription testifies, even in the private context of his journal, to a sense of collectivity. To do reading was a way of being white.

Not all whites were literate. The best literacy studies estimate that, of the free white males of seventeenth-century New England, roughly a third could not sign their names. After a long period of little improvement New England white men achieved nearly complete literacy in the middle of the eighteenth century. Among white women, on the other hand, only a third could sign their names before 1670, and even by the end of the eighteenth century that fraction had not risen to more than half. South of New England, even white males do not seem to have attained more than two-thirds literacy in the same period.[22]

Despite these differentials in the technology, print could represent the white community to itself, partly because more people could read than the statistics suggest. Ordinary patterns of education involved instruction in reading, especially reading of the Bible, for several years before instruction in writing was undertaken, and many students interrupted their educational careers before the second stage. Literacy statistics, which are almost invariably based on signatures of wills, marriage licenses, or other official records, give no indication of those who participated in the written without themselves being able to write. Many groups who do poorly in literacy figures—especially women—probably were able to read. For this reason the historian David Hall has argued that those who were able to read in some degree comprise the vast majority of white colonists, and that the print market was potentially very broad. To illustrate that point Hall has shown that some popular forms of print, especially devotional and sensational literatures, were extraordinarily common despite severe material limitations on the print market.[23]

Nevertheless, although women were reading printed goods in colonial America, very few of those goods were written by women. Nor is it the case that the gender barrier in letters dissolved when women took up pens to write. The important question is not access to writing, as a certain liberal humanism would lead us to expect, but rather the meaning of writing. Insofar as written contexts entailed dispositions of character that interpellated their subject as male, women could only write with a certain cognitive dissonance.

One curious symptom of this dissonance was a coding of the pen, of which the best-known literary example is Anne Bradstreet's "The Prologue." Like so much of her work, it thematizes the discrepancy between gender and medium and begins by abjuring the male subjects of civil history—too elevated, the poet writes, for her "mean pen." Sandra Gilbert and Susan Gubar have read this trope as part of a tradition of the literary metaphorics of creation—and a very problematic one for women writers—in which the possession of the pen signifies possession of the phallus.[24] For colonial Americans the connection had the force of self-evident fact rather than of literary metaphor. Even the shopkeeper Sarah Knight, adept at both commerce and writing, declares in her journal that the causes of divorce "are not proper to be Related by a Female pen."[25] Women such as Bradstreet and Knight were inscribed by an ideological link with the body. Despite the universalizing claims made by writing in its role as communication, these exceptional women felt themselves to be particularized in the given being of their bodies with relation to their pens. Holding pens, they entered a contradictory relation to the implicitly male community that was constituted in writing. In other words, the collectivity formation of written discourse meant that writing was gendered even where no outright prohibition from writing was in effect. To write was to inhabit gender.

The male collectivity formation of writing meant also that the metonymic link between the pen and the gendered body carried over even into printed discourse, where it might have been possible to abandon the trope. Ben Franklin, for example, declaring in 1732 the winner of a riddle competition in his *Pennsylvania Gazette,* makes a point of noting that the winning entry was "wrote by a *Female Hand.*"[26] More striking is the preface to the first *South Carolina Gazette* in that same year. There, when the printer hopes that the paper might be "some little Incitement to abler Pens," he and his male readers enjoy a conventional metonymic thrill. He particularly solicits writing on trade, which he says is the one subject that "every worthy Inhabitant of the Province" will find to have a "Claim to his [sic] Pen." Though the emphasis on hand-held instruments went without comment, the gendering of the instruments was not lost on an anonymous contributor in the next issue, who begins by apologizing: "This, Sir, I doubt not, but you'll think, comes awkwardly from a Female Pen."[27] The figurative pattern in these examples would seem trivial—a perhaps unfortunate conventional metonymy—did it not register an internal dissonance, or awkwardness, inhabited by women who wrote. For most women that awkwardness was resolved by not writing, which of course leaves no record for the historian.

Reading leaves no more record than not writing, but here again the fact that women *did* read does not tell us what its meaning was. Female farm children learning to spell out and recite the sacred text of the Bible were not performing the same act as a male merchant glancing at the latest commodity prices. Writing was a specialized skill primarily employed in the male-dominated realms of commerce and law; it was especially common for women to be taught reading but not writing. The case of Dinah Nuthead was probably not exceptional in this regard. The wife of a printer in late-seventeenth-century Maryland, she could not sign her name but was able to set type and run the press after her husband died.[28] The personnel teaching the different skills of literacy, moreover, were divided in the same way as their pupils. Increase Mather, remembering his education, records: "I learned to read of my mother. I learned to write of Father."[29] His experience was typical; to the very end of the eighteenth century, colonists distinguished between "woman schools" that taught children to read, and "masters' schools" that taught them to write. Here the terminology speaks, as it were, volumes.

Linguistic technologies were also saturated with class and social status, as can be seen in modern statistical reconstruction. Mid-eighteenth-century Virginia men with personal estates of £200 had a literacy rate twice that of men with estates of £100. Men in the clergy and the professions had a literacy rate of 90 percent or higher, and this figure decreases as one moves down the social scale from gentry to merchants, artisans, laborers, and farmers.[30] This would not have surprised anyone at the time, since everyone knew perfectly well that literacy functioned as a social distinction. More important than the statistical record is the registration of status in the immanent meaning of print for colonial culture. The *South Carolina Gazette* once led off an issue with a piece purportedly written by a cobbler, one "Ralpho Cobble," incensed by some encomia on education in the previous issue: "What do you tell us of yr Larnin & exampels of our Naboring colonees pish dont you no that Strangors were alwase perferd here To All digintys And molyments before any of Us Old Standerds." Orthography reminds the printer's gentlemen subscribers that their class is a natural feature of language. The editorial voice of the *Gazette* goes on to remark that "from the *Head* of *Science,* to the *Foot* of *Mechanicks,* there may be drawn a proportional Degree of Service to the Community."[31] Yet even in pointing out the self-evident social distinction of letters, the mock exchange in the *Gazette* nervously registers a potential resistance to the hegemony of letters. And not for the last time.

No one had a relation to linguistic technologies—speaking, reading, writing, and printing—unmediated by such forms of domination as race, gender, and status. Every printed artifact came saturated with the distinctive qualities of communities. Few groups in colonial society successfully incorporated the use of letters as part of their constitutive self-understanding: chief among these were the clergy, the Southern gentry, and the seaport merchants. Yet even for these groups, though the use of printed goods distinguished them advantageously from other colonial groups, the same goods could continually represent their marginal relation to other communities of the empire. For instance, unlike later periods, in which print acquired the ideological character of local and everyday phenomena, print in the early eighteenth century was distinguished for the fact of its distant origins, its ability to cross space and time in a way that made it represent the exotic. So the same Philadelphia merchant who distinguished himself from his wife and clerks by his familiarity with letters would in turn find himself inscribed in the imperial periphery by a print discourse that everywhere recorded its emanation from distant parts.

This secondhand authority of the provinces was reproduced by the colonists themselves. Most early colonial newspapers devoted their prime space to imperial and foreign intelligence (often of military character) rather than to domestic affairs. News from Muscovy and Hungary often occupied the front pages, while the tiny amount of local news was generally relegated to small type just before the advertisements. Local news could be had through hearsay faster than the weekly newspaper could print it, and until the colonists developed an ideological preference for seeing it in the paper rather than hearing it on the street, they turned to print mainly for advices from abroad. Dividing both media and news along the same axis classifies the spoken with the local and the printed with the exotic. Crossing space in a perceptibly alien way could thus be taken as natural to print.

The early papers are not divided by sizable headlines, and it seems likely that they were read through rather than glanced at for a selective reading.

Moreover the early presses, like other capitalized trades of the period, were almost always in the seaports; and printers had a very special relationship with merchants and ship captains. The normal errands of maritime commerce were the only channels for transoceanic news, and papers announced ship arrivals more regularly than any other kind of local news. The exotic reference of print came about in a commercial context, and newspapers were a kind of metacommodity—objects of trade that described trade itself. Reading the foreign advices, one would have recognized that print discourse derived its authority and material from the shipping trade. Built into the difference between printed news and street speech was a phenomenological topography of the seaport world that could be thematized as foreign reports.

There was only one kind of printed artifact that could have been regarded as an everyday secular object, a piece of the standard routine of early-eighteenth-century society. That was the legal form. Some colonies had passed laws at the turn of the century requiring the use of printed forms in all official transactions (Maryland, for example, did so in 1700). Soon they were available in an astonishing variety: summonses, writs of attachment, deeds of transfer, apprentice indentures, customs receipts, surveyors' certificates, tax assessment forms, land grants, powers of attorney, military supply requisitions, returns, executors' warrants, vouchers, bills of exchange, bonds, debentures, election decrees, jury summonses, petitions for military discharge, complaints for suits in equity, recognizance appeals, commissions civil and military, post-rider oaths, special warrants, bills obligatory, mortgages for slaves, bills of lading, oaths of allegiance, and more. The most prestigious legal forms might be engraved in London, but one of the clearest advantages for the colonists in having domestic printers was the ability to have the simple forms cheaply available.

At a time when legal affairs were usually transacted without professional lawyers, printed forms were thought useful insofar as the common-law tradition had developed a set of formulas, the exact following of which had legal value. Accordingly, printers advertised their forms as the "correctest," and legal forms as a genre remained very stable throughout the century. Because most of these forms required the manual insertion only of a name, or perhaps also an amount, their use did not require a high degree of literacy. It may have been largely through legal forms that nearly illiterate artisans and tradesmen in the seaport towns began to regard the use of printed objects as natural to their own legal and economic world. What is more, the printed forms metonymically represented the arena of imperial administration. The handling of these forms constructed for the colonists their relation to networks of power uniting the colonies and deriving from the English courts.

New England

Printers and readers were more numerous in New England than elsewhere. But, as Kenneth Lockridge has argued, high literacy in early New England did not result in the modernizing orientation toward letters. Printing seems to have been put to conservative uses.[32] Certainly the special tradition of Puritan culture conferred its own features on print and writing. Books that were read in the devotional tradition had a strong public value in the New England towns, where in fact it was not uncommon for committees to inspect each home to make sure that it had a Bible.[33]

The reading of these works was a technology of the self. Cotton Mather, for example, records in his diary the uses of the German pietists' writings: "I would endeavour as in Reading their Books, I find the Passages of a raised and noble Piety occurring, to pant and strive after a lively Impression thereof, on my own Mind. And in this Way I would seek a particular praeparation for Services which I may do, in the coming on of the Kingdom of God."[34] The ideal that Mather articulates here contains a norm for subjectivity: reading, ideally, is a way of internalizing that is simultaneously a feature of literacy and a feature of the sacred order. He takes it as a moral imperative for himself but also for the community: "In visits to credible Families, I will bespeak little Studies and Book-shelves for the little Sons that are capable of conversing with such things; and begin to furnish their Libraries and perswade them to the Religion of the Closet."[35]

The religion of the closet prescribes not only that books will be useful, but that their utility will lie in a practice of internalization. In the official text of the Massachusetts laws the colony's citizens were reminded, "When Laws may be read in men's lives, they appear more beautiful than in the fairest Print, and promise a longer duration, than engraven in Marble."[36] On the basis of the same perception, one minister could write, "The life of *Reading*, is in the *performance* of our duty in what we learn. *Words* are but *empty sounds*, except we draw them forth in our *lives*. *Printed Books* will do *little good*, except Gods Spirit print them in our hearts."[37] Implicit here are assumptions about printing technology that differ radically from those underlying John Adams' history of enlightenment. Sacred internalization renders the nature of print in such a way that the publication of broadsides or newspapers could only be seen as inferior uses accidental to the godly effort to "print" the divinely ordained laws "in our hearts." In this case we do not see individuals emancipated by print; instead, it is the individual who is printed from an authoritative stamp.

In the diary entry just quoted, Mather used the same figure to connect the nature of print with its normative effects: he speaks punningly of the "Impression" that reading should make on his mind. I want to make a strong claim about this metaphor as an indicator of the meaning of print in Puritan culture. At the very least, the idea of an authoritative stamp—as opposed to far-flung distribution, let us say—is the standard metaphoric use that Puritan rhetoric makes of printing. Such metaphors cannot be sharply distinguished from the objective facts of printing, for there are any number of ways in which printing might be distinguished from other technologies, and to describe it as a definitive impression has as much validity as any. The rhetoric of impression names the literal and defining features of the print medium in a way that already defines the social value of print. Here the emphasis is on the perfect reception by the copy of a master original. Puritan typography and Puritan typology, in other words, could be mutually reinforcing. Insofar as print is construed, valued, and used according to the perception of a relation between type and antitype—a relation that obtains both between copy and original as well as between text and animated reading—it expresses the character of authority. Constituted in the context of this symbolic logic, print seems eminently suited to the devotional text. One would not construe the distinctive features of the medium in the same way if the object were a shipping report.

Perceiving a relation between private reading and the religion of the closet, Mather became a tireless promoter not only of his own innumerable screeds, but of devotional literature of all kinds. "There is an old *Hawker*," he once wrote in his diary, "who will fill this Countrey with devout and useful Books, if I will direct him; I will therefore direct Him, and assist him, as far as I can, in doing so."[38] With such help, the Boston and Cambridge presses produced a moderate but steady stream of cheap broadsides, devotional steady sellers, execution accounts, sensational reports, and almanacs—all of which combined in various degrees the rhetorical pleasures of leisure reading with the disciplinary discourse of sacred exegesis.

The Massachusetts presses also produced a different kind of trade, often in conjunction with the European Protestant market: learned theological works produced and mainly consumed by the ministerial class. Such works differ from the popular trade not only in their subject matter or in their typically higher price, but in their mode of consumption. These are the works that were accumulated to form the libraries essential to the status and collective identity of the clergy. Learned lawyers and other nonclerical men of letters were rare in New England until James Otis' generation, and the popular, cheap literature consisted almost entirely of ephemera or a relatively small number of steady sellers. The New England library as a substantial collection, therefore, was clerical, and ministers well understood the relation between bibliotechnical capital and professional authority. Mather, for one, was seldom so happy as when he was able to purchase the library of a deceased fellow minister. Edward Taylor, unable to buy many books because of their expense and his remote residence, laboriously copied a library of books which he carefully bound.[39] The discourse that comprises the theological works of the clerical library is highly self-referential, and the books appear to have been read in an intensive and cross-indexical manner—digested for sermons, cited for authority, attacked in polemic. The theological literature exhibits the discursive mode of the library, which can itself be understood as a metonym for the corporate clerisy.

It has often been claimed that New England was an oral society.[40] In an important sense this is true, though not in the way that is usually meant. The conventional distinction between oral and literate societies, in which oral means *pre*literate and innocent of the exploitation that comes through writing, I would reject as sentimental and ideological.[41] It conceals norms not only about language, but about personhood and social relations. New Englanders, far from being ignorant of letters, used them with an intensity equalled by very few other cultures in the world at the time. Yet in an important ideological way it was an oral society. New Englanders accorded a disciplinary privilege to speech and in most contexts insisted on seeing writing as a form of speaking. A case in point is the response of Obadiah Gill and his collaborators to Robert Calef's skeptical treatise on the witch trials:

> Is there any among the Children of men, that have Sold themselves to serve the Interest of Satan to purpose? Let it be their Study by their *Slanders* to Blast the Reputation of those, in whom the Honour of God, and of His Religion, and the Salvation of Souls is much concerned. This we take to be the Grand Aim and End of all that Robert Calef can call his own, throughout his whole *Treatise*. And now, vent thy malice; speak what thou hast to Accuse them of; they shall come off with flying Colours.[42]

Gill here demonstrates a desire to consider his writing not only as speech, but as speech in a setting of exemplary and disciplinary personal presence. He wants to imagine the exchange of pamphlets as an unmediated relation between persons, in which the godliness invested in himself and the ministers will dictate the outcome. Hence the command to Calef—"speak what thou hast"—which creates a fictive scenario of speech in order rhetorically to cancel any sense of practical liberty that the print medium might occasion. The same vocative scenario can be seen governing Cotton Mather's practice to the end of his career—notably in the smallpox inoculation controversy, where he emphatically represents his opponents as assaulting his person. He once remarked that his sermons would be more powerful if "Preached a Second Time in the way of the Press."[43] And although he tells us that he gave away his books by the score, he also notes that when giving a book away he liked to instruct the recipient: "Remember, that I am speaking to you, all the while you have this Book before you!"[44]

This disciplinary fiction was part of the trade politics of print. Calef, after all, had been forced to send to England to have his attack on Mather printed, and a similar piece by Thomas Brattle evidently circulated only in manuscript. A group of disgruntled ministers in Boston charged in 1700 that the printer Bartholomew Green was so "in aw of the Reverend Author"—Increase Mather, Cotton's father—as not to print anything hostile to him.[45] Whether the accusation is entirely true or not, such struggles over personality and access to print demonstrate that an ethic of personal presence serves as the ground of print. Mather's defenders say of the charge that "It was highly rejoycing to us, when we heard that our *Book-sellers* were so well acquainted with the Integrity of our Pastors, as not one of them would admit any of those *Libels* to be vended in their shops."[46] The critical ministers and the Mathers agree in seeing the printing of a work as an act in a relation between specific persons, and the possibility that print might function as a public mediation is not even entertained.

In 1722, as a new set of print practices was only just emerging, the Reverend Thomas Symmes published a sermon which included a preface that comments extensively on the scene of print in New England society. The chief advantage of the "Art of Printing," he explains, is that by its means, "as many of the eminent Servants of God *being dead, yet speak unto us;* so many other worthy Persons, and especially . . . the Ministers of the Gospel are still blest with Opportunities of rendring their Usefulness more *extensive* and *durable*."[47] The attributes of extension and durability are the classically distinctive features of writing, and print's superiority to script is seen as lying mainly in its greater extension. Extension and durability determine print as a derivative of speech that introduces to the immediacy of speech the dimensions of space and time. In other forms of print discourse, writing's dimensions of space and time appear as exoticism and antiquarianism; here Symmes's terms for those dimensions—extension and durability—bear connotations less of curiosity than of ministerial power.[48]

Symmes encourages his fellow clergy to make more use of print. In a revealing moment he explains that the reason they do not is that they hope to "escape the scourge of the tongue." If the scourge of the oral is the restraint on the press, it is also the validation of the press. Symmes argues that no one need fear superfluous or bad publications, for such works "we are under no obligation in the World to patronize, admit under our roof, or touch with one of our Fingers."[49] Space and time, in the Puritan ideology, do not sever print from the speaking body and its fingers—they bring it inexorably under a metonymic discipline. Because New England culture structured print in this way, print discourse had not become the basis for the community's self-representation—as it would be for John Adams and his contemporaries—except in its covert identification with the community of white males.

The typological and ministerial virtues of print were only one symbolic context for understanding print. I have already indicated that the world of seaport commerce gave printing a set of features that could hardly be incorporated with those picked out by Symmes, Mather, and their fellow clergy. And since the way print was construed always had consequences for imagining society and its norms, there were stakes of power in these symbolic differences. The New England printing trade and its cultural settings were anything but monolithic; the trade, for example, displayed a much greater specialization than in the Southern colonies. As early as 1700 a book-buyer in Boston would have had a choice among nineteen booksellers and seven printers. Unlike Virginia, where book owning remained a sign of wealth and distinction, New England had some kind of printed artifact for almost all white families. As David Hall points out, in the same period in which the *Virginia Almanac* was printed in press runs of 5,000 copies (and even this figure is much larger than that of the average press run), New Englanders were buying 60,000 copies of a single almanac and supporting several others.[50]

We like to associate print with general distribution, but the same popular press that put almanacs in the hands of so many New England farmers was also decentralized and heterogeneous. Widely circulated titles were published by means of loose agreements among a number of printers and booksellers, none of whom alone would have had the kind of commercial network of transportation and marketing that is taken for granted by our more modern notion of a publisher. Because almanacs were produced on a schedule, and because their audience included many people who would not have bought any other book, they represent the peak of the book trade's organization. Uniformity was not at a high premium for other kinds of books. Some of the most widely dispersed titles, for example, were what Hall calls "steady sellers"—books usually of a devotional character that remained in print year after year and can be found in households of very little wealth. But these texts have little stability from edition to edition, since each printing was worked up cheaply by a small-time printer trying to reach a local market and would vary depending on what sources the printer had on hand and what tastes in his customers he anticipated.

The localism of the decentralized book trade meant that many texts circulated in a more or less "popular" fashion, meaning that the book market was capable of articulating a counterpublic print discourse in broadsides and cheap pamphlets. Those in position to represent the order of colonial society—especially ministers—occasionally expressed some anxiety about this counterpublic potential. Cotton Mather wrote in his diary in 1713 that "the Minds and Manners of many People about the Countrey are much corrupted, by foolish Songs and Ballads, which the Hawkers and Peddlars carry into all parts of the Countrey."[51] Unfortunately, we know relatively little about this literature—how much of it there was, what all of it was like, who made it, and how it was perceived and read by those who bought it. The counterpublic literature of broadside ballads, devotional books, and sensational pamphlets never articulated a public threat, depending as it did on an invisible worthlessness for its very existence. Not only did it have to be cheap in order to be hawked in the countryside, but in order to be counterpublic (and thus "corrupting"), it had to be "foolish," that is, without status and without public reference. Yet it was precisely this extraneous relation to claims of public value that Mather found disturbing. Accordingly he spent a considerable part of his writing and publishing career in an effort to match the public discourse of theodicy with the reading tastes of the sensational literature, striving for a seamless representation of the world in printed discourse.

An illustration of just how little status and authority many books had can be found in an anonymous broadside poem of 1731—a cheap popular artifact, which describes the cheapness of popular artifacts. Titled "Father Abbey's Will," the doggerel broadside lists the possessions that are sup-

24

posed to have been bequeathed by Matthew Abdy, an aged sweeper and bedmaker employed by Harvard, to his wife. Included are:

> A ragged Mat
> A Tub of Fat
> A Book put out by Bunyan,
> Another Book
> By Robin Rook,
> A Skain or two of Spunyarn.[52]

Here Abdy is an object of comic condescension for his poverty, yet his possession of two books is regarded as not incongruous. A literature without prestige was easily imaginable.

A different kind of cultural authority is visible in this broadside, as well as in the many surviving wills that follow its pattern for listing books. Virtually any New Englander who possessed devotional books such as *Pilgrim's Progress* would also have owned some cheaper kinds of print, such as the ever-present almanacs or broadsides like "Father Abbey's Will." These cheaper artifacts are not mentioned in wills. Their owners almost never went to the expense of having them bound for preservation, as they did for other kinds of works in an age when books were typically purchased in sheets. We consider the cheap artifacts ephemera because they were not considered by New Englanders to be eligible components in the construction of the archive of cultural tradition, any more than they have been considered eligible for the normative archive constructed by literary history.

One of the most important features of the colonists' relation to letters was the ability of certain printed objects to count as wealth. And the close relation between the economic wealth of books and their "cultural" wealth is evident in the ambiguity of the word "heritage." Inheritability was an ambiguous value in books in that it defined cultural tradition and capital at the same time, and was accordingly determined as much by allusion as by bindings and wills. It was and is also a paradoxical value since, in order to count as cultural wealth for the individual, a book must predicate the death of the individual. It is not valued either for its practical use—as, say, a farrier's manual would be for a farmer—or for its exchange, but for the possibility of its surviving the owner. Because of that possibility, because a book owner negates his own life in valuing a book, owning a book symbolically represents a degree of self-consciousness and independence. In the colonies this was markedly less true of manuals, almanacs, newspapers, pamphlets, and broadsides than it was of books in religion, history, and biography. One reason for the difference is that these categories of discourse were able to count as wealth insofar as they were able to thematize the death of the individual.

For New Englanders inheritability was most clearly determined by the sacred reference of a devotional literature, although in the Northern as in the Southern colonies a historical literature had the same potential. Works in the sanctioned discourses of theology and history were by no means all that the colonial presses produced; they are what have survived. Their potential for survival was both a condition of their discourse, which attained self-referentiality by presupposing the death of the individual, and of their material value for the owners whose independence was won by a self-negating investment. Perhaps for the same reason, most of the cheap broadsides that have survived, by far, are funeral elegies. In the main, however, the counterpublic literature of foolish songs and sensational accounts achieved its independence from the centralized forms of cultural authority by abjuring inheritability and, with it, the self-referentiality of a definite tradition.

The Southern Colonies

South of New England, where the press developed more slowly, it took on a different set of characteristics. Printing appeared in Philadelphia in 1685, and at the same time in Maryland, though in the latter colony it would continue only intermittently. For the first three decades of the eighteenth century there was no press in Virginia or the more Southern plantations, and consequently no newspapers or magazines. What print there was in these colonies was imported. Not until 1730 did Virginians persuade the Annapolis printer William Parks to establish a press and bookstore in Williamsburg. Books were still inaccessible to most people, literate or not. Even as late as the 1760s Smollett's *History* would have cost a Williamsburg resident the equivalent of thirty hogs.[53]

In this setting the extension and durability that defined print for Americans decidedly took on the character of the exotic and the antique. Book-buying was the province of the wealthy, since imported printed goods were costly, and the great libraries of the Southern colonies were, almost without exception, those of the landed gentry, not the clergy—though smaller collections were common enough among ministers and lawyers.[54] The necessity of importing the books for these libraries no doubt contributed to their function as a social distinction, since social distinction took the form of visible luxury rather than intensive pious reflection. Library building, like tea drinking, was part of a symbolic culture of regulated luxury. While Mather's library of 7,000 volumes or so probably lay in stacks and in chests, William Byrd II housed his 3,625 tomes in twenty-four black walnut bookcases.

Despite the scarcity of print, there were many different possible relations to print and writing for colonial Southerners, as has recently been emphasized by Rhys Isaac's history of Virginia.[55] Letters could have a prominent role even in the lives of the illiterate and semiliterate. The extreme case was that of slaves, since a slave was required to carry a letter written by his owner simply in order to travel. For whites who could read falteringly, but could not write, books provided enough of a glimpse into other ways of thinking and living as to be a reminder of the distinction between the two domains. Laws were still read aloud at the courthouse to the assembled citizens. In the Anglican liturgy, as well as in the traditions of recitation and spoken commentary surrounding the Bible and common-law judgments, the text was both tied to oral performance settings and employed to underwrite the authority of those settings. Letters thus appeared in intermediary connections between the high culture of learning and the other traditions of the community. Had letters been confined to the silent reading and writing of gentlemen such as George Wythe, they would have been easy to avoid.

As in New England, Southern society was organized by a performative order of speech. The meanings of speech and its privilege, however, were different in the South, chiefly because of the deferential order of status in which the gentry played a pivotal role. As Charles Sydnor so vividly pictures in *Gentlemen Freeholders,* the gentry relied for much of their authority on an exemplary speech, emphasizing their local interests by means of an agonistic self-representation. In common parlance, a man "carried his election," and the phrase meant more than mere success. "There was an implication," as Sydnor puts it, "that success was deserved and earned by energy, force of character, ready information, manly presence, and courage."[56] Campaigning for office in such an environment was not a matter of oratorical eloquence, and speech-making seems to have been rare during election campaigns.[57] If eighteenth-century Virginia was not oratorical, however, that was not because it was script-dominated but because its orality presided over the most mundane levels of interaction. Campaigning meant going among residents, inquiring about wives and children, simulating the immediate, conversational relation of a neighbor.

27

So great was the oral composition of the gentry's power that the elections themselves were conducted orally. Candidates faced the courthouse chamber, freeholders delivered their votes orally, and clerks paid by each of the candidates recorded the votes. Frequently the candidate would respond personally to each voter. In one election recorded by Sydnor a Mr. Buchanan entered the courthouse and was asked by the sheriff how he voted. When Buchanan announced that his preference was for John Clopton, Clopton replied, "Mr. Buchanan, I shall treasure that vote in my memory. It will be regarded as a feather in my cap for ever."[58] Clopton's invocation of his memory as a reference locates the value of Buchanan's vote within an unmediated relation between the two men (affection and loyalty versus alienation and enmity) temporally scaled by the lifetime of the single man.

On the other hand, as Rhys Isaac demonstrates, the gentry's authority within the general community had as much to do with script and print as did their authority among professionals and tradesmen. The unlettered assumed that writing belonged to a higher order that did not conflict with the oral tradition, and the difference in plane of reference between literate and illiterate authorized the social hierarchy of the genteel and the common. The extra-local reference of literacy, Isaac explains, was incorporated by the gentry as an aspect of character:

> The quality that most nearly epitomized what was needed in a gentleman was "liberality." This word was rich in connotations deriving from its Latin root: first and foremost, it denoted *freedom* from material necessity and the grubbing for subsistence that poverty entailed; second, it meant *freedom* from the servile subjection that the quest for satisfaction of material want imposed; third, it evoked *freedom* from the sordid subordination of considerations of honor and dignity to calculations of interest that lack of independence was presumed to involve; and fourth, most relevant to [the] discussion of print and social authority, it was associated with *freedom* to elevate the mind by application to the authoritative books that contained the higher learning (as in the expression "liberal arts"). Ultimately the idea of "liberality" referred to a certain disposition in the soul that all these freedoms made possible—the disposition to undertake important responsibilities in the community at large.[59]

The different meanings of liberality bear important relations. The value of the gentleman's willingness freely to take responsibility had to be grounded in the paradox of disinterest coupled with common interest.

The republican notion of freehold, by identifying real property with both independence and localism, was the core of that paradox.[60] The local allegiance of the freeholder was vouched for in the extensive oral perform-ances by means of which the gentleman familiarized himself with the less wealthy. A more substantial familiarity, however, could compromise the claim to disinterested independence and concerns particular to the broader commonwealth. The different referents of liberality—wealth, indepen-dence, and learning—all allowed the gentleman to stand above the merely local, to predicate his identity upon freedom from the kinds of private interest that would compromise his public commitment. It was to this liberality that writing testified in the society; particularly in its character as learning, writing gave evidence of breadth of mind, of extra-local com-prehension. It could do so precisely because of its antique exoticism in the Southern culture of literacy.

The social position of the Virginia gentry at that time—not unlike that of their English counterparts—was a complex mediation of orality, writing, and print—a mediation that took place under the categories of familiarity and liberality and that further required certain traits to be seen as natural to letters. The gentry identified themselves by means of oral performance with the populace and the locality of freehold; by means of learning with law and the clergy; by means of print with an authoritative public realm and with the freedom of freehold as demonstrated by extra-local concerns. The importance of this context for print can be illustrated by the first object to come from the newly erected Williamsburg press, a poem called *Typographia* by John Markland, celebrating the virtues of print. Markland begins by celebrating all that writing imports from with-out and from the past; as though to exemplify formally writing's ability to resurrect the foreign and the ancient, he opens with an epigraph from Cicero: "Pleni sunt omnes Libri, plenae sapientum voces, plena Exemplorum vetustas; quae jacerent in Tenebris omnia, nisi Literarum Lumen accederet." (All literature and the voices of wisdom abound with ancient and noble examples that would lie in darkness if the light of letters did not fall upon them.)[61] In the context of the oration from which the quote is taken, Cicero's notion is a norm for letters. He is contrasting the useful literature of public life with the private indulgence of the bookish recluse. Markland drops the distinction, implying that letters just *are* beneficial for their extension and durability.

In the poem that follows Markland articulates the nature of writing in accordance with the import economy of printed goods. What is most interesting about the poem is that it presents letters as distinguished through the anthropomorphic equivalent of their extension and durability. Writing, in Markland's view, transcends context, and that transcendence corresponds to aspects of character. He shares Cicero's emphasis on the exemplary content of literature; for both, what useful literature is *about* matches what it *is:* a way of having broad vision and detachment from local objects of attention, which are implicitly regarded as ignoble. Thus the phrase *literarum lumen* has the resonance of a liberal education.[62] As Markland continues:

> Happy the *Art*, by which we learn
> The gloss of Errors to detect,
> The Vice of Habits to correct,
> And sacred Truths, from Falsehood to discern!
> By which we take a far-stretched View,
> And learn our Fathers Vertues to pursue,
> Their follies to eschew.

Markland's "far-stretched View" is the psychological equivalent of the material circumstances with which he identifies print. In connecting the far-stretched view with "our Fathers Vertues," he grants a moral authority to the stance associated with the use of print. But Markland puts greater emphasis on the place of exemplary virtue in the past, making print the vehicle of a specifically ancestral example. The idea invokes the value of inheritability, a powerful component of colonial classicism, and one that implicitly appreciated a certain part of Parks's stock. The disposition toward inheritable knowledge in the consumption of print is a distinctive character trait. By describing the character of virtue by means of the far-stretched view, Markland associates the vehicle of print with the nature of exemplary virtue. The same temporal distance that constitutes "our Fathers Vertues" as an authoritative precedent makes print the appropriate means of access to that precedent, and the moral view that recognizes the fathers' virtues is acquired by the physical viewing of print. *Typographia* thus rhetorically assures the patrons of Parks's press that their favors are not wasted: by their use of print they naturally align themselves with the character of authority.

Transformation

It is not my intention to chronicle the full range of the printing in colonial America. Rather, I have sought to demonstrate that different ways of determining the nature and value of letters were available in different contexts in New England and the Southern colonies. I have sought not to speak of "print culture," as though to attribute a teleology to print, but to indicate some of the competing symbolic contexts of print. None of them, however, corresponds to Adams' vision of print. We have not yet seen print routinely opposed to authority, identified in its nature with a popular struggle or with emancipatory reflection, or forming the basis of a protonationalist consciousness. The forms of print discourse that have been examined so far have been stable if not homeostatizing. Adams' rhetoric would therefore seem to indicate a new condition for print.

Not until the middle decades of the eighteenth century did the printing trade begin to resemble the scene of circulating information and critical discourse that Adams depicts as natural to it. I have called attention to the regional and contextual differences in ways of determining print in order to suggest, in part, that the development of a public print discourse could not have derived from the nature of print, as is often suggested. The point can be strengthened by noting the lag between the establishment of printing in the colonies and its use for the tasks that Adams describes. The colonial printing trade had been around for a long time by the early eighteenth century; the oldest colonial press had been in operation since 1639. The date is not early in the history of printing (Mexico City had already had a much more active press a century earlier) but it was early for provincial printing in the English world. At the time of the Restoration only three towns in the realm outside of London had presses: Oxford, Cambridge (England), and Cambridge (Massachusetts). In 1662 York was added to the list. Then Boston in 1674, Philadelphia and St. Mary's City (Maryland) in 1685, and New York in 1693. When the restrictions on the press were repealed in England in 1695 the colonies had more towns with printers than England did.[63]

But these colonial presses had also been relatively inactive. Most seventeenth-century colonists were quite content—insofar as we can tell—to do without a press. On several occasions when printing was introduced it was immediately discouraged, sometimes by royal governors, but also by elected assemblies.[64] The early artisans printed no newspapers or magazines. They seldom concentrated their capital or developed broad enough markets to produce big editions or large volumes. In the main they were booksellers or general shopkeepers, retailing not only books imported from London but also stationery and a variety of unrelated goods. In Andrew Bradford's Philadelphia printing shop one could find, in addition to printed goods: molasses by the barrel, whalebone, goose feathers, rum, corks, chocolate, peas, snuff, tea, "very good Pickled

Sturgeon," beaver hats, patent medicines, a harpsichord, spectacles, and quadrants.[65] Most printers' income came from a combination of such general sales, a few imprints, and a good deal of job printing, such as blank legal forms and official publications subsidized and controlled by the colonial governments.

By 1765, however, print had come to be seen as indispensable to political life, and could appear to men such as Adams to be the primary agent of world emancipation. What makes this transformation of the press particularly remarkable is that, unlike the press explosion of the nineteenth century, it involved virtually no technological improvements in the trade. To the end of the eighteenth century, printers were using a wooden flatbed hand press that had scarcely changed since the German presses of the fifteenth century. The material constraints on the press—such as the scarcity of paper or the lack of the skill to cast type domestically—remained in force until the end of the eighteenth century. Nevertheless, printing changed both in character and in volume, after 1720 growing much faster even than the population.

Number of master printers	1720	1760
Boston	6	14
Philadelphia	1	9
New York	1	5
Elsewhere	1	14
Total	9	42

Source: Stephen Botein, "Meer Mechanics and an Open Press: The Business and Political Strategies of Colonial American Printers," *Perspectives in American History* 9 (1975):127–228.

Thrown into relief by the Stamp Act, figures such as the ones in the accompanying table begin to suggest the resonance of Adams' 1765 historical narrative. Yet the figures would not interest us if they recorded only more printers doing the same job printing. The importance of this expansion is that the trade was now involved in different tasks. The dramatic change had begun at the time of the establishment of newspapers, for only then did colonial printing become a substantial industry, rivaling and communicating with the European book trade. And only then did colonial printing begin to sustain a continuous local discourse. In the decades before Adams and the Stamp Act, the dynamism of the printing trade lay in new contexts of print discourse in commerce and politics. They became the arena in which print would be reconceptualized—and, with it, those dimensions of politics and subjectivity entailed by Adams' vision of republican enlightenment. When Adams politicized the Puritan "Religion of the Closet," his revision articulated the realignment of linguistic technologies and power that integrated print with an emergent republican paradigm as the proper medium of the public.

· *II* ·

The Res Publica *of Letters*

> It is worthy of remark that newspapers have almost en-
> tirely changed their form and character within the period
> under review. For a long time after they were first
> adopted as a medium of communication to the public,
> they were confined, in general, to the mere statement of
> *facts*. But they have gradually assumed an office more
> extensive, and risen to a more important station in soci-
> ety. They have become the vehicles of discussion in
> which the principles of government, the interests of na-
> tions, the spirit and tendency of public measures, and the
> public and private characters of individuals are all ar-
> raigned, tried, and decided. Instead, therefore, of being
> considered now, as they once were, of small moment in
> society, they have become immense moral and political
> engines, closely connected with the welfare of the state,
> and deeply involving both its peace and prosperity.
>
> —*Samuel Miller,* 1803

WHEN JOHN ADAMS describes print, he assumes it to be coextensive
with the public sphere. For the previous generation of colonists, publishing could be a public activity, but not in any special or privileged way.
The difference marks the structural transformation of the public sphere as
well as of the relation between letters and the subject. We can begin to
assess the transformation by noting that, in the two different relations to
discourse, the category of the public plays different roles. Before the middle decades of the eighteenth century, and also in ongoing contexts of
customary law, the political sphere of the colonies depended on its continuity with common social exchanges. But in the discourse of Adams'
later perspective, a public sphere had come to be distinguished by definition from the common exchanges of society and did not depend on an
entire congruence between its norms and those observed in custom. Because it was distinct from personal relations, it could be the arena for
adjudicating conflicts even over basic norms, as in sectarian religious conflicts.[1] The difference between the two models of the public sphere marks
one of the most profound and consequential developments of the

eighteenth century. As Adams' narrative shows, the difference in the public sphere was also a difference in the print medium. I take the connection to hold generally: medium and political structure are identical with respect to the question of what it means to speak publicly, and a history of letters requires a history of the political conditions of utterance.

The older model of the public as continuous with custom and natural order can be seen in a sermon preached in 1731 by Samuel Whittelsey, *A Public Spirit Described & Recommended.* Not untypically, Whittelsey defines a public spirit as one "that is truly & heartily Concern'd for the good and welfare of others."[2] The sphere in which this kind of public spirit functions is daily life, and although Whittelsey goes on to discuss the specialized business of government, his central premise remains a continuity between that business and common interactions, between public and spirit. The exemplary case of the public sphere is the daily practice of religion: "It is Religion that unites and ties the several members of the Society together" (9). Far from being an impersonal sphere of political decisionmaking, publicness is a mode of sociability as subjection in an ideally nonnegotiated social order, allowing judgment to "run down as a River, and Righteousness as a mighty Stream" (11).[3] And whereas, for Adams, public activity has a critical intention with regard to power, for Whittelsey public activity and critical intentions are categorical opposites: "A Contrary Spirit is a Base Spirit" (29).

To a public sphere of such a customary type print discourse holds a more or less arbitrary relation, capable equally of confirming or distorting the norms of public spirit. So for the early colonists, being public did not entail a special communicative context such as publication, and publishing did not have the meaning of making things public. In 1709, for example, Cotton Mather drew up in his diary a list of resolutions, including a set of resolutions to perform "In my public Circumstances." He resolves, under that heading, to pray and to make "careful Visits, in my Flock." It is also in this context that he writes, "And I would compose and publish many *Essayes,* accommodated unto the Interests of Christianity in the Land; such as may find out all Sorts of People, in the several Wayes, wherein they may be sett athinking on such Things, as may be for the Glory of God."[4] Insofar as publishing is public, it is as an extension of personal visitation. What marks Mather's entry into his public capacity is not writing as such, but rather his authoritative ministrations of which writings are only instruments. Because publication is as remote as possible from collective decisionmaking, political debate does not appear as an appropriate genre for Mather's writing.

Expressly political publications are exceptional in the print discourse of the colonies before 1720. One of the rare examples can reinforce the point: a pamphlet precipitated by the 1689 revolution against the Andros regime in Massachusetts. It begins by wishing its nonexistence: "It is the Unhappiness of this present Juncture, that too many Men relinquish their Stations of *Privacy* and *Subjection,* and take upon them too freely to descant upon affairs of the *Publick*."[5] Citizenship, ideally identical with adherence to stations of privacy and subjection, will not normally involve political publication. Of course, Puritan Massachusetts did have institutions and modes of discourse for political affairs: town meetings, magistracy, sermons, and the like. The structure and legitimacy of these institutions depended on their continuity with the mode of sociability called public spirit, and thus on their *not* taking the form of interested debate or collective conflict resolution. Published debate could take place, but only as an index of failure in public affairs, a poor substitute for a public spirit strangely forgotten in a moment of crisis.

A public print discourse did develop, however, beginning in the years just before 1720 in Boston and shortly thereafter in the other urban seaports. In every instance the emergent mode of publication entailed a reconceptualization of the public sphere. Articulating a new representation of the political order, this print discourse restructured relations of power. At the same time it established new meanings for the practices of writing, printing, and publication—transformations that were simultaneous with that of the public sphere not by chance, but because they constituted the new public sphere.

The relation can be illustrated in the example of Maryland. Maryland was not the first colony to develop a print political discourse, and one had, after all, appeared in London at the end of the seventeenth century. A public discourse was not the sort of thing that, once invented, could simply be exported. Precisely because it entailed new determinations of power, subjectivity, and language, a public discourse emerged in each instance only as the result of fundamental change and social struggle. On the other hand, the public sphere of print developed in Maryland only in relation to its development in other quarters of the empire, especially London and the seaports of the more northerly colonies, with which Marylanders had experience through trade, through migration, and through the importation of print.

Maryland had had printers as early as 1685, but not for political publishing. In fact, William Nuthead, who had already been forbidden to print in Jamestown some years earlier, was jailed in Maryland in 1693 for printing proceedings of the legislature. He was then ordered never again to print anything relating to public affairs, so he and his widow printed mostly blank legal forms. (When Nuthead died in 1695 his debtors, some sixty in number, were almost all sheriffs, clerks, or justices.)[6] By 1725, however, it had come to be understood—at least by some in Maryland—that the establishment of a public discourse would be a good reason for bringing another printer to Maryland. That year the Assembly decided now to print its own proceedings, a task for which it had to go to Philadelphia. The book, when it appeared, bore a preface complaining that without a press Marylanders "have scarce had any Opportunity of Judging whether they were Served or Prejudiced by their Representatives; whether their Constitution was maintained or prostituted, whether their *English* Liberties were Asserted or Neglected by them." Indeed, the preface continues, many delegates "who have, by an Ingenuous Honest Conversation, justly Recommended themselves to the Choice of the Electors, have not known what was the Constitution of their Country." The preface here establishes a double perspective for the utility of public discourse: print will function for freeholders as activity in the civic sphere, and for representatives as the medium of authoritative instruction. "But 'tis hop'd from this beginning and the provision that is made for having a Press amongst us, the Gentlemen of the Country will more readily fall upon this useful kind of Learning."[7]

William Parks, the English provincial printer who was brought to the colony shortly thereafter (and who later moved on to Williamsburg and printed *Typographia*), depended on the political value of such thinking for the success of his press. His immigration was arranged by the Assembly, especially a delegate named Thomas Bordley who was the probable author of the preface. Parks was made postmaster, and the Assembly awarded him a grant for the publication of the colony's laws. In addition to that book, which appeared in 1727, Parks published such works as *The Acts of Assembly* in 1726, Daniel Dulaney's *The Right of the Inhabitants of Maryland to the Benefit of English Laws* in 1728, and Henry Darnall's *Just and Impartial Account of the Transactions of the Merchants of London* in 1729. The last item grew out of a controversy over tobacco regulation, one that throve in the pages of the *Maryland Gazette,* Parks's chief source of income.[8] Obviously, the context for much of Parks's printing was that of imperial relations, and the benefit of having these works in printed form lay mostly in the way they defined a transatlantic sphere of representation. At the same time, however, the development of this print discourse transformed the local political world of the imperial periphery.

In 1727, shortly after Parks's establishment in Annapolis and early in the tobacco controversy, he printed a pamphlet called *A Letter from a Freeholder,* responding to a letter in the *Gazette.* (Unfortunately, the early issues of the *Gazette* itself are not known to survive.) As though to register resistance to the idea of public printed discourse, the tract opens with an apology for publication: "I am very glad that a Gentleman who is a Friend to his Country, (as I am firmly perswaded the Author of the late *Letter to the Printer* really is) has communicated his Thoughts to the Publick, concerning a thing so much desired and so much wanted as a *Tobacco-Law* ... And I am in Hopes that others, excited by the same generous Motive, will follow so laudable an Example, that by the Communication of Mens Thoughts and Sentiments to each other, such Methods may be taken for the Regulation of our Staple of Tobacco."[9]

For the author of the pamphlet, communication in print is not ancillary to a public sphere or a reflection of it, but rather is its ideal version. Apparently taken with the novelty of the form, the author goes on: "As I am of Opinion with the Author of the Letter, that aiming at the Good of ones Country, is a sufficient Apology for publishing a Man's Thoughts; so am I clearly of Opinion that it is the indispensable Duty of every Man to do it, with Sincerity and Freedom; and that he ought not to suffer any private Views or Ends (inconsistent with the common Good) to byass or influence him; and that not being Master of a correct Stile, or Propriety of Expression, is no Excuse for being silent on so important and pressing an Occasion" (4). Here the notion that every man ought to publish reveals that the author assumes a restricted community of white propertied males. But in this scenario he also imagines a new set of relations among persons, discourse, and the political order, though many of these relations are necessarily assumed rather than explicit.

Most obvious is the notion that men, who had after all been exchanging opinions all along in other formats, should now have a specialized discourse for that purpose. What would be the advantage of such a (meta)linguistic codification? How and to what purpose shall a public discourse be demarcated from other cultural forms and linguistic environments? The pamphlet's rhetoric shows us first that, purged of "private Views or Ends," it will be a discourse in which publicity will be impersonal by definition. Persons who enter this discourse do so on the condition that the validity of their utterance will bear a negative relation to their persons. These perspectives are not to be separated: the impersonality of public discourse is seen both as a trait of its medium and as a norm for its subjects. Moreover, a special feature of the political order will follow, since the government can no longer remain indifferent to this independent public discourse, but must regard its relation to the public discourse as a criterion of its legitimacy. A complex network of assumptions appears here in order to render the printing of this pamphlet normal, and for the rest of the century the presses would creak in elaborating it.

The new assumptions exemplify what Jürgen Habermas analyzes as a structural transformation of the public sphere—from a world in which power embodied in special persons is represented before the people to one in which power is constituted by a discourse in which the people are represented.[10] Habermas is careful to observe that the political public, in what he calls the bourgeois public sphere, is specifically a reading public. In this connection we can see the importance of the emergence of a public discourse for the history of letters. And we are not considering simply an emergent reading audience or a new genre; the people who read these pamphlets, after all, were presumably the same people who read other things, such as bills and Bibles, before. And the political tract (as genre) antedates printing, as was understood by its many eighteenth-century practitioners, who never tire of invoking their classical and early modern predecessors. What is more to the point is that the public sphere requires a special set of assumptions about print. It requires an articulated relation between assumptions about print and the norms of a specialized discursive subsystem. For the Maryland author and other contributors to the public discourse, the very printedness of that discourse takes on a specially legitimate meaning, because it is categorically differentiated from personal modes of sociability. Mechanical duplication equals publishing precisely insofar as public political discourse is impersonal.

Before examining the principles of this discourse, let us continue to pursue the Maryland author's own understanding of the new public order. He depicts the conditions of his pamphlet's utility, appealing jointly to the nature of representative government and to the act of printing:

It is the Opinion of some very learned Men, that something useful and improving may be collected from the meanest Productions: The Bee gathers honey from all sorts of Flowers to encrease the common Stock, and our Assembly is the common Hive into which every Man's Thoughts and Sentiments ought to be carried, and in which those that are good and useful in themselves ought to receive Life and Vigour . . . The Usefulness of Mens publishing their Thoughts with Candor and Sincerity on the present occasion, will further appear by this consideration, that the Legislators may by examining and comparing Mens Notions and Sentiments, find out all or the chief Advantages and Inconveniences to the People attending a Tobacco-Law.

As in the 1725 preface to the Maryland *Proceedings,* published debate is here presented as public from two different perspectives: freeholders are seen as actively engaged in the civic sphere by their participation in discourse; and legislators find their representative functions in that same discourse. The pamphlet claims the relevance of both perspectives in its full title: *A Letter from a Freeholder, to a Member of the Lower House of Assembly.* These twin perspectives of participation determine the text as an exchange between identifiable persons. In the colonial period by far the most popular genres for political debate were the epistolary pamphlet and the dialogue.

Yet it should be noted that an indispensable tension is visible in the pamphlet's rhetoric. The important thing about this pamphlet and others of its genre is that, although the relation between two correspondents defines the value of participation, that relation cannot be adequate to the medium. The pamphlet is not a personal letter, and *must* not be, in the conditions of the public sphere of representational politics. Writing's unrestricted dissemination appears here as the ground of politics because in its very contrast with personal presence it allows a difference between public discourse and private correspondence. Freeholder and member alike encounter the exchange *not as a relation between themselves as men, but rather as their own mediation by a potentially limitless discourse.* That is why their exchange is not just written, as the pose of correspondence already implies, but also printed in the form of a pamphlet. A consciousness of the medium is carefully sustained, not only in the explicit metacommentary here, but equally in the formalized diction and mode of exposition. And that consciousness of the medium is valued precisely because it remains unreconciled with the conventions of personal exchange.

The meaning of public utterance, for both men, is established by the very fact that their exchange can be read and participated in by any number of unknown and *in principle unknowable* others. No catalogue of empirical readers will exhaust the implied sphere of this discourse. The resulting form of mediated relation (which is not to imply that other relations are unmediated) was to become the paradigmatic political relation of republican America. The assumptions that made it possible could doubtless be translated to oral settings, as long as people agreed to behave as though they were being supervised by an indefinite number of others, any one of whom might occupy their own position irrespective of status. This univer-

salizing mediation of publicity, though possible in any number of contexts, would continue to find its exemplary case in printed discourse. The
more powerful the political norms of the relation became, the more print
discourse would seem special and important.

The surplus of the letter over the relation of correspondents is determined not as the free play of language—indeed, it requires a perfect faith
in the determinacy of meaning—but as the condition of a norm. Following Habermas, we may call this norm (the principle of supervision,) "that
very principle which demands that proceedings be made public." [11] On
the basis of this principle, and in the understanding that its address is a
spectacular transaction, the *Letter* is able to conclude with a reference to
communication that has the force of a threat:

> Thus, Sir, I have given you very candidly my Thoughts on the Pro-
> posals for a *Tobacco-Law;* and I am so far from making any Apology
> for the Trouble I have given you, that I tell you in plain and honest
> *English,* that it is your Duty (if you find any Thing in these my
> Notions, or in those of any other Persons, that shall be communicated
> to you, useful to the Publick,) to endeavour to the utmost of your
> Power, that the Publick may receive the Benefit of 'em; And, that if
> you are byass'd by any private or partial View, prejudicial to your
> Country's Service, you betray the Trust those you represent have
> reposed in you; but I hope for better Things from you, and that you'll
> behave your self as becomes a good Patriot, and an honest Man; upon
> which Terms, and no other, You may always depend on the Vote
> and Interest, as well as the sincere, and hearty good Wishes of, Sir,
>
> Your most humble Servant,
A Free-holder.

There is more involved here than the cantankerousness of an anonymous
author. The avoidance of privacy in the closing remarks is authoritative
because of the principle of supervision that conditions the public sphere
of print discourse. Supervision, in this cultural context, is both a legitimate
threat and the immanent meaning of printedness.

The principle of supervision is a paradoxical kind of discipline. In an
important sense the public official cannot answer to it as a person, by
proving his godliness or his gentlemanliness, because validity in the public
sphere of print discourse holds a negative relation to persons. The *Letter*
does not threaten the Assemblyman in his person—indeed, it warns him
to discount "any private or partial View." Because of this abstractness that
defines the norms of publicity, the same principle of supervision that

disciplines the public official also appears as empowering. It gives the legislator his capacity to represent the whole of the public rather than persons. At the same time, it is balanced by a contradictory emphasis on participation. The pamphlet depicts a freeholder instructing a representative, and a representative legislating for the freeholder; this component of individual participation does not disappear from the pamphlet's rhetoric, even though instruction and legislation are only valid to the extent that they are distinguishable from the personal dimension. The generic pose of correspondence maintains that dimension, while the recognition of printed dissemination (the recognition that correspondence is only a pose) expresses the negation of persons necessary for legitimacy.

As a condition of legitimation, the negation of persons in public discourse is equally important as the principle of supervision. To distinguish this specifically political assumption from the negativity of the symbolic in general, or the universality of truth claims in general, I shall call it the principle of negativity.[12] It is a ground rule of argument in a public discourse that defines its norms as abstract and universal, but it is also a political resource available only in this discourse, and available only to those participants whose social role allows such self-negation (that is, to persons defined by whiteness, maleness, and capital). And although the negativity of persons in the public sphere appears in the form of a positive trait—virtue—it is at this point in the republican tradition that virtue comes to be defined by the negation of other traits of personhood, in particular as rational and disinterested concern for the public good.

We may find the principle of negativity explained in the language of the time by a later contributor to the same tobacco debate. Writing in the pages of Parks's *Maryland Gazette,* one "P.P." defends himself for having published anonymously in the public controversy. He had been accused of cowardice and of insolence because he had brought forth, in what is called an "unprecedented Method," accusations against "a Gentleman"— and that "before the whole Country, in the most public Manner."[13] In a social order of deference and customary law, such action would be most scandalous. But "P.P." argues that persons are irrelevant in the discourse of the public sphere where, he says, assertions are assessed by readers for just reasoning. Public writing can therefore be contrasted with personal testimony, in which "it is absolutely necessary to know the Person of the Witness." "Now P.P. does not pretend," he says of himself, "to know any thing, of his own Knowledge, of the Conduct of any of the [tobacco] Merchants; what he chiefly relies on, is what is publish'd, and has been seen by the Generality of People, as have his Inferences."[14] P.P. here validates his writing by exempting it from any link to himself, a tactic nicely amplified by the use of the third person in naming himself. It is nonetheless a personal tactic and claim, a skillful posture that can be described as a kind of cultural capital. This personal tactic of depersonalization both requires and enables a specialized subsystem of public discourse.

Curiously, P.P. recommends that his accuser read several publications under fictitious names that, by means of their fictive personae, were able to avoid the resistance of "Personal Prejudice." This extra detail about pseudonyms reminds us of the importance of print, as it is here construed, in enabling the virtue of the citizen by the very fact that writing is not regarded as a form of personal presence. The difference between the private, interested person and the citizen of the public sphere appears both as a condition of political validity and as the expression of the character of print. We have already seen that the illimitable readership of print discourse becomes important as the correlative of public supervision; here the apparent absence of a personal author in printed language has become important as the correlative of the principle of negativity. As we shall see, the public discourse of the colonies is marked by a distinct preference for fictitious personae, a preference that expresses the general principle of negativity in representational politics.

P.P. was forced to articulate and defend these constructions because the public discourse of print was still emergent in conflict with other determinations of the public, of personhood, and of language. Many Marylanders were newly encountering such norms of polity and discourse when those norms were being clarified in the course of the tobacco debate, and the institutionalization of print discourse there was not yet secure. Neither the new paradigm of print nor the new paradigm of politics took the field instantaneously, though they appeared together since they made each other mutually intelligible. Moreover, as we might guess from the prominence of imperial and commercial issues in the Maryland public debates, the emergence of the public discourse was not simply a local phenomenon. In the same period similar events were taking place in cities such as Philadelphia and Charleston. For the gentry of the Southern colonies in particular, the development of public debate in print could be a way of keeping in contact with the English, and its spread, though gradual, was unimpeded.

The Boston Currency Crisis

In Boston, where the customary public sphere of Puritan society was more intensely organized, and where a corresponding tradition of printing was already established, the emergence of printed debate took place only in struggle. Since the brief crisis following the dissolution of the Andros regime, manifestly political printing in Massachusetts had consisted almost entirely of the governor's edicts. A newspaper was established in 1704; bearing the bold legend, "Published by Authority," it reproduced edicts of the governor and his imperial superiors, but contained virtually no local political news, much less debate. In 1714, however, a conflict suddenly veered into print with the publication of a handful of pamphlets. It subsided only temporarily, returning in a more critical form by 1720, when political pamphlets were published in then-undreamed-of numbers and occupied the town's attention. Late in 1719 a second Boston newspaper was founded, to be followed in 1721 by a third in the same town (though it was only the fourth in all of colonial America). One writer in the latter paper observed early in 1722, "Letters (I don't mean Learning) grow upon us daily; we have Weekly three News-Letters, and sometimes as many little Books or Pamphlets (I don't say Sermons) published."[15] These developments institutionalized the public sphere of print discourse, though that discourse continued to compete with other modes of legitimation.

As in Maryland, the transformation of the public sphere in Boston began in relation to the market. The central dispute in the Boston crisis was the creation of a currency. A group of merchants, plagued by a chronic monetary shortage that imperial policy had long aggravated, were struggling to establish a new currency of either private or colonial issue. When the Boston merchants first began planning a private bank for the issue of a currency in 1714, the attorney general viewed their project as that of an illegitimate body politic. He accordingly filed a brief in council in August of that year that produced an order that "the Projectors or Undertakers of any such Bank, do not proceed to Print the said Scheme, or put the same on Publick Record, Make or Emit any of their Notes or Bills, until they have laid their Proposals before the Generall Assembly of this Her Majesties Province . . . And that this Order be Printed in the Weekly News Letter."[16] For the council, the control of commerce belonged to customary authority. And so did print: the interdiction against printing assumes an official status for printed texts such as that of the interdiction itself. When the merchants continued to meet and discuss their plans, the attorney general published a pamphlet denouncing the scheme. Indignant that the merchants were "openly carrying on their *Bank*," he argued that all such authority must derive from the crown.[17]

The merchants, who had already reprinted a pamphlet describing a currency scheme, began writing their own pamphlets, thus treating print discourse not as an official channel of customary authority but as a second dimension of the political—an arena of debate distinct from the constituted authority of office. In one pamphlet they describe the interdiction against printing their scheme as "very hard, in that they were denied the benefit of the Press," but they maintain that the ban applied only to the final proclamation of the scheme and not to the debate of its formation.[18] Thus was inaugurated a new public debate in Boston. Many of the pamphlets that followed were distributed free by their sponsors, and most were circulated aggressively. One pamphlet plays on that fact by beginning with a comic scene: "My good Neighbour *Rusticus* quite tir'd out with the *dispersion* of the *Distressed State* from Vill to Vill (like the Circulation of a Country Brief for the Common Charity) came at last puffing to my door, and desired me to Read, and give my thoughts upon it."[19] Another writer claims to have had someone else's pamphlet thrust into his hands on the Exchange.[20] It became common for each pamphlet to review its predecessors. By 1720 a pamphlet called *Reflections upon Reflections* could be stating the obvious when it said that "various Schemes, & projections, and Sentiments of Men (as their particular Interests, and private views have led them) have been exhibited, and almost an infinite number of Pamphlets dispersed thro' the Country."[21]

That same pamphlet, however, goes on to lament the debate, which its author attributes to "such *furious Zeal,* and *Party warmth,* as has ended in Enmity." The idea of a political public of readers still seemed highly problematic. Nothing is more common in the pamphlets of the currency crisis than the theme that the debate itself manifests private and factional interests incompatible with the public good. The attorney general's argument, for example, is dismissed as representing only the "Court interest."[22] Another pamphlet appends cautionary postscripts defining "A Character of a Publick Spirit" as disinterested and "A Character of a Private Spirit" as selfish.[23] Each author denies having personal interests in the outcome. Moreover, each author strikes a defensive posture against the charge of partymongering. John Colman, leader of the merchants, concludes his major pamphlet with the assertion that he is "prejudiced against no Man": "It is the good & Happiness of my Country that lies upon my Spirits and hath Influenced me hereunto. I have no private *sinister* aim in pursuit separate from the good of the whole, but am animated only by a sense of the distresses of the Town and Country, for want of a Medium of Exchange."[24] A respondent felt similarly moved: "Thus, Sir, I have given you my Thoughts with a sincere aim at the Good of my Country; and without prejudice or affection to any Man, or Party of men."[25]

The antiparty theme, which was as prominent in Maryland or South Carolina or Pennsylvania as it was in Boston, has to be distinguished from the norms of a customary public. The latter were invoked by the *Boston News-Letter*'s appeal for people to shut up and lead "quiet and peaceable Lives."[26] Antiparty rhetoric would seem to be a version of the same appeal. But it is peculiarly double-edged. Antiparty rhetoric appears to invoke the earlier, customary norm of subjection insofar as it appears to oppose the existence of the debate itself. In actuality, however, it sustains the debate by providing the categories that would make an ongoing public debate thinkable. The language of resistance to controversy articulates a norm for controversy. *It silently transforms the ideal of a social order free from conflictual debate into an ideal of debate free of social conflict.* One pamphlet puts it this way:

> I wish from my heart that some Method may be found for our relief to prevent Party-making amongst us; it grieves me to see our Divisions which are daily increasing, and which tend only to our ruin; whereas if we would but Unite, and bare with one another in our different Apprehension of Things, debate Matters fairly, and lay aside all private designs, and Animosities, and believe that every Man's particular Interest is comprized in the General, and study sincerely the Publick Good, I am fully perswaded we might contrive ways to Extricate our selves out of these Difficulties, and be as flourishing a People as ever.[27]

This argument, apparently directed against public polemic, already presupposes the norms of public discourse—especially the principle of negativity, which appears here in the call to "lay aside all private designs and animosities." The tone suggests a conservative effort: divisions are increasing, but it is still possible to be "as flourishing a People as ever." The conservative posture, combined with the norm of unity, conceals the innovative character of the ideal of debate. The unity of this debating community will not, after all, be the same as the unity of the past society, since that society had been understood as unified only insofar as it was free of the "Divisions" that created debate.

Similarly, another pamphlet has it:

> The Gentlemen who have Printed their Thoughts on this Occasion, do (as far as I can discern) desire to see their Country in a Flourishing Trade, & Prosperous Condition, as they have seen it formerly; They differ indeed in their Conjectures about the Measures proper

to be taken at this Juncture for this End; But its much to be Lamented, that Gentlemen who desire the good of their Country, can't declare their differing sentiments, about the best Means to promote it, without falling under the Displeasure of those whom they study to serve.[28]

Though intelligible in a social order in which the debate seemed, at least to the governor and council, to be the loss of all public spirit and the degeneration of authority, antiparty rhetoric bore witness to the new discursive norms that constituted both a public sphere and an understanding of print. The use of certain kinds of texts had become natural to the political world.

The court party scarcely witnessed the transformation in complacent silence. The governor was unwilling to treat the semiotic environment of printed debate as special, and equally unwilling (what comes to the same thing) to register the norm of disinterested public debate. Legal proceedings were begun against John Colman, and in 1720 the governor requested new laws to "punish the authors of factious and seditious papers."[29] In effect, the governor wanted to treat the pamphlets in the new print war as the utterances of persons, holding a writer corporally responsible in exactly the same way as a speaker. The Assembly adopted the strategy of appearing to comply, while continuing to allow distribution of free and anonymous print. They also added a barb to their reply to the governor: encouraging the executive to bring authors to punishment, they especially suggested that he prosecute the author of a court-interest pamphlet which, they said, "grossly reflected upon" members of the house. The irony of their recommendation—which reminds the governor that the author he most wishes to prosecute for attacking the government is himself a pillar of the government and under attack by the governor—was a way of resisting the governor's desire to treat print as utterance. Speech, being immersed in the order of traditional power relations, left little room for the members of the Assembly to defy the governor. But they could defy him in allowing print to circulate under the rule of objects—treating pamphlets for the time being as a material commodity like any other—rather than under the rule of utterances. In so doing, the Assembly was not just evading the governor's authority, but implicitly locating power on different grounds.

The restructuring of power in the struggle over models of legitimation and discourse raises the question of who the agents in the struggle were, and what their interests in it might have been. In the eyes of the governor's party, the debate was a class problem, a view shared by the historian Gary Nash, who lays great stress on the episode. Nash sees in the currency crisis a turn toward populist politics. The pamphlets, he writes, "made direct appeals to the people, both those who enjoyed the vote and others who participated in the larger arena of street politics," and "were intended to make politics everyone's concern." According to Nash, print discourse was consumed by an artisan class that was not otherwise accustomed to adjudicating political affairs. "It was testimony to the power behind the printed word that even those who yearned for a highly restricted mode of politics were compelled to set their views in print for all to read. For unless they did, their opponents might sweep the field."[30]

Yet the difference between the old and new modes of politics was more than a matter of degrees of restriction. The pamphlets enact not so much an impulse of liberalization as the *abstraction* of the public, establishing the impersonality of its norms and the negativity of its citizens. Doubtless the transformation was motivated rather than arbitrary, and doubtless the self-understandings of economic classes were elements of its motivation. At the same time, the self-understanding of those classes, and thus their interests and nature, were at stake in the transformation. The currency dispute in Boston, like a similar dispute in Philadelphia, or like the tobacco-regulation debate in Maryland, gave a new identity to market society and legitimated new organizations of economy.

By seeing the debate as a turn toward populist politics, Nash also observes that the generalized public discourse potentially legitimated the participation of any class. This potential lay in the negativity that defined the citizen in the printed public discourse, since participation could be legitimate despite personality, faith, class, or other criteria of validity. Yet it would be easy to be misled by the potential of this principle of negativity, since it was incapable of extending itself by its own dynamic. Radical though the principle seems in retrospect, it did not in practice allow access to the public arena for women, or blacks, or Indians, or the unpropertied, or various persons classed as criminal. It was only because of the covert identification of print consumption with the community of propertied white males that public discourse came about in the first place. Because the same differentials of gender, race, and class allocated both citizenship, on one hand, and active literacy, on the other hand, freehold and discourse could coincide without necessarily entailing a liberalization of power. The posture of negation that served as the entry qualification to the specialized subsystem of public discourse remained a positive dis-

48

position of character, a resource available only to a specific subset of the community.

The principle of the citizen's negativity was not necessarily liberalizing as long as the covert distinction of the print community could be maintained, since in the new paradigm the print public could be equated with the political public. The principle of negativity, however, did mean that the constitutive distinctions of the political community had to *remain* covert. In situations where excluded groups were able to sustain a claim to discursive participation, the principle of negativity could be a powerful legitimating standard. In the case of Boston the currency crisis articulated the (white male) community of the market as society. In that situation (white male) artisans were politicized by print discourse, even though the abstraction of print remained incapable, by itself, of materially affecting lines of race and gender except by reproducing them in a masked form.

New York and the Zenger Case

As in Boston, the transformation of the public sphere in New York came about through the difficult emergence of a local print discourse, the difficulty of which was dramatized in a hotly contested political trial. What is particularly revealing is that it was the trial of a printer, John Peter Zenger, for seditious libel. The case has a certain notoriety in American legal history because it became the subject of nationalist legend in the nineteenth century. In this legendary history Zenger appears as a patriotic hero fighting for American liberties and founding the principles behind the first amendment. More recently the Zenger case has been the subject of a backlash among historians, who are now more likely to describe him as a poor pawn in a civic feud, a tradesman hired by the Morris faction because he was conveniently available, and one who played little more than a mechanical role in the events that now bear his name. According to the old Whig legend, Zenger's lawyer Andrew Hamilton was thought to have revolutionized liberty if not by inventing freedom of the press then at least by securing it on these shores. In the current historical literature it is sadly pointed out that prosecutions for seditious libel continued to occur on a regular basis. As late as 1798 the Alien and Sedition Acts could be passed without being impeded by the precedent of the Zenger case.[31]

Both the legendary history of the Zenger case and its debunking counterhistory share a set of modern liberal assumptions about the relation between the press and the law, as well as about the relation between persons and political discourse. It is assumed on both sides that the moral consciences of the colonists were equipped with an idea of free and unbiased mass media. In the Whig version the colonists are thought to have acted heroically on the basis of conscience by establishing the Zenger case as a precedent, while in modern legal history they appear to have betrayed their shabby ignorance and moral cowardice in failing to sustain the precedent. And for both Whig history and libertarian lament, freely competitive public debate is assumed to be the natural expression of political personhood. Because of such assumptions the historical literature typically misses the important developments in the public sphere that are exemplified in the Zenger case. If we stand back from the nationalism and preoccupation with precedent that have dominated this disagreement, it is possible to see the trial as an especially illuminating crisis in the joint transformations of print discourse and the public sphere. In particular, the trial reveals the stakes of power involved in the transformation.

The conflict leading up to the trial was one over the sources of law. William Cosby, in his turbulent and relatively brief career as governor of New York in the early 1730s, seemed to the colonials determined to play the role of the despot. He laid absolute claim to the spoils of his office; he treated the courts as administering justice at his pleasure, dismissing recalcitrant justices; he tried to avoid dependence on the General Assembly, and even attempted to rig elections; and he invoked imperial authority whenever customary legal and judicial procedures obstructed his plans. Such actions depended on a status-based model of legitimation that posited ultimate sovereignty in the crown—a model that until recently had been dominant in England and continued to organize many parts of the imperial administration despite the increasing importance of Parliament in English affairs. Local leaders in New York had different allegiances, in part to the traditions of common law, which gave them a high degree of local autonomy and made state administration dependent on local custom, and in part to the abstract norms and procedures of predictability that organized the emerging society of the capitalist market. Both the norms of custom and the norms of the market sometimes conflicted with the status model of legitimation on which the imperial administration rested.[32]

To an influential group of New Yorkers led by Lewis Morris, a Supreme Court justice whom Cosby had replaced, Cosby was a threat to their own local power and, more generally, to the system of customary law on which their power was based. Morris organized an opposition and sailed for London to plead for Cosby's removal. More consequential was the strategy of Morris' associates, the lawyers James Alexander and William Smith, who, in the fall of 1733, hired the almost unknown printer John Peter Zenger to establish a newspaper. Until that point there had been only one newspaper in New York: William Bradford's *New York Gazette.* A contributor to Zenger's new paper, the *New-York Weekly Journal,* would soon describe the *Gazette* as "a paper known to be under the direction of the government, in which the Printer of it is not suffered to insert anything but what his superiors approve of, under the penalty of losing £50 per annum salary and the title of the King's Printer for the Province of New York."[33] Implicit in this kind of language is a norm of public discourse, and in the long run the development of the emergent model of the public sphere would make far more difference in the structure of power than would Morris' London lobbying efforts. In the short term as well, both the content of the *Journal* and the norms of publicity implied by its discourse were recognized as a threat to the legitimacy of the governor's administration. Morris himself had published a pamphlet attacking Cosby, and the word in London was that the main count against his appeal to the ministry was his "writing his own Case & appealing to the Country."[34] Despite administrative resistance, as Alexander and Smith seem to have understood, the emerging power in the colonial periphery was neither the imperial sovereignty nor local custom, but the public of political discourse.

Conscious of the novelty of their opposition paper in New York, Alexander and Smith began in the *Journal*'s first essay to offer a theory of print that would at the same time be an antidynastic theory of legitimacy. "The liberty of the press," they announced in the first sentence, "is a subject of the greatest importance, and in which every individual is as much concerned as he is in any other part of liberty."[35] "Liberty" in the eighteenth century meant specifically civic liberty—not just freedom from restraint of any kind, but the power of exerting oneself in the civic sphere. The word resonated with the whole of republican political thought; even to speak of "the liberty of the press" was to treat print within a highly charged political language. The local appeal of this language was that it could articulate colonial resistance to administrative power. Alexander and Smith therefore stress that the utility of the press lies in its ability to challenge administrative abuse. Depicting an "evil minister," they argue that published reports of his actions, "by watching and exposing his actions," will bring him into censure.

What is transparent to us but scandalous to contemporaries is the assumption that the censure of readers is a legitimate way to coerce officials. Governor Cosby himself, in a letter to the Duke of Newcastle, referred to the "paper warr" launched by Alexander and Smith as an attempt to have the government "prostituted to ye censure of ye mob."[36] One hostile writer commenting on the Zenger case condemned those New Yorkers who mistook "the liberty of the press for a license to write and publish infamous things of their superiors."[37] The disagreement here discloses a structural conflict between two sets of assumptions: a social order in which "superiors" has a referent; and a discursive order in which the act of reading can be equivalent to the political act of censure.

In a social order based on status, such as that of colonial New York, it did not strictly matter whether the published censure of an official were true or not. Even if true, such publication would be regarded as the defamation of a superior. As John Peter Zenger would find out, English law held the truth of an accusation to be an *aggravation* of libel rather than a defense against it. Since more people would believe a true libel than a false one, it would do greater damage to the esteem in which officials must be held. Long before charges of libel were filed, however, Alexander and Smith were elaborating a concept of the social use of publication that would not only legitimate but require defamation. "When did calumnies and lies ever destroy the character of one good minister?" they ask. "If their characters have been clouded for a time, yet they have generally shined forth in greater luster."[38] The scrutiny brought about by critical publication validates the good official.

Clearly, the assumption behind this concept of publication is the principle of supervision, and the *Journal* authors express it in a remarkably revealing sentence: "The facts exposed are not to be believed because said or published; but it [publication] draws people's attention, directs their view, and fixes the eye in a proper position that everyone may judge for himself whether those facts are true or not."[39] While this sentence takes the principle of supervision as a presupposition, on the level of explicit content it offers a strikingly literal trope of supervision: a drawn attention, a directed view, and a fixed eye. The sense of sight is not necessarily more appropriate to the public world than any other sense is; yet the optic and spatializing metaphor of supervision became in eighteenth-century America the dominant way of conceptualizing the public. Like the earlier metaphor of the "far-stretched view" which we have seen in John Markland's *Typographia*, the *Journal*'s metaphoric supervision refers to a disposition of character that makes reading a valuable action. And it is the specificity of *reading* as the paradigmatic public action that lies behind the literalizing trope of supervision. The sentence unwittingly implies that when the virtuous citizen fixes his vigilant eye upon the civic scene, what he is looking at is a printed object. And because his gaze upon the material artifact of print is equivalent to the "popular examination" of officials, in Alexander's words, it follows that the press, in a republic with corrupt leaders, is naturally an opposition press (or, more generally, a regulative press).

The same sentence exemplifies the principle of negativity, to which the principle of supervision is closely related. "The facts exposed are not to be believed because said or published." The authority of published assertions is deferred to the validating inspection of the reading citizen. And because their authority is deferred, so is the responsibility for them. The *Journal* authors did not deny that there could be an abuse of the press, but they ambiguated the relation between such abuse and the responsibility of particular, authorizing persons. "I agree with [Bradford] that it is the Abuse, and not the Use of the Press, is blameable," one essay says. "But the Difficulty Lies who shall be the Judges of this Abuse . . . I would have the Readers Judges: But they cant Judge, if nothing is wrote."[40] The same deferred authority that results in the principle of supervision here implies the principle of negativity: political assertions can be made neutrally, since their validity will be determined by the impersonal judgment of the general readership. In this important sense, publication is no longer to be considered as personal utterance.

Bradford's *Gazette* was quick to challenge these implications. "Is the Art of Printing less criminal than Natural Speaking?" a *Gazette* author asked rhetorically. "Nature has given us the Liberty of Speech, but that will not protect a Man from having his Head broke, if he gives ill Language."[41] The governor, sharing the same desire to have somebody's head broke after the *Journal* printed some harsh criticism of his administration, and sharing the same skepticism about the negativity claimed by the *Journal*'s authors, had a charge of seditious libel filed against the printer. Zenger was taken to prison, where he remained for a full eight months before his case came to trial. The trial itself seemed destined to uphold the governor. To begin with, the judges were his hand-picked dependents. When Alexander and Smith, acting as defense counsel, challenged the legitimacy of the judges' commissions, the judges responded by disbarring them. Moreover, the legal case lay against Zenger. English law not only forbade evidence of truth as defense against libel charges, it decreed that the libelousness of a text was to be determined by the bench. Only the facts of printing or writing were to be determined by the jury, and Zenger's own journeyman and two sons were waiting in the court to testify that he had in fact printed the *Journal*. (Their testimony in any case would have been a formality; it is recorded that the jury knew this already, having themselves bought the *Journal* in Zenger's shop.)[42]

Zenger's new lawyer, the Philadelphian Andrew Hamilton, in the face of this seemingly closed case, pursued an entirely different line in the defense. Rather than defend Zenger on the terms constructed by the law, he conceded the relevant facts at the opening of the trial. Then, after the prosecution witnesses had been dismissed, he began an argument that in effect challenged the construction of political utterance that the prosecution case assumed. The first step in the defense was to introduce evidence about the truthfulness of the *Journal* articles named in the charges against Zenger. In doing so, he invoked the republican political principle that censure of an official is an exercise of virtue rather than a violation of status. But this line of defense was rejected by the court. Hamilton next turned to the jury, to whom he delivered a forceful appeal to decide not just the facts of the case, as precedent prescribed (and which he had already admitted), but the law of the case as well.

Hamilton's turn to the jury was powerfully overdetermined. Part of its strength lay in the appeal to custom and local tradition. The jury system, derived as it was from the common law and allowing a high degree of local consensual autonomy in the use of coercion, represented exactly the forms of power threatened by the growing imperial bureaucracy. Appealing to the jury to set the law, Hamilton was also appealing to the sociopolitical base of the original conflict with Cosby. But his arguments to the jury superimpose, on this appeal to custom and local autonomy, the substantially different discursive norms of the new public sphere. He justified the appeal to the jury in the same language of deferred authority, supervision, and negativity with which Alexander had described print. The exchange is worth following in some detail in order to see how this double appeal to custom and to publicity came about.

First, Hamilton baited the prosecution by asking for a definition of libels. The prosecutor's definition emphasized defamation, including that of language understood to be "ironical or scoffing." Hamilton responded:

> Ay, Mr. Attorney; but what certain standard rule have the books laid down, by which we can certainly know whether the words or the signs are malicious? Whether they are defamatory? . . . And what rule have you to know when I write ironically? I think it would be hard, when I say *such a man is a very worthy honest gentleman, and of fine understanding,* that therefore I meant *he was a knave or a fool . . .* Or

how can you know whether a man did not think as he wrote? For by your rule, if he did, it is no *irony,* and consequently no *libel.*[43]

Hamilton then seized on the word "understood" in the prosecutor's definition.

> Here it is plain the words are scandalous, scoffing and ironical only as they are UNDERSTOOD. I know no rule laid down in the books but this, I mean, as the words are *understood.*
>
> *Mr. Chief Justice.* Mr. Hamilton, do you think it so hard to know when words are ironical, or spoke in a scoffing manner?
>
> *Mr. Hamilton.* I own it may be known; but I insist, the only rule to know is, as I do or can *understand* them; I have no other rule to go by, but as I *understand* them.

None of Hamilton's argument so far did anything obvious to advance Zenger's defense, and Chief Justice De Lancey conceded the apparently trivial point.

> *Mr. Chief Justice.* That is certain. All words are libelous or not, as they are *understood.* Those who are to judge of the words must judge whether they *are scandalous* or *ironical, tend to the breach of the peace,* or are *seditious:* There can be no doubt of it.[44]

This exchange about interpretation set the stage for the climax of the trial. In the eloquent speech that followed Hamilton took the already conceded point about the test of understanding for irony or libel as an argument that the meaning of an utterance is deferred to its interpretation. He then in effect gave that principle a political meaning. Whereas Chief Justice De Lancey took the theoretical point to be consistent with his own role (he is clearly thinking about himself when he says "Those who are to judge of the words"), Hamilton argued that the only interpretation that could indicate irony or libel would be a socially general one. The relevant interpretation, therefore, had to be performed by the jury rather than the judge. "The law," he told the jury, "supposes you to be summoned *out of the neighborhood where the fact is alleged to be committed;* and the reason of your being taken out of the neighborhood is *because you are supposed to have the best knowledge of the fact that is to be tried.*"[45]

In Hamilton's courtroom performance, the jury's being taken "out of the neighborhood" refers ambiguously to their immediacy and to their mediation. He was clearly referring to their local roots, their embeddedness in the norms of custom and the politics of community. At the same time, he was referring to their representative plurality. Since the jury represents the neighborhood *in general,* their interpretation can be taken to indicate a properly social judgment rather than an interested one. Only in this latter sense could Hamilton's appeal to the jury conceivably follow from his argument about interpretation, especially since De Lancey, a New Yorker, could claim as much local knowledge as the jury members. The dependence of meaning on interpretation was thus understood in the Zenger trial as requiring a universality of judgment that militated against hierarchy. The success of Hamilton's performance, however, depended on his ability to conflate that implicit norm of abstract universality with the customary norm of local consensus. This delicate overdetermination made localism and universality indistinguishable and equally opposed to the hierarchy of imperial administration.

The rest is well known: the jury returned a verdict of not guilty. The courtroom broke into cheers for Hamilton, and he was carried jubilantly into the streets. (Zenger, meanwhile, had to return to prison for another night before he was released.) Regardless of whatever role it may have had in setting legal precedent, I take the Zenger case to be representative of prerevolutionary colonial politics in at least three ways. First, it demonstrates with clarity how the discursive norms of the public sphere required a specific understanding of print. A writer for the *New York Journal* in 1770 would make the connection clear in a way that had by then become commonplace. Citing the Zenger case as an illustration, he writes, "*Public grievances* can never be redressed but by *public complaints;* and they cannot well be made *without the Press.*"[46] Second, the case shows that the new discursive norms of print were articulated as a model of legitimacy that had revolutionary potential. The universality claimed by print discourse could be extended to an understanding of society as the agent of supervision. Third, the Zenger case shows how the success of that articulation depended on an overdetermined relation between publicity and custom. For forty years after the trial, resistance to the crown would increasingly be legitimated in the abstract and universalizing norms of public print discourse, though that resistance would be mobilized in the local politics of custom—an unstable alliance that, as we shall see, would break down after the Revolution.

In the same way, the norms of publicity often appeared in an unstable overdetermination with religion. As we saw earlier in this chapter, colonial religion involved an ideology of consensus and unitary authority. Its model of the public sphere presupposed an ideal of determinate truth and collective agreement. But the usual means of brokering such a consensus were already strained in the period of the Glorious Revolution.[47] And by the 1730s and 1740s they suffered considerable erosion in the face of the Great Awakening. For that reason recent historians have emphasized that the Awakening's religious conflicts were important in accustoming people to contention. What had been professional issues among the clergy became subjects of public discussion, often in print. When this happened, the norms of publicity were in tension with the norms of traditional religion. The Awakening therefore could have results similar to those of printed political debate, bringing about a critical break with the order of traditional authority. As Patricia Bonomi has pointed out, a central issue of the Awakening was "the divisibility, or as some argued the indivisibility, of ecclesiastical authority." The result was a "shift from collective to individual accountability."[48]

Bonomi also shows that themes from religious dispute could later be used in legitimating political resistance. As religious dispute became more normalized, colonists extended the norms of the new public sphere in place of the customary order of traditional religion. But important tensions remained. Even at the height of the Awakening and its contention, none of the evangelicals imagined dispute as a routine, normalized feature of the social order. Some of them understood the requirements of conscience as a minority right, allowing individuals to withdraw from customary associations. None, however, imagined such division as a normal condition of discourse. Yet that is just what the public sphere of print discourse presupposed.

A remark of Jonathan Edwards is a convenient illustration of this tension. He complains in 1735 that some converts were "*themselves* publishing their own experiences from time to time and from place to place, on all occasions and before all companies . . . [in] common *conversation*."[49] Here even Edwards worries that the new evangelicals will not be able to establish their own model of collective accountability, that conscience will not be mediated by the public order. What is published will now be as multiform as mere conversation. Edwards uses the word "publishing" in a sense now foreign to us because neither he nor the converts he writes about are governed by the norms of the new print discourse. By publishing he means the collectivization of truth. The act of publishing for him still implies, as on some level it does for all of the evangelicals, a norm of collective conversion and unitary authority. That is the norm, after all, that drives converts to convert others.

Religion and the public print discourse continued to operate under different versions of the metapolitics of speech. No matter how much religious contention the colonists experienced during the Awakening, religion continued to pull against the normalization of social division, eventually requiring a separation of church and state that would mark a key victory for the cultural forces of the public sphere. Nevertheless, while the norms of the public sphere were still emerging, they often appeared in an overdetermined unity with the Awakening's drive toward dissent and the rupture of traditional consensus. That apparent unity was no doubt crucial to the success of both.

The Public Sphere and Representational Polity

The overdetermined politics of the Zenger case also help us to see why it was not an unambiguous legal precedent. From the emergence of public debate in print until the Stamp Act, legislatures alternately imposed severe restrictions on the press and presented themselves as the defenders of the liberty of the press. They could defend in glorious rhetoric those who published criticisms of imperial officers, while peremptorily jailing those who published criticisms of representatives. We have already seen, for example, that in the case of the Boston currency crisis the Assembly gave the governor an apparently contradictory response to his claim that the pamphlets were libelous. That contradictory response—prosecute and don't prosecute—is typical of the behavior of legislatures with respect to print discourse, and although the doubleness of their actions is regarded by some modern historians as malicious hypocrisy, it is more properly seen as the result of the paradoxical relation between public discourse and political representation.[50] On one hand, the new role of the press entailed the principle of supervision, which exerted the force of discipline on legislators. On the other hand, that same principle of supervision empowered representatives by raising them from being parties in an Aristotelian alliance of orders to being the embodiment of the basic principle of the political.

Like so many other political developments in the colonies, the rise of the legislatures was parallel to a similar movement in England, for it was only in the middle decades of the eighteenth century that Parliament ceased to be an essentially conciliar body, protecting certain rights from the sovereign, and itself became the sovereign administrative body.[51] In the colonies as in England, the rise of the legislatures to such a representative sovereign status was gradual. Colonial society accorded relatively little of its coercive power to assemblies, to bureaucracies, or to positive law of any kind; most of the business of governing and coercion was done by the common-law institutions of the court system.[52] But the print public sphere was a different kind of social arrangement. Unlike common-law institutions, it did not require faith in consensus and allowed the legitimation of positive law. The legislatures, in their representative character, institutionalized the structural elements of the public sphere, and in their ongoing contests with imperial administrations the assemblies of most colonies promoted the press as a way of displacing criteria of legitimacy in their favor.

Paradoxically, we might say that the close relation between emergent legislative sovereignty and emergent public discourse was nowhere more clear than when legislatures responded to attacks on themselves by prosecuting for libel. Colonial accounts of the usefulness of the press—such as the essays in Zenger's *Journal*—invariably take the example of a corrupt administrative official rather than a representative. A legislative body, because it was representative of the people, was in an ambiguous position with respect to the people's action of supervision. Insofar as print discourse was understood as effecting a "popular examination" into the affairs of the public, legislatures could claim to be the agents, and thus not the objects, of that examination. That is why the Pennsylvania Assembly could claim in 1757 that as a representative body they could not be the objects of republican supervision: "A sheriff may be corrupted, a jury packed, a court who hold their commissions during pleasure may be influenced; but it is unnatural to assume that the representative body of the people should be partial, corrupted, or do injustice."[53] The ambiguity in the relation between legislatures and supervision was all the greater as customary authority was strategically conflated with publicity. Legislatures increasingly were learning to present themselves as the agents of publicity, but they also wanted to challenge the administrative machinery in the name of local custom. When criticism of legislatures was published, publicity and custom suddenly separated with respect to the authority of the representatives. The representatives were often unprepared for the supervision that was the basis of their legitimacy in the emergent public sphere, being more familiar with customary grounds for the legitimacy of their authority.

What made the tension especially acute for delegates was that the new criteria of publicity were spelled out not only in the official publications of the legislature, nor in unofficial debates about legislative action, but also in a growing campaign literature. Many works of this kind were broadsides, cheap and easy to post in traveled areas or on tavern walls.

Others were pamphlets, often very successful in setting the agenda for local discussion. A sample of their titles indicates their purpose: *To the Freeholders & Freemen* (Philadelphia, 1727); *A Letter to the Freeholders and Other Inhabitants of the Massachusetts-Bay* (Newport, R.I., 1739; another pamphlet of the same title appeared in Boston in 1749); *A Letter to the Freeholders and other Inhabitants of this Province, Qualified to Vote for Representatives in the Ensuing Election* (Boston, 1742); *A Letter to the Freemen and Freeholders of the City of New-York* (New York, 1750); and *A Letter to the Common People of the Colony of Rhode-Island* (Providence, 1763). As this discourse grew, representatives more and more defined themselves by the strictures and empowerments of its spectacular terms.

Beginning in 1715, the Massachusetts Assembly had its votes and debates published. In 1721 Elisha Cooke, a leading Boston merchant, inaugurated a very literal version of print supervision when he drew up a set of instructions for the representatives from Boston, had it printed, and submitted it to the town meeting for approval.[54] In the late 1720s a dispute between the Massachusetts Assembly and the royal governor over the fixing of the governor's salary developed into a question of the publicity of representation. The Assembly, denying the salary, took the position of the defender of the people's liberties. With some prefatory gestures toward discretion in making sensitive affairs known, it published an account of the dispute with the texts of the exchanges. The Assembly expressed high confidence that the people of the towns would read the material, "which at most," it claimed, "can be but a few hours Work." The governor called the strategy an attempt to "cry up the Knowledge of the Country People"; and indeed, although the publication was conceived in a power struggle internal to the government, it was justified as an appeal to the people for instructions.[55] This legitimating appeal was more than a mere tactical maneuver, since it legitimated the Assembly's power only by deriving it from a public discourse in which the representatives offered to be supervised. As one historian points out, the dispute "helped determine the meaning of representation," as the legislature developed its representative character as the ground of its distinction from the executive, and the ground of its opposition to the executive. By the time of the Stamp Act crisis, the same historian writes, the Assembly would present itself "as an agent of public opinion."[56] In such processes the legitimation criteria of the new print discourse were built into political institutions, governing political relations in a wide range of official and unofficial contexts.

Far from being a minor adjustment in the rhetoric of and about officials, the rise of the public discourse was one of the decisive innovations of the

modern era. It enabled nothing less than the newly important differentiation between society and the state. This distinction, the premise of so
much eighteenth-century social thought, carried with it the set of related
distinctions classically studied by Weber, such as that between officer and
office. It is without doubt one of the main reasons why modernity and
printing have been associated ever since. Yet the decisive factor was not
printing in general, but the specialized discursive subsystem that was
articulated through special conventions for print. Only by means of a
public discourse could bureaucratic institutions develop, because state and
society became differentiated in the appearance of the principle of supervision, which in turn was imaginable only when a supervising agency
could be given definition in distinction from the appointed and elected
officials whom it would supervise. In the juridical practices of common
law, where legislative and coercive power lay in a jury system predicated
on ethical unity, no such boundary could be drawn.

What is this supervising agency? The literal answer might be the freeholders, except that as the occupants of the perspective of public discourse
any such freeholders are distinguished from the exercise of office which is
otherwise their capacity. In this sense the "public," "society," or "the
people" have only a negative existence in relation to the official embodiment of power. Subjects find themselves within these large categories as
private persons to the extent that the public discourse makes available to
them their privative relation to the state.

In another sense, however, society and the public acquired a positive—
though unrecognized—identity in the transmission of print. The public
was constructed on the basis of its metonymic embodiment in printed
artifacts. That is how it was possible to imagine the public supervising the
actions of officials even when no physical assembly of the public was
taking place. By midcentury, newspapers were being published regularly
in the major towns and were sustaining an abstract but local political
discourse. Pamphlets and broadsides were a familiar and normal feature
of politics. In their routine dispersion, and in the conventions of discourse
that allowed them to be political in a special way, these artifacts represented the material reality of an abstract public: a *res publica* of letters.
Important consequences followed both for the public and for print. Unlike the public of the customary order, which was always incarnated in
any relation between persons and which found its highest expression in
church and town meetings, the public of print discourse was an abstract
public *never localizable in any relation between persons.* By the same token,
print became publication in a newly privileged way, since it was only in

print discourse that one could make things public for the now abstract public.

The coexistence of dispersed printed objects took on a political meaning because these objects were understood to be generally recognized by others. In their readability they held tangible promise of a universal mutual recognition. Yet the dispersed readability of printed objects could not have had this promise until it became the feature of a specifically political discourse, for only then could the simultaneous reading of printed objects have the meaning of social interaction as the readers' mutual recognition. It must be emphasized also that the mutual recognition promised in print discourse was not an interaction between particularized persons, but among persons constituted by the negating abstraction of themselves. The impersonality ascribed to printed objects was the condition of their promise as a discourse of political interaction.

Printed artifacts were not the only metonym for an abstract public. Currency and commodities in general were also important. It was not accidental that the public debates of print discourse took shape in relation to emergent forms of currency and commerce. Public discourse articulated a society of which the North American colonies were only the furthest periphery, a society of commerce and regulation that had developed from the great early Renaissance fairs to the markets of international commerce. Printing in Western culture has always owed much of its character to the fact that it developed as a trade within this world of the fairs and the markets. Printers sold their products as goods and advertised other goods. They also printed the experimental new paper currencies of the eighteenth century, as well as the increasingly detailed public trade reports. Early colonial newspapers were often frankly founded for the promotion of trade, and most of the early public discourse of print is devoted to the regulation of trade.[57]

As the public discourse developed, the market and the public came to be capable of mutual clarification. A common theme in the procurrency pamphlets, for example, is that an issue of currency will benefit all citizens, even those who are not debtors or merchants. The argument is based on the premise that market agents, though real, are in principle not identifiable in advance. (The same premise underlies one pamphlet's assertion that the projected bankers would have to "let their Books lie open for any Man in the Province to Subscribe his Sum.")[58] Given the context of the emergent perceptions of print, the print readership also represented an audience that was real but in principle not identifiable. The value of print and the value of currency equally required the potential for inexhaustible transmission, while the character of publication and the character of economic exchange equally required norms of impersonal relations. Public discourse and the market were mutually clarifying, then, in both their positive and negative characters: positive, because both public and market were metonymically realized in printed, mass-produced artifacts; negative, because the private subject finds his relation to both the public and the market only by negating the given reality of himself, thereby considering himself the abstract subject of the universal (political or economic) discourse.

The economy of discourse resulting from this mutual articulation was the decisive feature of print capitalism. I take the term "print capitalism" from Benedict Anderson's provocative study of nationalism. For Anderson, print capitalism was the historical development that made possible the emergence of the transcendent, imaginary communities of nations.[59] Unfortunately, his brief book leaves his suggestion relatively undeveloped and the term undefined. Observing that books were the first capitalized commodities, Anderson goes on to argue that their readers—especially the readers of novels—labor to imagine a community of which they are a part even though the identity of that community does not allow a local proximity. The community of readership is a corporate body realized only metonymically, and this imaginary community, in Anderson's view, is the elemental form of the nation. In the articulated relation between print and capitalism that the Boston and Maryland debates illustrate we can see that Anderson's term is more apt than he himself has shown. The imagination of community constructs the political nation not just indirectly, through novels, but directly, in the creation of the public sphere.

Republicanism as Metadiscourse

Any historian of the period will have noted that all the examples of public discourse I have given are also examples of republican rhetoric. In the practices of print discourse the American creoles elaborated a public sphere by means of their elaboration of the conceptual vocabulary of republicanism, and vice versa. Elaborating the republican vocabulary filled the need continually to make and remake a fit between the public discourse and the social world. Republicanism in this context means more than the republican political arguments advanced in printed debates. It is what J. G. A. Pocock calls "the language of republicanism": a conceptual vocabulary that made the whole range of republican political arguments possible.[60] By the same token, republican ideology was also an ideology of print in that its central categories—at least in the colonial American version of republicanism—were articulated in, and thus given meaning within, the symbolic practices of publication. We have already seen several examples: for one, the antiparty rhetoric of the Boston currency crisis simultaneously gave meaning to the practice of publishing and to the republican norm of disinterest. To honor the powerfully republican character of the arguments in the Zenger case, the city of New York gave Hamilton a gold snuffbox inscribed with republican mottoes (an act that was soon denounced from as far away as Barbados).[61]

Historians have observed, at least since Timothy Breen's *Character of the Good Ruler* and Bernard Bailyn's *Ideological Origins of the American Revolution,* that a powerful strain of republican rhetoric, associated in England with Whig or Country traditions, began to flourish in the colonies at about the same time as the Boston currency crisis.[62] Though the commonwealth tradition was scarcely unknown to the Puritans,[63] in the early eighteenth century the republican categories of Country politics rapidly took hold throughout the colonies to organize political interests and conflicts. Politics came to be conceptualized increasingly in terms of virtue and corruption, interest and disinterestedness, public and party, liberty and power. These categories were not simply those of learned argument but, more powerfully, those of cliché and common sense.

For this reason, nearly any example from the printed debates will also illustrate republicanism. Let us consider a pamphlet entitled *English Advice to the Freeholders, &c. of the Province of the Massachusetts-Bay.* Signed "Brutus and Cato," the pamphlet, which was printed in 1722 by James Franklin (no doubt with the assistance of his then apprentice brother), is a prime instance of print supervision in the emergent republican paradigm. It begins by noting the upcoming May elections and appeals with a rhetoric of urgency for the election of "Patriots," "especially in the *House of Representatives,* who are the *Guardians of the People's Liberty.*" The author is then able to add: "Remember (Countrymen) that Liberty is a Jewel of an inestimable Value, which when once lost, is seldom recovered again . . . One way to keep it, is, to chuse good Men to *represent* you; such as dare boldly exert themselves for the *publick Good,* by making Laws that will secure you from any Attempts that may be form'd to your Prejudice by succeeding Rulers" (3–4).

The general republican sentiments are presented as obvious and nonargumentative. Even supporters of the incumbent officials could concede the praise of active liberty and the ideal of the public good. Thus the speaker says only, "Remember . . ." Within this profession of the obvious lies a whole set of interpretive categories and normative assumptions about power and personhood. To begin with, the cliché represents liberty as imperiled by rulers and requiring rigorous civic exertion against their ever-threatening encroachment. The assumptions that make this cliché intelligible include a notion of place-holding as corruptive, of virtue as active but disinterested participation in the civic sphere, and of the opposition between general concerns and private interests. Where such rhetoric had been traditionally oppositional in the English context, for the North American creoles it could define the colonial situation in the administrative empire generally, a fact that would later be of some consequence.[64]

In this context, referring to the civic exertions that preserve liberty was also a way of thinking about the public discourse itself. Every citizen (read: white, landowning male) is assumed by the pamphlet's author to have an interest in monitoring the actions of rulers with a critical intention. Though ultimately this interest will require the election of public-minded representatives, an even clearer way of monitoring the ever-renewed threat to liberty is through discourse of the kind embodied by *English Advice*. This is how the principle of supervision comes into being. I have treated it as single principle, whereas in fact it was enunciated through a wide range of very different assertions about politics. There is a common element to these republican clichés about liberty, power, and corruption—one that allows us to summarize them as the principle of supervision: together they form a cultural understanding of the desirable uses of print. Republican rhetoric and the discursive conditions of the public sphere rendered each other intelligible. In the very act of giving advice about liberty and power, the pamphlet provides the categories of its own utility. In this sense, colonial republicanism can be described as a metadiscourse.

It is doubtless for this reason that the traditions of republican rhetoric most favored in the colonies were those that developed as a metadiscourse of printed debate in England. The most popular republican texts in the colonies included works such as *The Spectator* and, perhaps even more importantly, *Cato's Letters*.[65] Both were periodical series, and both incorporate their ongoing—even routine—appearance in print as an assumption about political legitimacy. For Addison and Steele, and even more for Trenchard and Gordon, political publication is far from being a deviation from social order produced by crisis. What they fear is not a society riddled with political publications but a society without them. This normative routinization of print discourse underlies the very idea of the serial essay. The first *Spectator* boldly advertised: "To be Continued every Day." Even though colonial printers were limited to weeklies, the serial essay became almost universally adopted as the showpiece of American newspapers.

The authors of these British essays, like those of their American counterparts, devoted their labors to the elaboration of terms that would allow continuous, normal, normative publication. The character of the Spectator is himself designed for that function. Here is his famous introduction:

> I have observed, that a Reader seldom peruses a Book with Pleasure, 'till he knows whether the Writer of it be a black or a fair Man, of a mild or cholerick Disposition, Married or a Batchelor, with other Particulars of the like nature, that conduce very much to the right understanding of an Author.[66]

Though no republican political arguments have yet been advanced, the Spectator has already established the Country posture of disinterested examination. His *nom de plume* (one might as well say: *nom d'imprimerie*) makes him almost an allegorically literalized embodiment of supervision. The tone of the passage, moreover, is organized by the normative implication that personal identity, in all of its contingent "Particulars," ought not to dictate the value of a writing. That implication is all the more powerful insofar as we know the subsequent details of the characters' identity to be fictitious. The principle of the negativity of public discourse is thus made available through the Spectator's ironic detachment from the reader's curiosity and through the fictitiousness of the serial's characters. And the normative character of that principle is made available in the form of the disinterest of Country republicanism.

The first *Spectator* essay, with its introduction of the Spectator, appeared in 1711. Ten years later, on August 7, 1721, the first issue of the *New England Courant* appeared, with its own introduction:

> It's an hard Case, that a Man can't appear in Print now a Days, unless he'll undergo the Mortification of Answering to ten thousand senseless and Impertinent Questions like these, *Pray Sir, from whence came you? . . . Was you bred at Colledge, Sir?*

The printer's apprentice brother, Benjamin Franklin, would repeat the same theme yet again the following year, in his Silence Dogood papers, albeit in a more graceful and inventive manner. The pressurized tone of the *Courant*'s introduction—the pertness of "Impertinent"—may be taken as registering the resistance to civic discourse in Boston. James Franklin's rhetoric is the Country posture without the Country. Where

Addison and Steele could rely on the (assumed) class position of the gentry as a liberal vantage on the political world, Franklin from the start was forced to validate utterance in a world of print dominated by Puritan clergy. His introduction comes into focus if we remember the swagger of the authors who defended Cotton Mather against Robert Calef in 1701: "It was highly rejoycing to us, when we heard that our *Book-sellers* were so well acquainted with the Integrity of our Pastors, as not one of them would admit any of those *Libels* to be vended in their shops." Franklin's opposition to the familiar pastors comes in the imagination of a different norm for the vending of what he prints. That imagination or action is made possible for him by the Addisonian model, but the model in turn is transformed in the articulation. Participation in print now refers not to a class position above concern—the concealed model of the gentry's liberality—but to market-society negativity. The self-conscious artisan Franklin marshals it more aggressively against social distinction than Addison and Steele would ever have done.

Imperial Crisis

Because publication was articulated in colonial America as a condition of legitimacy, it should not be surprising that the growing legitimation crisis in the imperial periphery was manifested largely in printed discourse. The practice of Sam Adams, who wrote under more than twenty-five pseudonyms but rarely spoke in public, is in many respects typical of the colonial resistance. It was, as Bernard Bailyn has demonstrated, an intellectual's revolution. Even for most of those not directly involved in the intellectual polemic of the conflict, writing was the dominant mode of the political. Bailyn describes the scene in this manner:

> Every medium of written expression was put to use. The newspapers, of which by 1775 there were thirty-eight in the mainland colonies, were crowded with columns of arguments and counter-arguments appearing as letters, official documents, extracts of speeches, and sermons. Broadsides—single sheets on which were often printed not only large-letter notices but, in three or four columns of miniscule type, essays of several thousand words—appeared everywhere; they could be found posted or passing from hand to hand in the towns of every colony. Almanacs, workaday publications universally available in the colonies, carried, in odd corners and occasional columns, a considerable freight of political comment.[67]

Though Bailyn goes on to describe an intellectual's movement, his description is remarkable for its materiality. Texts, physically, are everywhere.

For the colonists that was exactly the idea. As Sam Adams was quick to realize, writing could blanket the colonies, appearing anonymously or under false names, giving the impression that, as Franklin put it, "the discontents were really general . . . and not the fiction of a few demagogues."[68] As in the Zenger case, the dispersion of print acquired a social meaning, allowing it to represent the generality in a way that was normative as well as convenient. This perception of printing was enabled by several aspects of its social context besides those of publicity. Print shops, in the colonies as in Europe, had long been centers for meetings and exchanges among those who traded in information. In the North American colonies much more than in any other area of the West, printers held a monopoly on the postal service, making them an important center of communication and public life at a time when the post roads were the main way of linking as an identifiable body colonies that occupied many times the area of England with only a fraction of the population.[69]

Even apart from the networks of postal conveyancing between print shops, the printers themselves constituted an intercolonial organization. Despite other colonists' localism and widespread indifference to the noncommercial affairs of other colonies, printers had developed a complex system of links—partly through their frequent migrations, partly through kinship alliances, partly because of the entrepreneurial practice (particularly developed by Franklin) of capitalizing journeymen to set up affiliated shops in other towns, partly by the habit of trading stock and business information, and partly by the trade practice of freely reprinting material from the newspapers of other towns and colonies. As Arthur Schlesinger notes, the few printers and editors who were to be found in Tory ranks came from outside the personal network of the trade.[70] Moreover, the printers created local networks of readers that could be linked, by means of the common and public discourse they were reading, to similar local networks elsewhere. Newspaper readerships thus became among the most important forms of political organization in the colonies.

It was therefore neither accidental nor inconsequential that, when the British government decided to impose its authority on the colonies, it came up with the Stamp Act. As the early historian David Ramsay noted, "It was fortunate for the liberties of America, that newspapers were the subject of a heavy stamp duty. Printers, when uninfluenced by government, have generally ranged themselves on the side of liberty, nor are they less remarkable for attention to the profits of their profession. A stamp duty, which openly invades the first, and threatened a great diminution of the last, provoked their united zealous opposition."[71] In the context of print ideology the Stamp Act was far more noxious than just any tax; it was an attempt by authority to curtail civic liberty.[72] Printers, lawyers, and merchants—the most literate members of colonial society and, in urban settings, the most powerful—stood to lose a good deal of money because of stamp duties. Naturally they resented it. But print had become so central to the routines of colonial life and had come so completely to be seen within the same concepts with which the political itself was thought, that the most literate classes could successfully claim that the entire realm of the public was at stake, and not just the pecuniary convenience of a few professions. The town of Worcester, Massachusetts, for example, instructed its delegates to "take special care of the LIBERTY OF THE PRESS," even though the town had no press or newspaper of its own.[73] And when the newspapers began attacking the government outright, though General Gage recommended suit for seditious libel, the Governor's Council decided that, "considering the present temper of the People, this is not a proper time to prosecute the Printers & Publishers."[74]

One poem that appeared in protest of the Stamp Act literalized an image of that series of ideological identifications between the press and the liberty of the republic. The result was a phantasmagoric dream-narrative in which documents appear as injured persons bewailing their woes.

> One Night, as I lay slumbering in my Bed,
> Dark Images crouded into my Head.
> I thought, as through the Town I walk'd alone,
> I, at a Distance heard a grievous Moan.
> Attention rous'd; I then approach'd more near,
> And found a Croud of PAPERS gather'd there.
> To each of them, as to the Prophet's Ass,
> A Tongue was giv'n to tell his wretched Case.
> I watch'd their mournful Words with vast Concern,
> Hoping the Cause, for which they met, to learn.
> They spoke by Turns: In this they all agree,
> To plead the Cause of *English Liberty*:
> And deprecate the Woe, which each one thought
> Would, by the *St—p A–t,* soon on them be brought.[75]

What makes it plausible for documents to appear as speaking persons is a profound ideological analogy between documents and persons, and the importance of that analogy in the construction of the political. To speak publicly is to do so as a printed text.

> "Oh!——
> Must I (the Bond cries) suffer the Abuse
> Of being st—pt, when I'm of so much Use
> To Men of all Professions, rich and Poor,
> Whose Property I daily do secure?
> Those that are honest, honest must remain;
> And he that tries to cheat, tries but in vain.
> While I exert my Skill the Rogue to catch,
> And all his false dishonest Motions watch,
> Must I be crush'd and fall a Sacrifice
> To cruel Tyr—y?

The Bond speaks as bond; it represents the connection between persons. It does so not only for the obvious reason that it was used in legal machinery, but also because its existence as material language endorses the particular language of materiality that is called property. The relation between the Bond and bonding, however, is somewhat more complicated than that analogy. The poem reverses the fact that people read with their eyes to depict, not people reading texts, but texts reading people ("all his false dishonest Motions watch"). While the text's materiality allies it to property, the text's visibility allies it to the supervision of publicity.

This visibility, which is seen to characterize all of society with regard to the political, is clearly a mode of discipline. The Bond shows a kind of republican vigilance, matched by "Summons" and "Writ" when they boast, "We've call'd the Debtor to discharge his Debt; / We many Rogues at Justice' Bar have set." The discipline of publicity is seen as bringing persons under the watch not of particular masters but of the social itself. The same qualities that integrate writing with social discipline, therefore, make it oppositional to Power:

> The *Probate Papers* next, with many a Sigh,
> "Must we be st—pt (with tender Accent cry)
> We who our Life and Breath so freely spend,
> The Fatherless and Widow to defend.
> And dare their needy and defenceless State,
> So boldly plead against the Rich and Great?"

Yet finally, after "Diploma," "Licence," "Paper," "Almanack," and all the others have had their say, the poem makes a last attempt to use the fiction of their speaking in order to bring them back into the good graces of Power. "The KING and *Parliament* vouchsaf'd to hear" the lamentations of the documents, and accordingly repeal the Stamp Act, even though the narrator wakes to find it a dream. The poem, then, uses the texts' speech in two contradictory ways: first to demonstrate how important writing had come to be in imagining political personhood, and therefore to show how insidious the Stamp Act was; and second, to allow for a gesture of reintegration, in which the social discipline of print culture could be seen as still compatible with royal authority.

Resistance to the Stamp Act was so widespread as to unite the colonists in opposition to the British for the first time, and though few were thinking of independence in 1765, conceptions of legitimate power and liberty were already beginning to lead the colonies toward fundamental resistance. "America" rather suddenly appeared as a symbolic entity.[76] The crisis surrounding the Stamp Act, moreover, had the effect of strengthening the identification of print culture and republicanism. The more anti-British sentiment grew, the more writing and print became the mode of resistance. And the more writing and print were used to mobilize the political, the more the political came to be defined in ways alien to the British legitimation of power.

It was in this context too that John Adams wrote the political history of letters with which I began this book. His essay, like the preceding poem, joins publication as a natural resistance to imperial sovereignty, and all of the potential for republican paranoia in that construction can then be called forth by the imperial assertion of sovereignty *over* publication. The medium takes on an almost talismanic importance, and the climax of Adams' history is a peroration on print that is addressed to its printers. Americans, he writes, have always taken care "that the art of printing should be encouraged, and that it should be easy and cheap and safe for any person to communicate his thoughts to the public. And you, Messieurs Printers [Edes and Gill, printers of the *Boston Gazette*], whatever the tyrants of the earth may say of your paper, have done important service to your country, by your readiness and freedom in publishing the speculations of the curious."[77] At this moment Adams' essay both describes and enacts a perfect reciprocity between republicanism and print, between citizenship and publication. That reciprocity caps a fifty-year history of transformation with a promise of inevitable progress through publication for the future.

In concentrating on the importance of republican culture and the structural transformation of the public sphere, it would be easy to lose sight of the meaning of these changes for the historical agents involved in them. It is all the more necessary to consider those agents since, with its emphasis on negativity, the public sphere of print gave a newly special existence to the individual. The citizen who brackets the particularities of his life in order to make entry into political discourse discovers in that very act that his particularities give him a special (though privative) identity. The categories of republicanism, which describe political life *as* the bracketing of particularities rather than as the fulfillment of status, in this way gave a new structural importance to the private individual of bourgeois society.[78]

Yet the individual remained problematic in the eighteenth-century public sphere because of a tension between the personalizing value of participation—virtue—and the negating universality of the discourse. Within this contradiction reason developed as a negative mode of subjectivity to articulate the private subject of the public sphere. In other words, the negative relation of private subject to the state and to the public discourse found expression in the negativity of the rational subject.

· III ·

Franklin: The Representational
Politics of the Man of Letters

He knew what he was about, the sharp little man.
He set up the first dummy American.

—D. H. *Lawrence*

BENJAMIN FRANKLIN'S career as a republican statesman centers on an inescapable difficulty: while the statesman's task is to embody legitimate power, the task of republicanism was to remove legitimacy from the hands of persons. In the new republican polity, as François Furet has remarked of the French context, "power would belong only to the people, that is, to nobody . . . The 'people' was not a datum or a concept that reflected existing society. Rather, it was the Revolution's claim to legitimacy, its very definition as it were; for henceforth all power, all political endeavour revolved around that founding principle, *which it was nonetheless impossible to embody.*"[1] The republican statesman, therefore, is in some measure a contradiction in terms: he is the embodiment of that which, by definition, cannot be embodied. How could such a contradiction be mediated or disguised? In the case of Franklin the answer lies in the involution of republicanism and print. To the extent that he succeeded in appearing to embody representational legitimacy, he did so by virtue of his career as a printer and man of letters.

In the epitaph he wrote for himself, Ben Franklin announces his peculiar relation to print in a dramatic way:

> The Body of
> B. Franklin,
> Printer;
> Like the Cover of an old Book,
> Its Contents torn out,
> And stript of its Lettering and Gilding,
> Lies here, Food for Worms.
> But the Work shall not be wholly lost.
> For it will, as he believ'd, appear once more,

> In a new & more perfect Edition,
> Corrected and amended
> by the Author.[2]

This epitaph has a metaphoric excess that makes it difficult to take literally. But that very excess *tempts* us to take it literally. Franklin delivers the conceit with a bravura air that deflects attention from the ostensible subject (death and the hoped-for resurrection). He draws us instead into a fantasy of being-in-print. What makes the trope compelling—too compelling—is that Franklin wrote the epitaph not for a gravestone, but for a page. He composed it at the age of twenty-two, continuing later in his life to produce holographs of it which he left with hosts as mementos of his visits.[3] In such circumstances the ostensible message of piety could only be eclipsed in the pleasure of a fantasy about print, a fantasy that Franklin trades from hand to hand as a mark of his wit. But the way the epitaph presents him as a text that lies here (on the page?) holds our attention even more than it would need to in order to exhibit his cleverness. The metaphor has a suggestive power that exceeds the familiar logocentric distinction between accidental substance (body, book) and plenary meaning (spirit, text).

The epitaph is disturbing because it treats print and life in equivalent terms: to live is to be published. At first glance the gesture of the epitaph defies the termination of death; on closer inspection, it poses a grave question about what it means to live. Such implications are all the more striking in a document composed in 1728—the year in which Franklin set up shop as a partner in a printing house—since the epitaph may be said to announce not his death, but his intentions for his career.[4] Embarking on a new enterprise in printing, he describes himself all too literally as a man of letters.

Nor is this an isolated moment in Franklin's career. We need only recall his now infamous habit, in the *Autobiography,* of referring to his mistakes as "errata." In a more extended way that habit repeats the identification between Franklin's life and his printed work. The entire project of the autobiography repeats and develops the central themes and assumptions of the epitaph. At the outset of the work, which had no clear generic precedent to serve as a rationale, Franklin returns to the themes of the epitaph to explain what he is doing.

> I should have no Objection to a Repetition of the same Life from its Beginning, only asking the Advantage Authors have in a second

Edition to correct some Faults of the first. So would I if I might, besides corr^g the Faults, change some sinister Accidents & Events of it for others more favourable, but tho' this were deny'd, I should still accept the Offer. However, since such a Repetition is not to be expected, the Thing most like living one's Life over again, seems to be a *Recollection* of that Life; and to make that Recollection as durable as possible, the putting it down in Writing.[5]

These introductory remarks are written at an early stage of the manuscript, when Franklin shows no clear intention to publish the work, considering it instead a private record for his son. Yet even here he is already describing it as a "second Edition." And already the autobiographical posture of self-objectification (life becomes book) has its meaning in the analogous self-objectification that is the posture of modernity. One's life can be repeated in the form of a book because life is already understood to have some of the features of books: authorial design, durability, corrigibility, and exposure before a public. Those features of Franklin's self-relation can be traced to the cultural assumptions of a certain print discourse. For that reason, although Franklin has been (at least since Weber's *Protestant Ethic and the Spirit of Capitalism*) the exemplary figure of modernity, his exemplary modern subjectivity can be read as a very special cultural articulation of printing.

Franklin's practice of regarding himself as "B. Franklin, Printer" partakes of the general revaluation of print that we have seen in eighteenth-century America. When Franklin was a child print was a negligible phenomenon, and most colonies had no press at all. That was soon to change, and his career corresponds in striking detail to the path of the press's expansion. In 1718, at the age of twelve, he was apprenticed to his printer brother James in Boston—just as the currency debates in that city were heating up. In that year and the following, he wrote two broadside ballads, now lost, which he hawked in the streets. (They sold "wonderfully," according to his later memory.) After printing the *Boston Gazette* for several months in 1719 and 1720, the Franklin shop began producing the *New-England Courant* in 1721. By this time the younger brother, now fifteen, was at the center of the print explosion in Boston.

More important is that Franklin quickly displayed an understanding of the character of that development. The *Courant* was aggressively republican and Whiggish, and soon ran into trouble. When, in the paper's first summer, James Franklin was imprisoned and forbidden to publish, the paper began to appear under Benjamin's name. The younger Franklin, whose Dogood papers had already begun to appear, used that serial persona to reprint, on the front page, the essay on the liberty of the press from Trenchard and Gordon's *Cato's Letters*.[6] He was already promoting the republican principles that would be the metadiscourse of a specialized subsystem in print.

Franklin moved to Philadelphia just in time to become involved, as a printer and writer, in a similar transformation of the political. His was the press that competed with Andrew Bradford's in the 1730s, and he wrote for Bradford's *American Weekly Mercury* in the 1720s until he established his *Pennsylvania Gazette* as its rival. He also followed closely the events of the Zenger controversy in New York, having known William Bradford from the time of his arrival in Philadelphia, and being a friend and ally of Andrew Hamilton. When two pamphlets were published attacking the arguments put forward by Andrew Hamilton in the Zenger case, Franklin printed James Alexander's replies in the *Pennsylvania Gazette*. He developed an elaborate network of printers—such as the Timothys of South Carolina—whom he supported in one kind of partnership or another; he also branched into related trades, such as papermaking and typecasting. He was both printer for the Assembly and clerk of the Assembly before becoming an assemblyman himself, and no one understood better than he the connection between public discourse and representative polity.

But the importance of print in Franklin's career is more than a matter of his having been involved in the local struggles through which the politics of print changed. He may be said to have embodied the written subject, to have lived within the structures of career and personality in a way that was profoundly shaped by the printed discourse of the public sphere, articulating a career for the subject of that discourse.

Franklin was the first American to fashion a career entirely of letters. All previous figures whom we sometimes describe as men of letters—the Mathers, Cotton, Edwards, Taylor—achieved their prominence in oral settings, usually as preachers. Only with Franklin was this not the case, and the differences were so determining as to make him a man of letters in an entirely different and more profound sense.[7] His career placed him in exactly those situations in which it had become possible to adjudicate political struggles by appeals to a neutral and rational ground of public representation, where citizens were called on to exercise civic virtue by placing the common good over personal interest. The print ideology of the public sphere, as we have seen, valorized the general above the personal and construed the opposition between the two in the republican terms of virtue and interest. It is at this point that Franklin becomes an

especially illustrative case, as his career best exhibits the paradoxical embodiment of print ideology in the personal. In an anonymous broadside
poem of 1756, for example, Franklin is praised as a perfect republican
citizen because he is "Void of all partial, or all private ends."[8] His virtue
is predicated on his absorption into generality. If it is difficult to see what
allowance is being made for Franklin's person when he is praised in such
terms (or, for that matter, in the terms of the epitaph), my argument here
will be that his career is preeminently that of the republican man of letters,
the citizen of print.[9]

We may assume that Franklin was relatively deliberate in articulating
the career of the man of letters, since he often remarks on the political
agency of print and frequently allegorizes the problem of the subject who
writes.[10] The epitaph is one example; more dramatic is the preface to the
1740 edition of *Poor Richard's Almanack*. Richard there inserts a document
purportedly authored by his competitor, Titan Leeds. The trick is that
Leeds is alleged by Richard to be dead, and the document has been written
by the dead Leeds through Richard's own hand:

> You will wonder perhaps, how this Paper comes written on your
> Table. You must know that no separate Spirits are under any Confine-
> ment till after the final Settlement of all Accounts. In the mean time
> we wander where we please, visit our old Friends, observe their Ac-
> tions, enter sometimes into their Imaginations, and give them Hints
> waking or sleeping that may be of Advantage to them. Finding you
> asleep, I entred your left Nostril, ascended into your Brain, found
> out where the Ends of those Nerves were that move your right Hand
> and Fingers, by the Help of which I am now writing unknown to
> you; but when you open your Eyes, you will see that the Hand
> written is mine, tho' wrote with yours.   (2:246)

This extraordinary fantasy of ghostwriting dramatizes a discrepancy between persons and texts. As in the epitaph of twelve years earlier, the
writing subject is necessarily cut off from the body. There is considerable
emphasis on the separation of the two, since the writing subject is an
incorporeal agent acting not only separate from the body but also to
violate it. In the epitaph the writing body is decomposed; in the preface
it is entered through the nose and handled like a puppet. This gap between
the person who writes and the person who lives is focused in the play on
"hand": "the Hand written is mine, tho' wrote with yours." The pun is
one of Franklin's ways of marking the difference between the man *of*

letters (the Hand written) and the *man* of letters (Richard's fleshy, manipulated hand).[11]

The same difference is marked by Poor Richard himself since he is the pseudonymous screen for B. Franklin, Printer. Some years earlier, the real Titan Leeds had accused Richard of nonexistence; in the preface to the 1736 almanac, Richard had been forced to defend his writing hand:

> They say in short, *That there is no such a Man as I am;* and have spread this Notion so thoroughly in the Country, that I have been frequently told it to my Face by those that don't know me. This is not civil Treatment, to endeavour to deprive me of my very Being, and reduce me to a Non-entity in the Opinion of the publick . . . [But] if there were no such Man as I am, how is it possible I should appear publickly to hundreds of People, as I have done for several Years past, in print? I need not, indeed, have taken any Notice of so idle a Report, if it had not been for the sake of my Printer, to whom my Enemies are pleased to ascribe my Productions; and who it seems is as unwilling to father my Offspring, as I am to lose the Credit of it.
>
> (2:136)

Richard is an anti-Quixote, an imaginary man of discourse vainly taking himself for real. As such he is the perfect screen for the Printer who is so unwilling to father his offspring, preferring to have them stray onto the page unaffiliated.[12] The games Franklin typically plays with his personae often take this form: a fantasmatic self-splitting or self-objectification that results in a concealed or absent agent behind a manipulated surface. What stake does B. Franklin, Printer, have in this fantasy?

Ben Franklin was not out of childhood before he was struggling with the issue of personhood and written discourse. He seems to have been quite self-conscious about living after the model of print. In what I take to be a crucial passage of the *Autobiography,* for example, he narrates his discovery that thought could conform to the manipulation of objects— a discovery that foreshadows the 1740 image of Titan Leeds's ghost manipulating the hand of Poor Richard. Franklin has just mentioned that "Prose Writing has been of great Use to me in the Course of my Life, and was a principal Means of my Advancement," when he begins the anecdote as a way of explaining how writing came to be so important to him. In the anecdote, he is engaged in argument by correspondence with his bookish friend Collins, when his father points out to him that "in elegance of Expression, in Method, and in Perspecuity," Franklin is being bested by Collins. At this point he comes across a volume of the *Spectator*.

I thought the Writing excellent, & wish'd if possible to imitate it. With that View, I took some of the Papers, & making short Hints of the Sentiment in each Sentence, laid them by a few Days, and then without looking at the Book, try'd to compleat the Papers again, by expressing each hinted Sentiment at length & as fully as it had been express'd before, in any suitable Words that should come to hand.

Then I compar'd my *Spectator* with the Original, discover'd some of my Faults & corrected them ... I also sometimes jumbled my Collections of Hints into Confusion, and after some Weeks, endeavour'd to reduce them into the best Order, before I began to form the full Sentences & compleat the Paper. This was to teach me Method in the Arrangement of Thoughts.   (1318–1320)

It is worth thinking carefully about this passage, because it portrays in some detail the often-remarked connection between texts—whether written or printed—and ways of thinking. Franklin claims to learn a certain rationality ("Method in the Arrangement of Thoughts") directly from handling textual artifacts. Being a type compositor and press worker by day as well as a writer at night, he has a keen sense of the duplicability of letters; here he sees that feature of letters as expressive of something in the nature of thought and discourse, marking a distinction between form and content. But what is most important about this passage, and holds the key to the significance of any link between print and rationality for Franklin, is that his picture of printed artifacts is structured from the beginning by an instrumental objectification. He does not just confront or see the texts; he handles them. And he handles them not for pleasure or for violence but in a strictly instrumental way. As a result, the link between texts and thoughts amounts to modeling the act of thinking after the manipulation of objects.

This kind of rationality, with its literal patterning of intellection after an instrumental relation to discourse, is quite different from the abstract thought for which New England was famous. By characterizing thinking itself as manipulation of thought, it postulates a manipulating self that does not coincide with thought, that is not even immanent in it. It assumes this absent agent in just the same way that print, so conceived, postulates a generative agent not immanent in it. Franklin's ideal of method in the arrangement of thoughts therefore reintroduces, on another level, the basic problem that he dramatizes through the persona of Poor Richard. In rational thought, who is thinking?

Franklin is famous for the sort of calculating rationality that he depicts here. And his rationality is often understood to make him representative of his historical moment. But how could something like rationality be contextualized? We can begin to answer that question by noting that although rationality, in the special sense exemplified here by Franklin, has an intersubjective dimension, it is primarily conceived as a private self-relation. That is why it seems difficult to contextualize: it is a feature of the individual and is usually assumed to be distinct from "context." But it is just this private, individual nature of Franklin's rationality that makes it relevant to a certain historical context.

Method in the arrangement of thoughts is something that Franklin teaches *himself.* There are two parallel self-splittings in that notion: the first divides the arranging and methodical agent from the subject who has thoughts; the second divides the teacher of method from the thinker who learns it. These splittings allow Franklin to have an internally privative relation to himself: neither way of describing his action or his thinking can comprise his "self." He can carry out actions of which he is both subject and object, and in which neither God nor anyone else participates. So his reason seems to be pure individuality. At the same time, it requires a thorough and normative self-division. And the latter is the key to its contextualization. Franklin's internal relation to self is fundamentally negative and critical. By adopting such a paradoxically privative posture (who is thinking?), he could fit himself to the negativity of public discourse.[13] His internalized, private understanding of rationality implies a set of properly social and public norms.

The remainder of the passage in the *Autobiography* clarifies what I mean. Franklin goes on to tell us that his rationalizing experiments with letters led him to the resolution of

> never using when I advance anything that may possibly be disputed, the Words, *Certainly, undoubtedly,* or any others that give the Air of Positiveness to an Opinion; but rather say, *I conceive,* or *I apprehend* a Thing to be so or so, *It appears to me,* or *I should think it so or so for such & such Reasons,* or *I imagine* it to be so, or *it is so if I am not mistaken.*—This Habit I believe has been of great Advantage to me, when I have had occasion to inculcate my Opinions & persuade Men into Measures that I have been from time to time engag'd in promoting.—And as the chief Ends of Conversation are to *inform,* or to be *informed,* to *please* or to *persuade,* I wish well meaning sensible Men would not lessen their Power of doing Good by a Positive assuming Manner that seldom fails to disgust, tends to create Opposition, and

to defeat every one of those Purposes for which Speech was given to us, to wit, giving or receiving Information, or Pleasure.

(1321–1322)

In this famous passage Franklin seems only to be recommending a rhetorical tactic. If you want to persuade, couch your language in modest and uncertain tones. But second thought discloses that the rhetorical tactic— or rather, the idea here presented of discourse *as* tactical—extends the object manipulation of literal intellection as a principle of social discourse. Just as the young Franklin arranged paper and type, and just as the good writer arranges words and expressions, and just as the rational thinker arranges thought, so also rational man arranges discourse.

The notion has a certain ambiguity. Franklin, like the "P.P." quoted in Chapter 2, repudiates *personal* authority in favor of a general authority based in a negative relation to one's own person. And that can be taken as a strongly universalizing claim to truth. At the same time, it is an inherently rhetorical principle; indeed, Franklin presents it as a theory of rhetoric. He claims that the rhetorical self-objectification he describes is eminently rational. But it is more than that. Rhetoric ceases to be duplicitous masking in Franklin's rationality because the negative self-relation of the instrumental rhetorician just *is* the structure of rationality. Rhetoric is rational because rationality is rhetorical.

It is not accidental that the particular tactic Franklin recommends as the example of rationality in discourse is the gesture of self-negation. "I conceive or apprehend a thing to be so or so"; "it appears to me," or "I should think it so or so, for such and such reasons"; or "I imagine it to be so"; or "it is so, if I am not mistaken"—these phrases foreground the self only to eliminate it from discourse; thought has validity not *because* it is vouched for by a self, but *despite* any relation it might have to a self. The self from the beginning appears in its fallibility, its negligibility, its evanescence. Any form of "Positive" assertion disgusts. It is as though the personal is, for literal intellection and rational society, a necessary postulation, nothing more.

I am not just willfully reading this problem out of the *Autobiography;* in his 1726 journal Franklin wrote,

Man is a sociable being, and it is for aught I know one of the worst of punishments to be excluded from society . . . I have heard of a gentleman who underwent seven years close confinement, in the Bastile at Paris. He was a man of sense, he was a thinking man; but being deprived of all conversation, to what purpose should he think? for he was denied even the instruments of expressing his thoughts in writing . . . He was forced at last to have recourse to this invention: he daily scattered pieces of paper about the floor of his little room, and then employed himself in picking them up and sticking them in rows and figures on the arm of his elbow-chair; and he used to tell his friends, after his release, that he verily believed if he had not taken this method he should have lost his senses.   (1:85–86)

The passage demonstrates that thought is unimaginable for Franklin without exchange or objects, that the personal is an insufficient context for thinking. The mere asking of the question, "to what purpose should he think?" implies an inseparability between thought and instrumental reason. Remarkably, the narrative satisfactorily substitutes for the act of thinking, as an example of the rational, the act of sticking pieces of paper onto a chair. The substitution presumes an analogy, and the common thread is that both reasoning and pinning scraps of paper are seen to conform to the same model of objectification. Thus, where one would expect to find the self, Franklin anticipates madness, and where one would expect to find nothing personal at all, Franklin finds reason.

The thinness of the personal might seem to be a problem for the civic vision of rationality. Since the virtuous citizen is one who surveys society from a detached perspective, detecting corruption, as one Philadelphia paper put it, in its "obscure Lurking Holes," he stands for the authority of the social. But how can he assert the efficacy of virtue without being endowed also with the authority of utterance? [14] In the extreme of republican print ideology, this is a nonquestion. Social authority, like truth, holds validity not in persons, but despite them; it is located not in the virtuous citizen nor in God nor in the king, but in the light of day, in the supervision of publicity itself. Thus print—not speech—is the ideal and idealized guardian of civic liberty, as print discourse exposes corruption in its lurking holes but does so without occupying a lurking hole of its own. It represents a public vision from a nonparticular perspective, as though the whole system of object-exchange could see.

Franklin's earliest extant publications, the Dogood papers, attempt to enact the translation of print rationality into civic virtue. Written during the height of the factional conflict in Boston, they present themselves as conspicuously written (each one begins: "To the Author of the *New England Courant*") and advertise themselves as public criticism and information. "I am naturally very jealous for the Rights and Liberties of my Country; and the least appearance of an Incroachment on those invaluable

Priviledges, is apt to make my Blood boil exceedingly. I have likewise a natural Inclination to observe and reprove the Faults of others, at which I have an excellent Faculty. I speak this by Way of Warning to all such whose Offences shall come under my Cognizance, for I never intend to wrap my Talent in a Napkin" (1:13). Or again, "I have from my Youth been indefatigably studious to gain and treasure up in my Mind all useful and desireable Knowledge, especially such as tends to improve the Mind, and enlarge the Understanding: And as I have found it very beneficial to me, I am not without Hopes, that communicating my small Stock in this Manner, by Peace-meal to the Publick, may be at least in some Measure useful" (1:13). Mrs. Dogood, that is, will be publicly useful to the degree that she is rational. She validates the combination of her letters' writtenness and their claim to usefulness by appealing to the authoritative vision of print: "A true and natural Representation of any Enormity, is often the best Argument against it and Means of removing it, when the most severe Reprehensions alone, are found ineffectual" (1:39). The Dogood papers propose to be such true and natural representations of "the present reigning Vices of the Town" (1:21).

In good republican form they oppose their own legible appeal to the corruption and dominating desire of arrogant men. "Among the many reigning Vices of the Town which may at any Time come under my Consideration and Reprehension, there is none which I am more inclin'd to expose than that of *Pride* . . . The proud Man aspires after Nothing less than an unlimited Superiority over his Fellow-Creatures. He has made himself a King in *Soliloquy;* fancies himself conquering the World; and the Inhabitants thereof consulting on proper Methods to acknowledge his Merit" (1:21). Mrs. Dogood's claim to have transcended pride (though she admits to having been proud before) is vouched for by her act of writing the letters, for they show her not to be "in Soliloquy." She incorporates into her text letters written to her as additional evidence that she is merged into the public discourse.

The subjects of the Dogood papers demonstrate the concatenation of ideas associated with print and civic virtue: liberty of the press (#8); the value of broad learning and the failure of restrictive and elitist institutions like Harvard to foster it (#4); the domination of women (#5); the pride of decorating the body in extravagant apparel (#6); the boundaries of reason in poetry (#7); religious hypocrisy as a mode of false power in social relations (#9); and so on. Because in each case they argue for the breadth of an undifferentiated social field against the restriction of the personal, the letters support in particular arguments their own claim to oppose true and natural representations against soliloquies. They are purely socializing texts. But what about their author, who has already admitted to having been proud as a girl, and who has moved from her country seat to Boston expressly for the purpose of airing her opinions? Would it not seem that the appearance of these letters *as* her opinions would vitiate their claim to be civic representations?

The fictional environment of the letters addresses these very questions. The letters are not of course by Mrs. Dogood at all, and the pretence that they are is the sixteen-year-old Ben Franklin's way of airing opinions without reference to himself. The fictionality of the Dogood papers validates their truth claims, but not because of any potency or value in fictionality per se. Mrs. Dogood's authorship is a ruse, the very transparency of which endorses neither authorship nor fictionality, but anonymity. These papers are those which, Franklin tells us in the *Autobiography,* he slipped under the door of his brother's printing shop at night for fear that they would be dismissed if his brother knew the author's identity. His fear that the contamination of the personal would occult the letters' value as civic representations takes remedy in the persona of the papers, but it also repeats itself thematically in the announcement of that persona. Following the model of *The Spectator*—which, as we saw in the previous chapter, had already been imitated by his brother—Franklin writes at the beginning of the first letter, "since it is observed, that the Generality of People, now a days, are unwilling either to commend or dispraise what they read, until they are in some measure informed who or what the Author of it is, whether he be *poor* or *rich, old* or *young*, a *Schollar* or a *Leather Apron Man,* &c. and give their Opinion of the Performance, according to the Knowledge which they have of the Author's Circumstances, it may not be amiss to begin with a short Account of my past Life and present Condition, that the Reader may not be at a Loss to judge whether or no my Lucubrations are worth his reading." Puritans would have found good reason to be unwilling to commend or dispraise an utterance without knowing something about the person making the utterance, since faith and status governed truth and value. Franklin invokes the still common assumption that the personal was the necessary guarantee of any statement only to defy that assumption with the screen of Mrs. Dogood's persona.

Mrs. Dogood's persona thematically repeats the same abnegation of the personal. Her "having no Relation on Earth" figures her literariness and the generality of her social function. This is especially true since she tells us that in lieu of relatives she has spent most of her youth "with the best of Company, *Books*." For Mrs. Dogood, then, the written quite literally constitutes the social. In the context of her writing's claims to police the social without the corruption of character, her name, Silence Dogood, takes on added importance as signifying not just a Puritan humility but a generality of person. It was thus supremely fitting—in relation both to the ostensible subjects of the Dogood papers and to the conditions of their production—that when Franklin ceased to supply them his brother entered the following advertisement in the newspaper: "If any Person or Persons will give a true Account of Mrs. Silence Dogood, whether Dead or alive, Married or unmarried, in Town or Countrey, that so, (if living) she may be spoke with, or Letters convey'd to her, they shall have Thanks for their Pains" (1:45).

Silence Dogood's silence, her final disappearance, makes narratively concrete what had been a condition of her virtue, as does her anonymous invisibility in her account of a moonlight walk through the streets of Boston:

> Here I found various Company to observe, and various Discourse to attend to. I met indeed with the common Fate of *Listeners,* (who *hear no good of themselves,*) but from a Consciousness of my Innocence, receiv'd it with a Satisfaction beyond what the Love of Flattery and the Daubings of a Parasite could produce. The Company who rally'd me were about Twenty in Number, of both Sexes; and tho' the *Confusion of Tongues* (like that of Babel) which always happens among so many impetuous Talkers, render'd their Discourse not so intelligible as I could wish, I learnt thus much, That one of the Females pretended to know me, from Discourse she had heard at a certain House before the Publication of one of my Letters; adding, *That I was a Person of an ill Character, and kept a criminal Correspondence with a Gentleman who assisted me in Writing.* One of the Gallants clear'd me of this random Charge, by saying, *That tho' I wrote in the Character of a Woman, he knew me to be a Man; But,* continu'd he, *he has more need of endeavouring a Reformation in himself, than spending his Wit in satyrizing others.* (1:41–42)

Roaming incognito through the town, observing "various Company," attending to "various Discourse," Silence narrativizes and personifies the civic vision of print, even as her narrative and her persona present themselves as part of that vision. Her ability to see without being seen is that of the republican reader, while at the same time she exemplifies the republican stoicism of publicness in the regime of supervision. Though assaulted by libels, she regards them with a "Satisfaction beyond what the Love of

Flattery and the Daubings of a Parasite could produce." It is, therefore, appropriate that opposed to her printlike silent anonymity should be the gossip about her person, the "Confusion of Tongues" generated by "impetuous Talkers." The talkers surveyed by her text wish to locate her in their speech. The first who claims to know her has "heard," or claims to have heard, some "Discourse" about Silence "before the Publication of one of my Letters."

The woman's desire to corporealize Silence, to identify her, is so aggressive as to take the form of a sexual fantasy. Silence, she has heard, was "a Person of an ill Character, and kept a criminal Correspondence with a Gentleman who assisted [her] in Writing." Silence's reputation for criminal correspondence is an extraordinary detail; it depicts an obsessional need in the oral setting to posit a body for writing. The woman posits, moreover, not just any body for writing, but a corrupt body, as though writing were necessarily a degeneration. The identification of writing with illicit liaison also appears in the puns on "ill Character" and "criminal Correspondence," which, immediately preceding the phrase, "a Gentleman who assisted me in Writing," cumulatively suggest that the latter may itself be sexual slang on the order of "criminal Correspondence." Of course the joke is on the gossiper; since Silence has already noted that the gossip is taking place in mixed company, and since the subject of the letter as a whole is patterns of courtship, we are meant to see the woman's "random Charge" as a sexual maneuver exposed in the light of Silence's writing.

A gallant then remarks that he knows Silence to be a man writing "in the Character of a Woman." His comment, by reversing the genders, dismisses the sexual scenario—or, rather, confuses it in such a way as to convert that vivid erotics of correspondence into a muted suggestion of the autoerotic, the man writing in the character of the woman. That suggestion is further hinted at by the language in which she continues: "But he has more need of endeavouring a Reformation in himself, than spending his Wit in satyrizing others." In this case, however, a further complication arises in our knowledge that Silence is neither man nor woman, but a sixteen-year-old boy. Through an elaborate and witty scenario, Franklin suggests that to "satyrize" others and to satyrize himself can be consonant because, despite the care with which he has larded the passage with sexual innuendo, neither act has a corporal object. The sexual references are there because for Franklin writing is reproductive; they are confused into a bodiless autoeroticism because the reproduction of writing is general and continues without the corruptive body it associates with the oral. In one respect Franklin inhabits a major contradiction in print discourse. He has access to its voice only on the basis of a gendered body, with its *vir*tue and its privilege of freehold, but as citizen-in-print he must negate even the particularity of gender that his citizenship requires. In another sense this is but the earliest version of what we have already witnessed in the 1736 preface to *Poor Richard's Almanac*: Franklin the printer, "unwilling to father [his] Offspring," diffuses his person in print behind the screen of another.

The most important point about the passage is that Franklin envisions writing as the scene of pure socialization, and even of a social erotic, paradoxically because it is freed from the localization of the personal, the bodily, the corruptible. It is not that he envisions the elimination of self, and least of all does he envision self-denial.[15] In one *Busy-body* essay he speaks strongly of "innate Worth and unshaken Integrity." But what he proposes is that innate worth and integrity be seen as such only when they are seen as reproducible. The paradox is that the personal is founded on and valued within the pure reproduction of the social, not, as is usually assumed, the other way around.

Equally illustrative of this paradox is the frame narrative of Franklin's best-known piece, "The Way to Wealth." Far from being the simple catalogue of capitalist maxims it is often taken for, the essay is a complicated ventriloquist act, projecting its aphorisms into repetitive screens of fictitious personae. They appear first as Poor Richard's. But the beginning of the essay offers one of Franklin's usual jokes about Richard's fictitiousness.

> I have heard that nothing gives an Author so great Pleasure, as to find his Works respectfully quoted by other learned Authors. This Pleasure I have seldom enjoyed; for tho' I have been, if I may say it without Vanity, an *eminent Author* of Almanacks annually now a full Quarter of a Century, my Brother Authors in the same Way, for what Reason I know not, have ever been very sparing in their Applauses; and no other Author has taken the least Notice of me, so that did not my Writings produce me some solid *Pudding,* the great Deficiency of *Praise* would have quite discouraged me.
>
> I concluded at length, that the People were the best Judges of my Merit; for they buy my Works; and besides, in my Rambles, where I am not personally known, I have frequently heard one or other of my Adages repeated, with, *as Poor Richard says,* at the End on't; this gave me some Satisfaction, as it showed not only that my Instructions were regarded, but discovered likewise some Respect for my Authority; and I own, that to encourage the Practice of remembering and repeat-

ing those wise Sentences, I have sometimes *quoted myself* with great Gravity.

Richard then narrates having overheard his maxims being delivered by the equally fictitious Father Abraham. The layered screens vividly detach the worth of the maxims from the "Authority" allegedly behind them. That kind of detached utterance can only be made by a rational subject, who internalizes its negativity. Richard's vain petulance about not being credited for his productions shows him not to be such a subject. But the internalized negativity of the rational author Franklin, the author unwilling to acknowledge his offspring—is parodically mirrored in the picture of Richard quoting himself. Richard's own productions return to him from another, even from "the People" in places where he is "not personally known." And in the same way, his words return to him from himself. Though his writing is in general circulation, he clings to the desire for acknowledgment as author. But the inverted quixotism of this desire is the counterpoint of the negativity being enacted by Franklin, here and at every point in his career, through the projection of his personae.

Franklin might seem to be mocking our notions of integrity. Yet I take him to be ironizing an *incomplete* rationality rather than the ideal of sincerity itself. He reconceives sincere worth and integrity as deriving from rational discourse. They are positive traits of character only insofar as they exhibit the *resources* of negativity. The point can be illustrated by the description of that man of worth and integrity in the *Busy-body,* who is introduced only as "Cato": "He appear'd in the plainest Country Garb; his Great Coat was coarse and looked old and thread-bare; his Linnen was homespun; his Beard perhaps of Seven Days Growth, his Shoes thick and heavy, and every Part of his Dress corresponding. Why was this Man receiv'd with such concurring Respect from every Person in the Room, even from those who had never known him or seen him before? It was not an exquisite Form of Person, or Grandeur of Dress that struck us with Admiration." [16] The answer will turn out to be virtue, here rendered visible by the very *disregard* that Cato has for his own person. And although Franklin was as fond of fine cloth as the next man, he too could adopt the Catonic costume when he needed to appear the man of virtue, especially in France.

Print ideology as formulated by Franklin and others, by incorporating the republican tradition of political thought, was to shape the course of American political behavior and American writing for the remainder of the century. But print ideology was also to shape lives and careers. It may be difficult to imagine how that could be. What would it mean, one might wonder, to live out the contradictory imperatives of self-repudiation and self-validation as Franklin describes them? Franklin explicitly imposed the structure of print rationality on his career from an early date, with regard both to rationality of character and to rationality of life progression. He wrote in his journal when he was twenty:

> Those who write of the art of poetry teach us that if we would write what may be worth the reading, we ought always, before we begin, to form a regular plan and design of our piece: otherwise, we shall be in danger of incongruity. I am apt to think it is the same as to life. I have never fixed a regular design in life; by which means it has been a confused variety of different scenes. I am now entering upon a new one: let me, therefore, make some resolutions, and form some scheme of action, that henceforth, I may live in all respects like a rational creature.[17]

Unfortunately the full plan is no longer extant. But we can see from this preamble that Franklin thought of his own life with the detachment with which one arranges objects, thus bringing career under the structure of rationality. Life, in his rationality, conforms exactly to the model of writing, even as Franklin writes the model of his life. The notorious perfection chart and self-examination scheme of the *Autobiography* are more than a printer's convenience; they represent a reconception of what it means to live—not just because Franklin did live in accordance with such rationalizing documents (as he says in the *Autobiography,* "I always carried my little Book with me" [1390]), but because those documents for him exemplify reproducible generality: "tho' I never arrived at the Perfection I had been so ambitious of obtaining, but fell far short of it, yet I was by the Endeavour made a better and a happier Man than I otherwise should have been, if I had not attempted it; As those who aim at perfect Writing by imitating the engraved Copies, tho' they never reach the wish'd for Excellence of those Copies, their Hand is mended by the Endeavour, and is tolerable while it continues fair & legible" (1391). Franklin's famous ambition of perfection is formed on the model of print, on the submersion of the personal in a general reproduction.[18]

Life has become reified as the object of design; by comparison, the previously supposed immediacy of oral relations appears as "a confused variety of different scenes." But when one lives "in all respects like a rational creature," who is living? When one's life is thus objectified, must it not be a shadow screen for an "I" postulated behind it, designing? We seem to be in the presence of a crippling contradiction in the rational.

But it is this very contradiction on which the rational founds itself, for by the paradoxical logic of literal intellection, though the "I" must be entirely occulted as the designing agent detached from any of the phenomena from which its existence is inferred, it is also seen as perfectly transparent, so that Franklin can speak of his plan as the condition necessary for "sincerity in every word and action—the most amiable excellence in a rational being." Not to be any particular man is not to be a "Partyman," and not to be a Partyman is to possess a character of integrity.

Franklin's career of public involvement was the articulation of what was implicit in his Plan of Conduct. For although that plan only announced the intention of designing his life the way one would design a piece of writing, in the social context of that announcement the analogy guaranteed for the career the same civic publicity that it allotted for writing; even private virtue was imagined in terms of civic visibility. It followed that the life most consistent with the model of writing would be the public life, but—and this is crucial—a public life uncontaminated by particular aspirations, party affiliations, dependencies on governments and ministers, influences of powerful men, and the like.

From the outside such rationality ironically bore a strong resemblance to the self-centered cunning of officeholders to which, as part of a print ideology, it was opposed. Franklin's political enemies make the point for us. They portrayed him as lecherous and greedy, but above all as "designing"; a common theme in anti-Franklin literature is the connection between his self-concealing designs and his manipulation of letters. A good example is a 1758 pamphlet allegorizing local politics in scriptural style. In the allegory Franklin is "Adonis the scribe": "And Adonis the scribe was a learned man, after the learning of the Jews; for he had read over the seven volums [*sic*] of the *Talmud,* containing the dreams and visions of those who hated truth; and from thence he learnt to say the things that *was not.*" Adonis, furthermore, is accused of imitating Jacobs, whom he loves as David loved Jonathan: "For *Adonis* the scribe took the dictionary of *Jacobs* the translator, and he interleaved it; and whatever he catched, in talking, or reading, or——sleeping, he popped it down, saying, Now are we as one, O my brother *Jacobs!* for my knowledge is as thy knowledge, and thy knowledge is as my knowledge." [19]

The pamphlet quite vividly depicts a Franklin whose real self is secret or void, concealed behind a screen of misleading texts. It can be seen as the flip side of the broadside quoted earlier, which praised Franklin for being "Void of all partial, or all private ends." Similarly, a 1764 broadside proclaimed:

Yet tutor'd by the Flying Post
The Gazettes, and the Post-Man,
Each Fancies he can rule a host
Or steer a Fleet with most Men.

. . . . .

Therefore the Prudent *Dutch* should Use
All Female soft Perswasion,
To draw F——n from raising News.
To mind (his occupation)."[20]

The broadside is typical of attacks on print ideology, as well as those on Franklin's person, for it fixes in two ways on Franklin's role as printer, publisher of the *Gazette,* and postmaster. First, it depicts Franklin's dissemination of print as part of a leveling tendency, and as effecting a false pretension on the part of the common people to belong to the realm of the public. Instead of being misled by the general nature of print, the broadside tells them, they should mind "their betters." Further, the broadside imposes a class stigma on Franklin's origin as a "leather-apron man," suggesting not only that print discourse encourages leveling but also that Franklin the printer (mere mechanic) manipulates that tendency in print in order to arrogate political power to himself.[21] "Post" and "Post-Man" share alike in the perversion of the public.

The strongest and most famous denunciation of Franklin came in 1774, in the so-called Cockpit confrontation with Alexander Wedderburn. Again, Franklin's manipulation of letters was the occasion. He had obtained by secret means some incriminating letters written by Thomas Hutchinson, then governor of Massachusetts. He had then sent them from London, where he was acting as agent for the Massachusetts Assembly, back to a group of influential men in the colonies, that they might know what Hutchinson had been writing in private about colonial affairs. Though the letters for the most part stated only what Hutchinson had already written publicly, the effect of their circulation was highly inflammatory, and eventually they were published. The colonials thus spread written evidence that their governor had privately advised such things as "There must be an abridgement of what are called English liberties." The publication of the letters exacerbated colonial discontent to the point that the Assembly addressed a petition to the royal government to remove Hutchinson from the governorship.[22]

Ironically, Franklin was the Assembly's agent at that time, so it fell to his lot to present the petition. Between the time of the letters' circulation and the hearing before the Privy Council, however, two other parties to the affair—both ignorant of Franklin's hand in it—engaged in a near-fatal duel about the responsibility over revealing and publishing the private correspondence. Franklin was forced to admit his role in order to avoid another duel. He justified his disclosure of the letters by arguing that they were public correspondence about public matters. Naturally the admission made him the focus of the anger of the ministry, who were already agitated by colonial intransigence.

Enter Alexander Wedderburn. Wedderburn was already on the upward trajectory of a career that would make him Lord Chancellor and an earl, though not too long before he had been dismissed from the Scottish bar for insulting the Lord President in the courtroom.[23] His skills in this case were to take Franklin as their object. His defense of Hutchinson's position as governor centered upon the argument that Hutchinson had been the victim of Franklin's unscrupulous schemes to incite rebellion. And Franklin, Wedderburn suggested, schemed in this manner primarily in order to have *himself* made governor. Wedderburn addressed a crowded and highly anticipated hearing before Privy Council; the audience included Burke, Priestley, and the young Bentham among its common ranks. In that charged setting, he heaped such invective on Franklin's head as to make the "Cockpit" fully deserving of its name.

> I hope, my Lords, you will mark (and brand) the man, for the honour of this country, of Europe, and of mankind. Private correspondence has hitherto been held sacred, in times of the greatest party rage, not only in politics but religion. He has forfeited all the respect of societies and of men. Into what companies will he hereafter go with an unembarrassed face, or the honest intrepidity of virtue. Men will watch him with a jealous eye; they will hide their papers from him, and lock up their escrutoires. He will henceforth esteem it a libel to be called *a man of letters; homo* trium *literarum!*
>
> (21:48–49)

Wedderburn's scapegoating constructs an agonistic force for the authoritative oral setting. The florid periods of his self-consciously oratorical denunciation enact what they describe, simply by constituting an exemplary orality backed by law—an orality that both stands in opposition to and disciplines the vagrancy of the literal.

The wit with which Wedderburn substitutes "thief" (Latin *fur,* hence "homo trium literarum," man of three letters)[24] for "man of letters" hangs on a reversal of the relation of man to letter. Whereas the man of letters finds his identity, or loses it, in letters, the man of three letters suffers the imposition of writing that is exterior to his person. It is consistent with the fact of his own authoritative speech and with its opposition to Franklin's literate transgression that Wedderburn conjures an image of bodily disfiguration: "I hope, my Lords, you will mark (and brand) the man." The brand restricts the written to the body, thereby furnishing the furtive manipulator of texts with a localized identity. Since identity in official orality is a disciplinary category, the body is specifically the body of the outcast.[25] By such logic Wedderburn portrays Franklin as being henceforward unfit for company because of the embarrassment of his face. And it is in the service of the same subordination of the written to the oral that he depicts private correspondence, hidden papers, locked escritoires.[26]

The faceless designing of Franklin's literal manipulation can appear only as a contradictory combination of impassivity and evil purposes or, in Wedderburn's words, "the coolest and most deliberate malevolence":

> [Here] is a man, who with the utmost insensibility of remorse, stands up and avows himself the author of all. I can compare it only to Zanga in Dr. Young's *Revenge*.
> "Know then 'twas—I:
> I forged the letter, I dispos'd the picture;
> I hated, I despised, and I destroy."
> I ask, my Lords, whether the revengeful temper attributed to the bloody African, is not surpassed by the coolness and apathy of the wily American? (21:49–50)

"It was a year of fine harangues," wrote Horace Walpole at the memory of Wedderburn's speech.[27] What is telling about the harangue is that the terms in which Franklin was most vitriolically condemned—his apathy, his wile—were the exact inversion, in a paradigm of imperial orality, of the virtues imagined by Franklin for rationality in a paradigm of print. His use of the material circulation of print in the service of oppositional republicanism (the morning after the hearing he told Priestley that, given another chance, he would have done everything in the same way), though exemplary of civic virtue in the ideology of print, was for the authority of orality the most heinous of crimes.

But if Franklin was being abused before the assembled peerage of the British Empire for his coolness, apathy, deliberate plotting, and wile, he did nothing to deny the charge. The *Public Advertiser* reports on February 2, 1774, that "The Doctor seemed to receive the thunder of his [Wedderburn's] Eloquence with philosophic Tranquility and sovereign Contempt." According to one witness, Franklin "stood *conspicuously erect, without the smallest movement of any part of his body.* The muscles of his face had been previously composed, so as to afford a placid tranquil expression of countenance, and he did not suffer the slightest alteration of it to appear during the continuance of the speech in which he was so harshly and improperly treated.—In short, to quote the words which he employed concerning himself on another occasion, he kept his 'countenance as immovable as if his features had been made of *wood.*'"[28] Declining to take the stand, Franklin endured Wedderburn's hour-long harangue impassively. He thus turned the tables on Wedderburn, implicitly proposing the very detachment for which he was being castigated as an exemption from that castigation. Like Silence amid the impetuous talkers, Franklin maintained secrecy and inscrutability because, when the imperial oral setting yielded to the specialized subsystem of public printing, those same qualities would be transformed into the integrity of a public virtue. "On this occasion it suited the Purposes of the Ministry to have me abused," he wrote. "And having myself been long engag'd in Publick Business, this Treatment is not new to me, I am almost as used to it as they are themselves, and perhaps can bear it better . . . [W]hat I feel on my own account is half lost in what I feel for the publick."[29] The incident greatly recuperated Franklin's colonial reputation, which had suffered in the mid-1760s, and did much to inflame revolutionary sentiment.

It was not a mere flourish, then, when one writer recorded the Cockpit affair as follows:

> Sarcastic Sawney, swol'n with spite and prate
> On silent Franklin poured his venal hate.
> The calm philosopher, without reply,
> Withdrew, and gave his country liberty.[30]

The ethic of silence and withdrawal is a salient feature of the lived form of rationality, a transformation of agon within the structures of print discourse; and silent Franklin's withdrawal is in a very strong sense equivalent with the conferral of liberty. And if it be objected that his image as this sort of "calm philosopher" is a calculated one, we should remember that it is precisely the nature both of liberty and of calm philosophy to be a calculated image.

The extent of Franklin's willingness to pursue this paradox is stunning enough in the Cockpit affair, but even more so in its coda. On February 16, 1774, eighteen days after the confrontation with Wedderburn, the following letter appeared in the pages of *The Public Advertiser:*

> The Admirers of Dr. Franklin in England are much shocked at Mr. Wedderburne's calling him a Thief; but perhaps they will be less surprised at this Circumstance when they are informed, that his greatest Admirers on the Continent agree in entertaining the same Idea of him. As an Evidence of this, I send you a Copy of a poetical Stanza, which is engraved under his Portrait prefixed to the late French Translation of his Work, in two Volumes, Quarto.
>
> I shall also send you an Attempt of a Translation of them, that the English Reader may be able to judge of the Similarity between the Idea of Mr. Wedderburne and that of the French Philosopher, with whom all the Philosophers in Europe intirely concur. It will even be seen that Foreigners represent him as much more impudent and audacious in his Thefts than the English Orator (though he was under no Restraint from a Regard to Truth) has ventured to insinuate. I am, Sir, Your humble Servant,
>
> HOMO TRIUM LITERARUM
>
> Il a ravi le feu des cieux,
> Il fait fleurir les arts en des climats sauvages.
> L'Amerique le place a la tete des sages,
> La Grece l'auroit mis au nombre de ses Dieux.
>
> In English.
>
> To steal from Heaven its sacred Fire he taught,
> The Arts to thrive in savage Climes he brought:
> In the New World the first of Men esteem'd;
> Among the Greeks a God he had been deem'd.

The letter is anonymous, but the audacious wit by which the theft of letters is revalued as promethean suggests Franklin as the author. If he wrote the letter, it would be his only direct response to Wedderburn. But who else could have taken up the signature "Homo trium literarum"? Franklin's appropriation of the epithet is itself a theft and therefore ironically proves the truth of the epithet. "Ironically," because the same theft also warrants his revaluation of the epithet, exemplifying his ability to locate himself in letters, free of strictures, anonymous and first of men at once. The letter of "Homo trium literarum" thus resembles the epitaph with which we began in this chapter, since it too indulges with remarkable literalness a fantasy of being-in-print. And the vaguely postmodern tone of Franklin's super-irony here may be attributed to the very rigor of his modernity, to his at times untempered pursuit of print negativity.

For the same reason, if the character of the man of three letters appears here in the form of a joke, we must remember that the stakes are high. Some four years after the Wedderburn affair, Joseph-Siffred Duplessis would paint his famous portrait of Franklin, the frame of which would bear the bold, simple legend "VIR." It might seem that only a poor pun unites the three-letter man of Duplessis' portrait to the man of three letters named by Wedderburn, but the logic that would justify such a pun has been provided by Franklin himself. In Franklin's career the virtuous citizen of the republic *(vir)* attests to his virtue by constituting himself in the generality of letters; if the designation of manipulator *(fur)* is made appropriate, so is the exemplary and general status that makes possible the designation of "VIR" rather than "Franklin." The poet who claimed that the calm philosopher's withdrawal bestowed liberty upon his country had disclosed the central truth of Franklin as man of letters: his career is designed at every level to exploit the homology between print discourse and representative polity. He cashes in like no one else on the resource of negativity. The logic of his career is the logic of representation.

Its closest analogue may be the fictive speaking voice of the written constitution, that bizarre invention in which Franklin took a hand. "We, the People," like B. Franklin, Printer, Richard Saunders, Silence Dogood, and the Homo Trium Literarum, speaks only in print, and for precisely that reason speaks with the full authority of representative legitimacy. It is with the Constitution, therefore, at the climax of Franklin's career, that his lifelong effort to locate himself in the generality of republican letters finds its embodiment. In his well-known speech to the convention, Franklin submerges his own voice to the motion for unanimous passage, authorizing as his own the voice of the document, as publication comes literally to constitute the public in yet another pseudonymous text.

· *IV* ·

Textuality and Legitimacy in the Printed Constitution

FP 039,40

official
hermeneutics → judicial
                review??

republicanism

yet review seems
central??

lacks or
official   hermeneutics — if it hv ones
                            (rf it is
                            suspicious?
                            see p.70
emerge of
liberalism

IN OUR SOCIETY, outfitted as it is with unprecedented technologies of discipline, the forms of coercion are innumerable. The supreme means of deriving force over the will of others, however, is to win the appeal to a written text. Let us consider this state of affairs. Why is the ground of legality, and thus of coercion, an official hermeneutics of a written text? What establishes *its* legality, and what is the significance of its textuality? The question is complicated because the Constitution's textuality was an issue even before conflict over the text's meaning was institutionalized in the role of the court system. The act of writing constitutions had been an American innovation, and in the case of the federal Constitution of 1787 at least, one that took place only on the assumption that the constitutional text would be a printed one. The subject of this chapter, therefore, is the meaning of the writtenness and printedness of constitutions in the culture of republican America, and of the relation between textuality, so considered, and the changing criteria of legitimacy that produced our official hermeneutics.

—an vr.
p.109
"all"

cf 110

p.114

How
"official"—
no
controversy
interpretive
procedure?

For Americans of the Revolutionary period the written constitution was a way of literalizing the doctrine of popular sovereignty. That literalization was a complex strategy, giving substance to the people's authority but doing so only through the agency of writing. It was a deeply problematic strategy, since the sovereignty of the people obviously is not identical to the official hermeneutics entailed by the constitutive text. On the other hand, if popular sovereignty seems to be a doctrine beyond question in our society, I shall argue that its literalization articulated its already problematic nature. The writtenness of the Constitution mediated a central and paradoxical problem in revolutionary politics: that of sovereignty in a legal order, or, more generally, the legality of law.

The British too had believed their polity to be founded, in theory, on the sovereignty of the people. Sovereignty lay in Parliament, or the king-in-Parliament, but it did so because all Englishmen in their capacity as subjects were represented there and could be said to have consented to Parliament's laws. The imperial crisis leading to the Revolution came about when Americans, refusing their consent to the laws of Parliament, denied that they were represented there. In doing so they disclosed a tautology deployed in England to legitimate the order of law: although what gave authority and legality to parliamentary law was its claim to represent the people, the only warrant for its claim to represent the people was parliamentary law. No one questioned the appeal to sovereignty; it was axiomatic that law required some authority for its legality. But since Americans were denying that they themselves, in representation, were the authority for law's legality, it became obvious that parliamentary law was its own authority. The American rhetoric of contestation, which identified parliamentary law as arbitrary power, thus derived its categories and its power from the British rhetoric of legitimation.

Working out that rhetoric of contestation could be dangerous. Since it was (and could only have been) worked out within the paradigm of representational legitimation, having identified the tautology of representational politics left the Americans with a heavily invested challenge to the legitimacy of their own governments. Recognizing that their challenge to the British was not just a challenge to particular rulers but to the fundamental validity of a legal order, the Continental Congress, on May 15, 1776, issued a decree calling for suppression of the authority of the Crown and for the establishment of new state governments, "on the authority of the people." A peculiar crisis ensued. Extant governments, like Parliament, already claimed the authority of the people in their representational character, though their claim to that authority became problematic because revolutionary politics depended on rejecting the circularity of such claims. But it also seemed that any *legal* procedures for claiming the authority of the people would have to be void along with the rest of the Crown-derived legal order. Far from being a lawyer's debate internal to law, this was a political crisis involving the legality of law. In a time of increasing military violence and crowd actions, the legal order as a whole was losing legitimacy.

In Philadelphia, as soon as word had spread of the May 15 decree, a pamphlet called *The Alarm* appeared, asking the hard question of who the "proper persons" could be to establish a government, "on the authority of the people," and what could be the proper "mode of authorizing such persons?" The Assembly was claiming that right, but as *The Alarm* pointed out, the Assembly derived its legal warrant from the proprietary charter, the authority of which was now void. Were the Assembly to suppress the authority of the Crown and institute the authority of the people, it would be suppressing its own authority and instituting its own authority; thus the Assemblymen might be "continually making and unmaking themselves at pleasure" (1). The Assembly, in other words, was not legal enough precisely because it was already legal.

For all the splendor of the argument, one has to wonder what ideal standard is being invoked against the Assembly. The very posing of the problem in *The Alarm* offers us the spectacle of a legal order trying to legalize itself. "It is now high time," the pamphlet says, "to come to some settled point, that we may call ourselves a people; for in the present unsettled state of things we are only a decent multitude . . . We are now arrived at a period from which we are to look forward as *a legal people*" (3). From decent multitude to legal people—how could this transformation come about? Better yet, how could it come about without law being there already?

The crisis symptomatized an irresolvable problem in the sovereignty of the people. The sovereignty of the people had to be appealed to as the ground for a legal order, but it could only be represented from within that legal order. As James Otis had put it in 1764, "An original supreme Sovereign, absolute and uncontroulable, *earthly* power *must* exist in and preside over every society; from whose final decisions there can be no appeal but directly to Heaven. It is therefore *originally* and *ultimately* in the people."[2] Originally, ultimately—but in the meantime? One reason why the American Revolution has struck many observers as not being very revolutionary is that the Americans insisted at every point on the continuity of law; new governments could not be established by fiat.[3] The common-law tradition continued; as a sphere of customary law rather than of positive, bureaucratic law, it required no original authority and could even be said to be authoritative *because* its origins lay beyond memory.[4] What required original authority was a state apparatus and the legal order in which it would operate. In this sphere of positive, bureaucratic law, revolutionary rhetoric insisted that law had been abrogated. Some in New Hampshire, for example, believed that once royal prerogative was annulled, "they never were a body politic in any legal sense whatever."[5]

There is a delirious theatricality about such claims. The American crisis of law was acting out, through time, the eighteenth century's narrative of legitimation: the social contract. Once law had been relegalized by the

Massachusetts constitution, for example, an orator named Thomas Dawes proclaimed that the people had successfully "convened in a state of Nature." "We often read," he said, "of the original Contract, and of mankind, in the early ages, passing from a state of Nature to immediate Civilization. But *what eye* could penetrate through the gothic night and barbarous fable to that remote period? . . . And yet the people of Massachusetts have reduced to practice the wonderful theory." By enacting the founding of the legal-political orders that would represent them, the people would render the origin within history, and the transcendent source of law as its present practice.[6]

The crisis is revealing because the difficulties encountered in generating law from nature are symptomatic of difficulties in the legal order's claim to transcendent justification—that is, to law's character of duty as opposed to force. Many of the period's most vexing problems, such as the problematic character of popular sovereignty, continue to haunt law's account of itself. As H. L. A. Hart argues in *The Concept of Law,* the people cannot be said to lay down the rules, and thus to be sovereign, because "The rules are *constitutive* of the sovereign . . . So we cannot say that . . . the rules specifying the procedure of the electorate represent the conditions under which the society, as so many individuals, obeys itself as an electorate; for 'itself as an electorate' is not a reference to a person identifiable apart from the rules."[7] Hart concludes that a legal system cannot have a sovereign, an origin of law not itself legally constrained. It can have only rules.

Hart argues against sovereignty because he identifies it with coercion, with an account of law as orders backed by threats. Sovereignty, to him, is that point at which legality must derive from orders backed by threats, or, what comes to the same thing, from politics. His solution, however, will be subject to the same problem. Hart argues that primary rules, such as statutory law, are made law by means of secondary rules—rules of recognition that enable certain people under special conditions to establish law. According to these terms, Americans of the Revolutionary period were trying, in their debates about constitution-forming, to establish the secondary rules. But what rule of recognition allows one to establish or adjudicate or even reproduce a rule of recognition? Rules, as Hart himself remarks in another context, cannot provide for their own interpretation (123). It follows that the legality of law is not itself guaranteed by law or rules. The effectiveness of any claim to be operating according to rules depends in the last analysis not on autonomous or self-modifying rules, but on the politics of rhetoric in which rules are reproduced and altered. Hart struggles to imagine a self-contained and self-authorizing system of legality because, for him, if law's authority derives from the contingencies and irregularities of political culture, it can no longer be exempt from the character of coercion.

Eighteenth-century Americans had the same dream of a self-contained system of positive law. Where Hart dreams of law regulated by its own regularity, Americans pictured law justified by its derivation from the will of the people. The legal-political order would be transcendent in its authority but immanent in its source. The trick was to see how law could be given to the people transcendently and received from it immanently at the same time. Like Hart's, *The Alarm*'s solution for the legal origination of law was predictably disappointing. The committees of inspection, "agreeable to the power they are already invested with," were to call a convention for the drafting of a constitution. The pamphlet regards the authority of the committees as unproblematic, a tendency which should not be astonishing since at some point the authority of law must always be seen as "already invested." Similar crises in other colonies were resolved in similar ways. The 1778 Massachusetts constitution, for example, was voted down primarily because it originated in the old House of Representatives and not a special convention; two years later a convention-drafted constitution was adopted. Only a national pest like Noah Webster would follow the critique to its conclusion, pointing out that a convention must inevitably be "chosen by the people in the manner they choose a legislature."[8]

If the argument for constitutional conventions lacked a legal and theoretical consistency—and no argument for the legal establishment of law *could* have had such a consistency—the question of how they were legitimated could only be answered politically. Why, having mounted a brilliant challenge against the Assembly's claim to originate law, did *The Alarm* simply turn around and accord that right to conventions established by virtually the same legal procedures? The explanation lies in one of the most brilliant insights in Gordon Wood's history of the period. Given the colonial tradition of extralegal conventions, says Wood, the new constitutional conventions could fill their legitimating role precisely because of their inferior legality. Formed in imitation of assemblies, the conventions had long been denounced as subversions of law. They could therefore be described, as Tom Paine describes them in *Common Sense,* as "some intermediary body between the governed and the governors, that is, between the Congress and the people."[9] In the political culture of revolutionary America the convention was sufficiently dubious to appear unconstrained by law; thus it could stand in the place of the sovereign.

But this is also where writing comes in. Paine's notion that the constitu-

tional conventions would stand between "the governed and the governors" is an invocation of the contract theory of written law, in which bills
of rights or charters or the Magna Carta were supposed to embody agreements mutually constraining rulers and ruled. Yet, as Wood points out,
"bills of rights in English history had traditionally been designed to de-
lineate the people's rights against the Crown or the ruler, not against
Parliament which presumably represented the people" (272). The bizarre
new American project of writing charters as fundamental law for all government aimed at removing the circular legitimation of representative
assemblies. But the constitutions, themselves generated "on the authority
of the people," prescribed the procedures for claiming the authority of the
people. By constituting the government, the people's text literally constitutes the people. In the concrete form of these texts, the people decides
the conditions of its own embodiment. The text itself becomes not only
the supreme law, but the only original embodiment of the people. In this
act of literalization, the meaning of the charters' writtenness has been
transformed; no longer merely a better way of keeping records, writing
gives original existence to its author. Ecriture would save the republic.

Because the notion of writing constitutions stems from the legitimating—and, by the same token, delegitimating—tenet of popular sovereignty, it shares a history with crowd actions, extralegal conventions, and
the intense localism of community assemblies in the 1770s and 1780s. Yet
these latter movements, though motivated by the desire to maintain political sovereignty in the people rather than in the kind of supreme institution that Parliament had become, were distinctly outside the legal order.
They were perceived not as manifestations of the sovereign body, but as
the breakdown of government altogether. In these contexts "the people"
functioned as a legitimating signifier that did not entail the regularity of
law. It interpellated subjects into a political world without interpellating
them into the juridical order.[10] In some regions, such as Vermont and
the western counties of Massachusetts, people began regularly to disobey
the courts, and they defended their action through rigorous republican
constitutional theory. Undesirable as this delegitimizing result was for
American revolutionaries, it was the practical fulfillment of the necessary
conditions under which the signifier of "the people" could *legitimate* a
juridical order.

Like any signifier the people could never be realizable as such. Yet in
the revolutionary years a wide range of collectivities—especially local assemblies—were able to recognize themselves, in action, as the people.
Moreover, they were often able to sustain that self-identification legiti-

mately in their dealings with other, similarly identified collectivities. This should not surprise us, since a people recognizing itself as the people is like a king recognizing himself as the king; we do not have to indulge in a sentimental populism to see these groups as realizations of the people. The difficulty of doing so is that our society's representational polity rests on a recognition of the abstract and definitionally nonempirical character of the people. It is the invention of the written constitution, itself now the original and literal embodiment of the people, that ensures that the people will henceforward be nonempirical by definition. The opacity of signification has become a political fact.

By means of their customarily extralegal status, the constitutional conventions repeated the revolutionary realizations of the people so that writing could be summoned, from a position not yet law, to become already law. It could do so partly on the very grounds of a traditional logocentric anxiety: whereas in speech, persons, hearing themselves speak, are present to themselves and responsible for their language, writing migrates from persons arbitrarily. Rousseau cites this determination of language in order to argue for the necessity of speech for any realization of the people in a republic. "I maintain," he writes in the *Essay on the Origin of Languages,* "that any language in which it is not possible to make oneself understood by the people assembled is a servile language; it is impossible for a people to remain free and speak that language." The classical republics survived because "Among the ancients it was easy to be heard by the people in a public square." Writing, by contrast, is the mark of modern corruption: "Popular languages have become as thoroughly useless as has eloquence. Societies have assumed their final forms: nothing can be changed in them anymore except by arms and cash, and since there is nothing left to say to the people but *give money,* it is said with posters on street corners or with soldiers in private homes; for this there is no need to assemble anyone; on the contrary, subjects must be kept scattered; that is the first maxim of modern politics."[11] As Derrida observes of Rousseau, "Praise of the 'assembled people' at the festival or at the political forum is always a critique of representation. The legitimizing instance, in the city as in language—speech or writing—and in the arts, is the representer present in person: source of legitimacy and sacred origin."[12]

The Americans who prevailed in the constitutional movement regarded their task not as getting rid of representation, but of deriving representation in the first place. The presence of the people to themselves in oral assembly was for them not legitimate enough precisely because it was recognized as the *source* of legitimacy. As source, or sovereign, it was by definition not legally constrained. The speech heard by the assembled people, in the words of the Boston *Independent Chronicle,* could only come from men "with the *vox populi vox Dei* in their mouths."[13] In this view the vox populi, in order to be the vox Dei, cannot be in anybody's mouth, because the owner of that mouth, as the embodiment of the sovereign, would not be a constrained subject. The people in assembly do not follow legitimate procedure in laying down the law, and they could not do so unless someone could lay down the law of legitimate procedure to the sovereign—but then *that* agency would be sovereign, and thus not following legitimate procedure. What was needed for legitimacy, the Americans came to believe, was the derivative afterward of writing rather than the speech of the people. By articulating a nonempirical agency to replace empirical realizations of the people, writing became the hinge between a delegitimizing revolutionary politics and a nonrevolutionary, already legal signification of the people; it masked the contradiction between the two.

Written constitutions, including the federal Constitution of 1787, completed a deployment of writing that had begun with the Declaration of Independence. The best account of that earlier deployment comes to us from the unlikely source of Jacques Derrida, in a set of prefatory and not entirely serious remarks at the University of Virginia during the Declaration's bicentennial. Derrida notes the paradox that documents such as the Declaration—or the Constitution—should be signed. "In principle," he observes, "an institution is obliged, in its history and in its tradition, in its permanence and thus in its very institutionality, to render itself independent from the empirical individuals who have taken part in its production." Nevertheless, "the founding act of an institution—the act as archive equally with the act as performance—must retain the signature within it." Derrida will attribute the felt need for the founding signature to "the structure of the institutive language." But for such a purpose, "whose signature could be legitimate?"[14]

Derrida observes that although Jefferson wrote the Declaration, he did so not in his own right but by delegation from the other delegates, who then revised his draft and put their names to it. But they in turn put their names to it not in their own right, but "in the name and by authority of the good people of these . . . free and independent states."

> By rights, then, the signatory is the people, the "good" people . . . It is the "good people" that declares itself free and independent by the relays of its representatives of representatives. One cannot decide—and it is all the interest, the strength, and the impact of such a declara-

tive act—whether the independence is stated or produced by this statement . . . Is it the case that the good people is already freed in fact and does nothing but acts out its emancipation by the Declaration? Or rather does it liberate itself at the instant and by the signature of this Declaration? . .)

Such then is the "good people" which is not engaged and only engaged in signing, in causing to sign its own declaration. The "we" of the Declaration speaks "in the name of the people."

But this people does not exist. It does not exist *before* this declaration, not *as such*. If it is given birth, as a free and independent subject, as a possible signatory, that can only depend on the act of this signature. The signature invents the signatory. The latter can only authorize to sign once it has arrived at the goal, so to speak, of its signature, in a sort of fabulous retroactivity. Its first signature authorizes to sign . . .

In signing, the people speaks—and does what it says to do, but in deferring it by the intermediation of its representations, whose representativeness is only fully legitimated by the signature, and thus after the fact . . . By this fabulous event, by this fable which is implicated in the trace and is in truth possible only by the inadequacy of a present to itself, a signature is given a name.   (20–23)

In this mention of the trace and the inadequacy of the present, Derrida's philosophical concerns become visible, and he will pursue his teasing remarks only in that direction, through a discussion of Nietzsche. Yet the paradox he identifies in the Declaration is perhaps not just a tease or a philosopher's puzzle, and Derrida indicates in passing a couple of ways in which it raises a serious issue. The puzzle of the relation between the authorizing people and the authorized signature that creates the people's authority, he remarks, "is not a matter here of an obscurity or a difficulty of interpretation, a problematic on the way toward a solution. It is not a matter of a difficult analysis that founders before the structure of implied acts and the overdetermined temporality of events. This obscurity, this indecidability between, let us say, a performative structure and a constative structure, is *required* in order to produce the effect sought for. It is essential to the very position of law [droit] as such, that one speaks here of hypocrisy, of equivocation, of indecidability or of fiction" (21).

Derrida suggests, in other words, that the paradox of the authorized and authorizing signature replicates the contradiction that we have observed in the notion of sovereignty. By saying that it is "essential to the very position of law as such," however, he means that the effect is not simply that of the founding moment produced by the Americans' theatrical claim that they had reverted to the state of nature. The word "droit," essential for his assertion here, denotes at once law and right, commandment and authorization to command. In the systems of positive law that characterize modern society—systems of law, let us say, not underwritten by God—law is defined by its derivation of authority from itself.

The contrast with divine authority may clarify the position of the written constitution as fundamental American law. In *Rights of Man,* Paine refers to the written constitution as a "political bible." It is no accidental turn of phrase. When the Declaration asserts that the states "are and ought to be" free and independent, Derrida notes that the "and," which "articulates and conjoins here the two discursive modalities of is and ought, statement and prescription, fact and law," occupies the position of God (27). "Are and ought to be" is like the divinely imperative and creative "Be," which human authority can approximate in an indicative "is" or a subjunctive "ought." For a legal system to derive its legality immanently rather than transcendently, therefore, requires the effect of textuality that collapses the two modes. William Nelson's study of the law in Massachusetts affords an interesting illustration of this point. According to him, prerevolutionary legislation was almost always justified by preambles that explained the continuity of the statute with common law. Beginning with the ratification of a written constitution, however, the legislature began to shift its self-understanding, so that by the 1790s "legislation was coming to rest solely on a 'be it enacted' clause—a naked assertion of sovereign legislative power."[15] The Constitution deploys that effect most notably in the preamble: "We the People . . . do constitute." Legality rides on the inability to decide whether the people constitute the government already—that is, in fact—or in the future, as it were by prescription.

In order to be the law to the law, however, the people must occupy this textual position themselves, and not through the relays of representatives who sign for them in the Declaration. For this reason it was of utmost importance that the legal-political order be constituted not just by a written text, but by a printed one. In the important 1776 pamphlet called *Four Letters on Interesting Subjects,* which along with *Common Sense* was among the first to argue for a written constitution, we read that "All constitutions should be contained in some written Charter, but *that* Charter should be the act of *all* and not of *one man.*" The specific negative reference here is to Pennsylvania's proprietary charter, granted by the Crown. Such charters are inappropriate models, the pamphlet suggests, because they emanate from the authority of persons, and are thus "a species of tyranny, because they substitute the will of ONE as the law for ALL."[16] Because it is not clear how any concrete act could be the act of all, (the obscurity of agency) in print was helpful as the enabling pretext for a constitution.

In *Common Sense*, Paine suggests that the people might charter their own government. This suggestion occasions the famous passage in which he imagines a solemn day for "proclaiming the charter," on which the charter will be brought forth and crowned so that the world will know that "in America the law is king." "But lest any ill use should afterwards arise," he adds in a revealing afterthought, "let the (crown) at the conclusion of the ceremony be demolished, and scattered among the people whose right it is." The political motives for this vivid image of the smashed and scattered crown would also determine the meaning of the printed artifact of the constitution. By the time of *Rights of Man*, Paine would be laying great emphasis on the constitution's printed condition, detailing carefully the procedures of printing proposed constitutions for the people's approval. Similarly, he notes with satisfaction that once approved in Pennsylvania, the state constitution had been properly scattered. "Scarcely a family was without it. Every member of the Government had a copy; and nothing was more common when any debate arose on the principle of a bill, or on the extent of any species of authority, than for the members to take the printed Constitution out of their pocket, and read the chapter with which such matter in debate was connected."[17] When every representative is able to pull the people out of his pocket to receive his charter, then is law law.

The (procedure of printing) the Constitution for reference was undergone twice during the proceedings of the federal convention (after the reports of the committees of detail and style), that each delegate might be sure of identical wording. The procedure guaranteed that the constitution would be a general creation. Franklin's motion for unanimity indicates the importance of (nonparticular authorship.) When his famous speech failed to obtain the assent of every delegate, Franklin proposed that the document be signed by "unanimous consent" of the states. By this stratagem, signing the constitution would not amount to endorsing it personally. Thus, whereas the climactic moment for the Declaration of Independence was the signing, for the Constitution the climactic moment was the maneuver that deprived signing of personal meaning. For the same reason, whereas the signed copy of the Declaration continues to be a national fetish, from which printed copies can only be derived imitations, the Constitution found its ideal form in every printed copy, beginning, though not specially, with its initial publication, in the place of the weekly news copy of the *Pennsylvania Packet*.

The Constitution's printedness allows it to emanate from no one in particular, and thus from the people. It is worth stressing, however, that this meaning for print is a determinate construction of political culture, not a transcendently secured logic. The Constitution derives from particular persons as much as speech or script do. We know their names—compilers, printers, and print-shop journeymen included. Only contingent structures of meaning ensure that such filiations will lack the status of the filiations of other kinds of language. Among these structures we may count the emergent paradigm of representational legitimacy, with its newly literal and literalizable notion of the sovereignty of the people. We may also include the republican metadiscourse of the specialized subsystem of public discourse, a paradigm that for several decades had informed perceptions of print in America.

Developed in practices of literacy that included the production and consumption of newspapers, broadsides, pamphlets, legal documents, and books, the republican ideology of print elevated the values of generality over those of the personal. In this cognitive vocabulary the social diffusion of printed artifacts took on the investment of the disinterested virtue of the public orientation, as opposed to the corrupting interests and passions of particular and local persons.[18] *The Alarm* is a good example of the continuity between the republican metadiscourse of print and the legitimacy of constitutional measures. It argues that one reason why the Assembly should be disqualified from writing a constitution is that its members have a "private interest" in the positions to be established under such a constitution. Offering itself as a contrast, the anonymous *Alarm* proclaims: "The persons who recommend this, are Fellow-Citizens with yourselves. They have no private views; no interest to establish for themselves. Their aim, end and wish is the happiness of the Community. He who dares say otherwise, let him step forth, and prove it; for, conscious of the purity of our intentions, we challenge the world" (3).

"We," however, do so anonymously, in print, while the doubtless corrupt challenger is imagined to speak and stand forth in person. Anonymity, in the republican culture of print, designates not cowardice, but public virtue. The arguments of *The Alarm* are vouched for by the claim to disinterested concern for the general good, which claim is in turn vouched for by the perceived conditions of the very medium in which it is made. And if such assumptions on the part of the unnamed "we" of *The Alarm* seem to be determinate features of a political culture, the same assumptions enable the unnamed "we" of the Constitution. They will also be seen animating the ratification debates, especially in the aggressive print campaign of the "Publius" who stands forth in the Federalist papers.

For all the power of the republican paradigm of print discourse, it hardly replaced the more familiar logocentric determinations of language. Readers of *The Alarm,* even while according validity to its rhetorical self-presentation, might have speculated about the authors' identities and private views. The same is true, as we know, of the Constitution. Its composers, unlike those of *The Alarm,* did not refuse to subscribe their names, though after Franklin's motion they deliberately ambiguated the significance of their subscriptions. It was not unusual during the ratification period for copies of the Constitution to omit the delegates' names, printing only the approved resolutions of unanimity. That the generality of the printed language be seen as more important than the signatures was crucial to the legitimation of the document.

Some of the document's detractors, from that time to the present, have insisted on reading its significance as determined by the private interests of those men. By the same token, many of the document's professed admirers also adduce, for their interpretations, views about the private interests of the subscribing individuals, though interests in this case are redescribed as intentions. Former Attorney General Edwin Meese, for one, considers the preamble's version of the Constitution's authority uncreditable. In his view, all official hermeneutics of the text should be governed by the intentions of the particular men who signed it on September 17, 1787, in Philadelphia—long before its ratification. Given the eighteenth-century republican understanding of the Constitution as fundamental law expressing the authority of the people, Meese's understanding of constitutional validity would transform the document into the kind of charter that *Four Letters on Interesting Subjects* calls tyranny. For, in the last instance, he derives authority from the will of the so-called founders—specifically, from the supposed mental contents of those founders—rather than from the people, the only legitimate founders. The Constitution would never have been ratified had it been perceived as the kind of document that Meese thinks it is. His brand of intentionalism could only take hold once a nationalist filiopietism had supplanted the radical republicanism that initially legitimated the constitutional order. The amnesia of that shift in legitimacy paradigms demonstrates the historical specificity of the cultural assumptions that allowed the printed constitution to embody the will of all.

The printedness of the constitution, in short, was understood as precluding *any* official hermeneutics, especially an intentionalist one that would accord privilege to the views of the delegates. As one South Carolinian put it in 1783, "What people in their senses would make the judges, who are fallible men, depositaries of the law; when the easy, reasonable method of printing, at once secures its perpetuity, and divulges it to those who ought in justice to be made acquainted with it."[19]

This last passage makes it clear that in allowing the expression of the will of all, the printedness of the Constitution not only underwrites, so to speak, the popular authorship of the Constitution—it summons the readership of the print audience to recertify it continually and universally. As with the authorship, the readership of the Constitution is more than a convenience or mere exigency; in an important sense it is structurally required by representational legitimacy. The same textuality essential to the constitution of law's authority inhabits equally the position of the subject under the law, in that it provides a necessary ambiguation of consent. Popular sovereignty, which avoids domination by allowing that all subjects of the legal order will take their place as the sources of law, requires a notion of consent, in which the people who give law vow that they will take their place as its subjects. The two parts of sovereignty and consent correspond to the compulsory and voluntary aspects of duty. To give law the character of duty republican political rhetoric insists on the foundation of politics in popular sovereignty and popular consent. Thus the predicament of sovereignty in the revolutionary period was everywhere implicated with a problem of consent. Much of the power of the constitutional innovation lies in its solution to the problem: with the Constitution, consent is to sovereignty as readership is to authorship.

Revolutionary rhetoric required Americans to be very good at using the word consent to mean both authorization and compliance at once. For example, when the *Boston Evening Post* proclaimed in 1765 that "the only moral foundation of government is, the consent of the people," it meant either that the consent of the people allowed an existing government to have a "moral foundation," or that consent allowed the existence of the government in the first place—or it meant both simultaneously.[20] On one hand, to say that people consent to the law is tautologous, since consent from this point of view designates what Weber calls "validity"—the belief in a norm by the members of a society. Consent of this variety does not confer any lasting authority on law, but just *is* the authority of law; it is either continually reproduced or law loses legitimacy. On the other hand, in a system of positive law and popular sovereignty, consent is adduced

to justify the enforcement of norms even where they are not believed—
that is to say, where they are not taken as duty—or those norms obviously
would not be law. But this second variety of consent is narrativized; it is
the moment at the origin of law in which the coercive character of law is
forsworn in advance. Unlike the voluntary aspect of duty, which by nature
cannot be instituted as positive law, authorizing consent is consent to
one's own coercion, contradiction in terms though that might be.

For the American republicans it was self-evident that a law could not
be law by reason of someone else's consent. In a letter to Madison in 1789,
Jefferson took this to mean that "no society can make a perpetual constitution, or even a perpetual law." Madison's response astutely realizes that a
doctrine of actual consent would not only prevent one generation from
legislating for another—this, it will be recalled, is Paine's justification for
revolution—but will prevent the majority from legislating for the minority. "Strict Theory," he observes, "at all times presupposes the assent of
every member to the establishment of the rule itself." But, asked John
Adams when he sensed the same implications, "Shall we say that every
individual of the community, old and young, male and female, as well as
rich and poor, must consent, expressly, to every act of legislation?" "I find
no relief from these consequences," Madison wrote, "but in the received
doctrine that a tacit assent may be given to established Constitutions and
laws, and that this assent may be inferred, where no positive dissent appears." Indeed, he went on, "May it not be questioned whether it be
possible to exclude wholly the idea of tacit assent, without subverting the
foundation of civil Society?" Madison, Adams, and Jefferson were under-
standably worried about this conclusion, because it retroactively denied
the legitimacy of the Revolution and, more to the point, left the present
order without transcendent legality. Every extant legal order—no matter
how tyrannical, corrupt, or irrational—is justified by tacit assent, which
is to say that no legal order is justified at all.[21]

The written constitution mediates this crisis in perpetuity—the only
way it could be mediated. In the preamble the reading citizen interpellates
himself—even herself—into the juridical order precisely at its foundation.
Whereas Meese's sacralizing intentionalism understands the foundations
of law to lie in the intentions of the patriarchs, the ongoing consumption
of the preamble in print makes the moment of foundation perpetual and
socially undifferentiated. Not only does it enact the consent of every citizen—male and female, old and young, black and white, rich and poor—it
also reads that consent as the transcendent grounds of subjection. We
might say that the printedness of the Constitution here restores to the

dutifulness of law the permanence that consent had narrativized. By the same token, the "we" of the Constitution—and this is essential for its legitimating effect—is speaking *to itself.* The evidently untraced origins and universal audience of the printed text allow the people always to be both authoring and reading, both giving and receiving its commands at once. Unlike Rousseau's general will, which similarly derives its obligatory character from the simultaneity of its common origin and common object, the printed constitution is a mechanism that translates the transcendent conditions of legality into a system of positive law. In this sovereign interpellation the people are always coming across themselves in the act of consenting to their own coercion.

I say "their" own coercion, but of course this is what the Constitution will not allow me to say. There is no legitimate representational space outside of the constitutive we. When someone calls out to the people, you will answer.[22] You inhabit the people, but this is not true of any group to which you belong, the people being the site where all lesser collectivities are evacuated. For this reason the preamble contributes to a nationalist imagination in the same way that Benedict Anderson has argued for novels and print in general.[23] By means of print discourse we have come to imagine a community simultaneous with but not proximate to ourselves: separate persons having the same relation to a corporate body realized only metonymically. The national community of the constitutional we is an aspect of the people's abstractness and may be contrasted with the intense localism of the popular assemblies which were its main rival for the role of the people.[24]

Some other spokespersons for the people noticed this hazard to their voices. In the ratifying convention in Massachusetts, for example, one Amos Singletary stood up and protested aloud: "These lawyers, and men of learning, and moneyed men, that talk so finely, and gloss over matters so smoothly, to make us poor illiterate people swallow down the pill, expect to get into Congress themselves; they expect to be the managers of this Constitution, and get all the power and all the money into their own hands, and then they will swallow up all us little folks, like the great *Leviathan,* Mr. President; yes, just as the whale swallowed up *Jonah.* This is what I am afraid of."[25] Singletary senses a danger, but he misrecognizes the threat posed against the illiterate by the new constitution. That threat does not depend, as he believes, upon the rapacity of the men of letters, but is established in the legitimation of the document itself, since the document's authority means that the kind of oral setting in which Single-tary participates will henceforth be secondary. To be accurate, we should say that the authority of the written constitution creates two hazards to the voice of the people. First, it enables the mediation of legitimacy by a relatively small class of the literate. Second, it establishes the denial of such mediation as the first condition of representative legitimacy—a denial made possible by the existence of the written text ceaselessly representing a silent people.

The new paradigm about which Singletary worries finds its exemplary "spokesman" (though neither speaker nor man) in one "Publius"—author of *The Federalist* and now known to be the collective pen name of Alexander Hamilton, James Madison, and John Jay. The very identity of Publius dramatizes the conditions of authority in representational polity, for Publius—like the People in "We, the People"—is emphatically a pen name, a composite voice made articulable only in his written pseudonymity. Throughout the ratification debate he was lauded or attacked only as "Publius" because he was not known by any other name. The highly literate men who lie behind Publius underscore the analogy between their spokesman and the People in the name they give him: Publius Valerianus, commonly known as Publicola ("people-lover"), was one of the founders and early consuls of republican Rome. In Plutarch's *Lives* he is lengthily compared to Solon as an exemplary lawgiver. In choosing the relatively uncommon pseudonym of Publius the authors of *The Federalist* punningly identify themselves with the public while also identifying themselves with the founding of polity and the institution of law.[26]

In keeping with the publicity suggested in the identity of Publius, *The Federalist* was produced in a barrage of print. Publius was not content simply to appear in print. Through various machinations he was able to appear simultaneously in four newspapers in New York and another in Virginia, with occasional appearances elsewhere to boot—a strategy of blanketing the public space of print that was warmly resented by his opponents.[27] That strategy no doubt reflects Publius' sense of the high stakes involved in his persuasive task; it can also be seen as corresponding to the claims of public representation implicit in his identity. Publius speaks in the utmost generality of print, denying in his very existence the mediation of particular persons.

For several decades before the Constitution, print had been acquiring the ability to serve as a means of imagining the public sphere. The simultaneity of the artifacts of political print discourse expressed the identity of this sphere which was no longer local. Eventually, although this abstract public sphere was articulated with republican categories of generality, disinterested virtue, and civic liberty, it would enable a modern national state that was more appropriate to liberal individualism. We can look forward beyond the scope of this book to suggest a way in which the deployment of textuality in the Constitution, though itself profoundly republican, marks the emergence also of a new mode of textuality.

The commission of sovereignty to its literalization in print required from American political culture a high degree of confidence in the transparency of language and the undifferentiated universality of print. "No man is a true republican," says *Four Letters on Interesting Subjects*, "or worthy of that name, that will not give up his single voice to that of the public" (386). The voicing strategies of the written constitution are registered here as the liberty of the social contract. In the decades after ratification, however, a liberal discourse of rights increasingly regarded the state as an institution for accommodating the conflicting claims of persons, and defined persons by their economic self-interest and their privative relation to the state. The republican ideology of print eroded, and an official hermeneutics emerged—only twenty years after our South Carolinian had argued that printing made the opinions of lawyers and judges unnecessary.

Between the legitimating drama of sovereignty that gave rise to the Constitution and the official hermeneutics that resulted from it, the meaning of the document's writtenness had been transformed. The transformation was not recognized as such, but was regarded as a restatement of republican principles. A good example is John Marshall's decision in *Marbury v. Madison,* where he appeals to the Constitution's writtenness in order to argue that hermeneutics gives the law exactly in the act of receiving the law.

> The powers of the legislature are defined and limited; and that those limits may not be forgotten, the constitution is written . . . Certainly, all those who have framed written constitutions contemplate them as forming the fundamental and paramount law of the nation, and consequently, the theory of every such government must be, that an act of the legislature, repugnant to the constitution, is void. This theory is essentially attached to a written constitution, and is, consequently, to be considered, by this court, as one of the fundamental principles of our society.[28]

It may seem paradoxical that Marshall's decision, which establishes the principle of judicial review, does so precisely by denying that the court can make law: "the courts, as well as other departments, are bound by" the written constitution. Official hermeneutics came into being on the condition of its own denial. It required both the drama of popular sovereignty and the republican faith in the transparency of print that seemed to make a hermeneutics unnecessary. Giving the law in receiving it, official hermeneutics repeats, albeit in a very different mode, the sovereign consent of the Constitution.

The salient point of difference is that official hermeneutics constructs a relation between the subject and the text that is registered as mediation. *Language, far from being transparent, has become in its ambiguity the site of social conflict, even while the resolution of that conflict must be received from an authority immanent in the language.* In a letter written in 1814 Gouverneur Morris expresses disbelief at the new state of constitutional textuality. For him, the existence of "a written constitution containing unequivocal provisions and limitations" should have eliminated all difficulty of meaning. Interpreting the Constitution, he writes, "must be done by comparing the plain import of the words with the general tenor and object of the instrument." He then adds, evidently in support of his position: "That instrument was written by the fingers which write this letter." The curious thing about Morris' remark is that he does *not* appeal to his intentions as founder, but to the act of writing as testament to the clarity of the written text. But because authority was now to be received from its already mediated condition, Morris' somewhat comical confidence in what might be called the indexical value of his fingers had become deeply anachronistic. Legality, under the bureaucratic nationalist state, is to be registered as an alienation within experience.

This relation to an authoritatively mediated hermeneutics is characteristically modern. I suggest that it helped to determine a newly representative relation between literary textuality and the nature of subjectivity in the bureaucratic nation. It was of no small importance that the years in which literary culture was established in this country were also the years of protracted constitutional crisis. In the official discourse of law and the state, as well as in the specialized discourse of an emergent literary culture, or even the theological discourse of the higher criticism, it became possible to locate in language the conflicted and mediated character of truth, nonetheless maintaining the authoritative character of that truth. Insofar as authoritative mediation had come to define the position of the subject in relation to the bureaucratic state, such discourses could mutually articulate the experience of that subject. They were all ways of understanding one's fateful immersion in social conflict as a naturally alienated dependence on interpretation. Constitutional hermeneutics, literary culture, and the higher criticism jointly helped to make language to liberal society what the market was to the liberal economy: authoritative but disembodied mediation of conflict among interested and conflictual subjects.

Thus, textuality came to be understood as rather more than polysemeity, which had long been recognized within scriptural hermeneutics. Texts began to be regarded as having incommensurable meanings, and it became possible to see that incommensurability as given and even as necessary. For this reason Poe's *Narrative of Arthur Gordon Pym,* published fifty years after the Constitution, is a more appropriate illustration of the textuality of official hermeneutics than is Morris' appeal to his fingers. Although Poe displays an obsession with textuality throughout his career, it is nowhere clearer than in this text. And since Poe brought to full development for the first time in America a discourse of the literary distinguished from other discourses precisely by its embrace of a naturalized textuality, there is good reason to regard the novel as a cultural landmark.

In particular, consider the unfingered text that has mysteriously but authoritatively materialized on the island of Tsalal. Pym and his companion, it will be recalled, find some markings resembling characters on the side of a chasm where the earth has flaked away. The circumstances prove to Pym that they could only have been produced by the work of nature. He also makes a set of drawings that show, from an aerial perspective, the shapes of the several chasms he has found. Not until the "Note" appended to Pym's narrative is it revealed that both the markings *and* the shapes of the chasms themselves are writing. We are not told who the agent of these writings is, and our knowledge of the agent behind the Note is ambiguous, since the Note points out that the pattern of the chasms had "escaped the attention of Mr. Poe." According to the Note, the markings Pym has found in the chasm combine an Arabic word meaning "to be white" with an Egyptian word meaning "the region of the south." And the shapes of the chasms, when read in an inverted map, constitute the Ethiopian word meaning "to be shady."[29]

It would be too simple to say that the meaning of these writings is left ambiguous. That they have reference, even authoritative reference, is clear. The novel appeared in the midst of a crisis over black and white in the region of the South, and its dominant episodes are about race and revolt. Nothing is clearer than that these messages refer to the political crisis of race in the union. At the same time nothing is less clear than *how* they refer to that crisis. This is not simply to say that Poe's ideas on racial conflict are difficult to infer. It is to say that what he has most carefully ambiguated is the textuality of the writings from which he solicits our inference. Another example can illustrate. An extra line appended to the

Note reads: "I have graven it within the hills, and my vengeance upon the dust within the rock." This line, the last in the book, is curiously unattributed. It is italicized to set it off from the speaker of the Note, but it is assigned to no one in lieu of that speaker. In such circumstances, and with a scriptural tone rare in this most untheological of writers, the last line in relation to the text epitomizes the nature of the texts that Pym and Peters have found on Tsalal. They appear from a general source, admit with difficulty of interpretation, are conflictually fraught, but carry transcendent authority as well.

The political crisis that forms the relevant context for these cryptic texts—race and regional conflict—hinged on the textuality of the Constitution. Webster's debate with Hayne had been seven years earlier, and in another three years Madison's newly released notes from the constitutional convention would be read as the key to national fate. In this context it should not surprise us that, although without an author—or rather *because* without an author—the writings on Tsalal bear the full prophetic weight of law. They are encountered both as fate and as the pure resonance of signification. It is the romantic scandal of hermeneutics, now to inhabit the law.

But this, as I have said, is to look beyond the scope of my book. Another problem lies closer at hand. If, as I have suggested, literary textuality can be seen as an aesthetic developed to fit the legitimacy of postrepublican, liberal society, what aesthetic could have developed to fit the preliterary culture of republican society? To ask such a question is to have created a problem for literary criticism, which typically predicates its inquiries into early national literature, like any other, on the assumption of liberal society's textual aesthetics. Early national, republican America stands as an interesting anomaly. The cultural conditions for valuing ambiguated textuality and giving it the resonance of modern experience had not yet developed. But the discourse of the public sphere also required a critical posture toward the personal and theological modes of authority that had previously grounded textual aesthetics and hermeneutics.

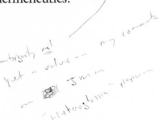

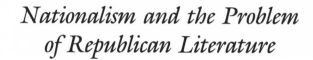

· V ·

Nationalism and the Problem of Republican Literature

TO CELEBRATE the ratification of the Constitution, the city of Baltimore held a parade. As in the ratifying pageants of other cities, the artisans of the printing trade took a prominent part. Some of them, costumed as Mercury, distributed copies of the Constitution; others carried objects that, in the words of the local paper, represented "Volumes, American Productions."[1] The printers' display of their "American Productions" was not unusual at a time when a rhetoric of commercial nationalism was growing everywhere. The phenomenon was more complex than it seemed. The printers had not just one image for the national value of their work, but two: the dispersed Constitution and the displayed volumes. These images convey distinct ways of thinking about the printing trade. By distributing the Constitution, printers could imply a powerful claim for the relation between print and power, offering themselves as the tangible reality for the scattering of the nation's foundations. But that image does not treat books as commodities; it does not value them as objects made and sold for private gain. So the printers also armed themselves with their wares as they paraded through the streets. But print's salability, so presented, might seem incommensurate with its claim to be the palladium of liberty; accordingly, the printers take pains to identify their commodities as bearing the distributive value of nationality. Even onlookers who would not or could not buy the books could in theory partake of them by virtue of their national production.

That rhetoric of nationalism burgeoned everywhere in the 1780s and 1790s, but nowhere more than in the printing trade. Writers began to talk of making specifically American books. So did printers, typographers, binders, papermakers, and lawmakers. The new federal Congress wasted no time in drafting its first copyright act, and several states had already enacted copyright laws of their own. Congress found other ways of contributing to nationalism in the trade, going so far as to impose heavy tariffs on imported books for private purchasers. The official tariff was 15 percent, and since customs charges and dealers' profits were figured on top of that amount, the law gave considerable incentive for American editions. The idea behind such policies did not seem to need argument: American printers, by reprinting foreign texts in new, cheap editions, would keep funds circulating at home. Domestic authorship had the same advantage; it was local manufacture.

How are we to take this nationalist rhetoric? There is a long and unchallenged tradition in criticism, familiar to every scholar of American literature, in which the 1780s and 1790s are seen as the period of American literature's newfound self-consciousness. Americans' post-Revolution fervor is widely taken as having led to a call for an independent culture, freed from servile colonial imitation of English models. It can then be lamented that so few American writers made good on that hope for national culture, or it can be claimed that they did. But that Americans of the 1780s and 1790s *wanted* a distinctively indigenous culture, of the kind that developed in the 1820s and 1830s, has never been disputed.[2] This critical cliché points toward an impressively common theme in the early national period, but I believe it misses the nature of commercial nationalist rhetoric. Republican Americans understood print and the nation as intimately related; but it is not clear that the relation obtained for them in a separate realm of cultural goods, beyond the public sphere.

When advertisements and subscription proposals tell readers that an author is American, they do not necessarily point to a link between traits of nationality and those of aesthetics; they merely solicit patrons' encouragement of the domestic trade, much as they might for the making of shoes. An example can make the difference clearer. In 1792 one printer proposed to print, by subscription, a novel called *The Hapless Orphan*, by "an American Lady." The subscription proposals promote the book as follows: "This work is an original *American* production. The facts are recent. The history is affecting. The sentiments are pure. The language is perspicuous and elegant. The lovers of virtue and polite literature are respectfully invited to lend their patronage to genius, and may rest assured that they will have no cause to repent of their encouragement."[3] The advertisement does not even attempt to connect the book's American production with its culturally distinctive virtues—recent facts, affecting history, pure sentiments, and perspicuous language. These could as easily be claimed for a foreign work. By calling attention to the American-ness of the author, the publisher provides an economic rather than aesthetic argument for its purchase. The purchasers of the book are asked to see themselves as contributing to, not consuming, the literature of the republic. And the "genius" that subscribers will "encourage" is ex-pected to be a source of civic capacity rather than the object of private appreciation.

The modern reader might be led by such an advertisement to expect a specially indigenous cultural good. He or she would then be predictably disappointed to find that the novel is written to accord with standards of appreciation that are not particularly American at all. But that effect of disappointment, which for decades has been the dominant tone in critical commentary on the period, has been produced by the prism of modern "literary" expectations. The benefits of American authorship, at least in the case of *The Hapless Orphan,* were defined at the time so as to be secured regardless of the book's aesthetic character.

But if nationalist rhetoric was not expressing a hope for a new, distinc-tively indigenous culture (and I will have more arguments that it was not), then what could its significance be? There is a problem here both for literary history and for the history of nationalism. What cultural assump-tions were necessary before people began to see "Americanness" saturating the cultural goods they produced and consumed? Nationalism had not reached that point in the United States by 1800. In some ways, although the nation-state was a product of the eighteenth century, the national imaginary was a product of the nineteenth. For in the republican period the nation continued to be imagined through the public sphere. As we have seen, that required a specialized subsystem of print discourse, and the printing trade was closely tied to the self-image of the republican nation. But for all books—considered now as private commodities—to be American, one had to have a new kind of national imaginary. One had to have a meaning for "American" that would be distinct from the special-ized public sphere. It had to be equally possible to speak meaningfully of American character, American doughnuts, American furniture, or Amer-ican hygiene. National value would have to be detached from public dis-course.

That in fact is what happened in the early nineteenth century. A national imaginary and a liberal ideology of literature arose together, because both divorced the public value of printed commodities from the public dis-course. In the 1780s and 1790s, however, that outcome was far from clear. Americans had a republican metadiscourse that identified print with the public. It came under increasing stress as newly aestheticizing and nationalist perceptions of books developed. But its transformation was neither guaranteed nor easy.

Nationalist rhetoric began in the printing trade before it began in aesthetic criticism. It allowed printers to extend the self-understanding they attained in the public sphere to the self-understanding implied by their practical activities as tradesmen. Because the nationalist rhetoric referred mainly to the political economy of the nation, it could apply equally to any and all stages of bookmaking. An extreme but indicative case was the 1807 quarto of Joel Barlow's *Columbiad*. Barlow and his publishers promoted the text as a national epic and billed Barlow as a genius of the republic. For promoters and reviewers alike, however, Barlow's authorship and subject matter were aspects of the more general fact that the quarto represented an American venture into the fine arts of bookmaking. American illustrators and engravers had been commissioned, and the American printers had exercised lavish care in the composition and correction of the text. (The master compositor is said to have offered a hundred pounds for detection of any error that escaped his proofreading.) The type itself, specially chosen for the project, was a domestically cast font that its founders appropriately called "Columbian." Even the fine paper came from a domestic papermaker who decorated his ream wrappers with portraits of American statesmen and the legend, "The American Arts Only Want Encouragement."[4] Nevertheless, the quarto *Columbiad* was a financial disaster, largely responsible for bankrupting its publishers. Priced at twenty dollars (unbound) in a period when that figure was greater than the total value of the average private library, and when few books cost even a quarter of that amount, the *Columbiad* rested its appeal on an uneasy alliance between republican pride and polite finery.

It was one thing to believe that the new republic required a thriving printing trade and the broad circulation of letters. It was quite another thing to treat a book as a luxury good or an end in itself. So although the publishing of the quarto may have been bad business strategy, the mistake points to a divided purpose that was also latent in the civic pageant of the Baltimore printers, with its separate images for commodities and the public sphere. There is even a note of the same division in the advertisement for *The Hapless Orphan*, which appeals somewhat ambiguously to "the lovers of virtue and polite literature." The traits by which Americans identified print in order to confer on it the value of nationality (virtue) were not those that would value books as cultural ends in themselves (polite literature). The rhetoric of republican nationalism can be sharply distinguished from the kind of literary nationalism that would become powerful in the 1830s, because republican trade nationalism did not entail a liberal ideology of the literary.

The Potent Hand of Literature

When Noah Webster argued in his 1783 *Grammatical Institute* that "America must be as independent in *literature* as she is in *politics*," he did not have in mind texts that would be cultural ends in themselves; rather, he meant all of the forms of written discourse and the uses of literacy. His dictionary gives the definition of "literature" appropriate for such an argument: "Learning, acquaintance with letters or books. *Literature* comprehends a knowledge of the ancient languages, denominated classical, history, grammar, rhetoric, logic, geography, &c. as well as of the sciences. A knowledge of the world and good breeding give luster to literature."[5] The very breadth of Webster's definition—comprising knowledge of all kinds of letters—was one of literature's most important connotations. The *Universal Asylum and Columbian Magazine* addressed its subscribers as "The Patrons of American Literature," even though those patrons subscribed to attacks on novel-reading rather than novels, political rather than critical essays, economic news rather than reviews, mechanical diagrams rather than engraved art, and scientific rather than literary speculation. In typical fashion, the page addressing the patrons of American literature is followed by a listing of current commodity prices for Philadelphia. If that seemed logical, it was because the term "literature" defined a way of looking at all of these subjects as continuous.[6]

Because "literature" described the entire field of letters in a way appropriate to the discourse of the public sphere, it could establish a national plane of reference for the printing trade. As the *Columbian Phenix* put it, "LITERATURE well or ill conducted, is the great Engine, by which all civilized States must ultimately be supported or overthrown."[7] Literature is possessed not just by persons, but by peoples. And when persons are said to possess literature in republican America, they are credited with citizenship rather than private culture. The value of literature is distributive rather than proper, general rather than private. Note the way literature arises in the political context of a Boston sermon of 1778, by the patriot Phillips Payson:

> The slavery of a people is generally founded in ignorance of some kind or another; and there are not wanting such facts as abundantly prove the human mind may be so sunk and debased, through igno-

rance and its natural effects, as even to adore its enslaver, and kiss its chains. Hence knowledge and learning may well be considered as most essentially requisite to a free, righteous government. A republican government and science mutually promote and support each other. Great literary acquirements are indeed the lot of but few, because but few in a community have ability and opportunity to pursue the paths of science; but a certain degree of knowledge is absolutely necessary to be diffused through a state for the preservation of its liberties and the quiet of government . . . Despotism and tyranny want nothing but wealth and force, but liberty and order are supported by knowledge and virtue.[8]

Like the John Adams essay with which this book begins, Payson's sermon asserts a politicized understanding of letters. The implicit tendency of that assertion becomes clear as he is led to emphasize the social *distribution* of letters. The political utility of literature, he sees, will not bestow value on "great literary acquirements" (which he accordingly does not pursue as a theme) but rather on what he calls their diffusion. "Nothing can so well promote the equality of rank, so much talked of and applauded yet so little known in republics," wrote another, "as the universality and the estimation of literature."[9]

The theme of the diffusion of letters would become one of the most prominent in the discourse of early national America. By 1796, when George Washington delivered his Farewell Address, this kind of rhetoric was so familiar that he was able to draw on commonplace but complex assumptions about the republic by appealing for a "general diffusion of knowledge." This phrase of course was hardly unique to America, being familiar to writers of England and the continent. Nor was it new in the early national period.[10] "Diffusion," moreover, was to have a long history. As late as 1867 Horatio Alger's *Ragged Dick* could allude to diffusion of literature as the occupation of newsboys. The persistence of the phrase in Alger's parody testifies to its familiarity. And that familiarity can be traced to republican rhetoric of the later eighteenth century, when it was used almost obsessively. I take the early national appeal of the phrase to be an index of the kind of nationalism appropriate to print, and the kind of print appropriate to the nation. As Zabdiel Adams put it in 1782: "An ignorant people will never long live under a free government. They will soon become slaves, or run into anarchy. This, therefore teaches the infinite necessity of diffusing intelligence among the body of the people."[11] It is by "the diffusion of useful knowledge," another writer explains, that "the prevalence of virtue shall be rendered secure."[12] The key terms for each of these writers, such as "diffusion," "literature," and "prevalence," all stand in opposition to private appropriation, especially as typified by the despot. "Information," Noah Webster wrote, "is fatal to despotism."[13]

Early national writers did not distinguish between the diffusion of science and the diffusion of literature, since both literature and science lacked as yet the associations of subject and method that would polarize them in the next century. For the most part, however, Americans preferred the term literature when speaking of diffusion. The difference between the two is that the term literature emphasized the model of letters, to which it literally refers. In the case of *The Worcester Magazine*'s appeal for the diffusion of the "spirit of literature," there is good reason for seeing the model of letters as an important subtext. Isaiah Thomas, the magazine's printer and publisher, had two years previously issued a book of specimen types in order to recruit business. The book was dedicated "To the Lovers of Literature, and Encouragers of Printing (The First and Best of Arts) in the Commonwealth of Massachusetts."[14] Literature here literally implies not just letters, but particularly the block letters that Thomas was offering for hire. The diffusion of literature clearly was to be undertaken largely through print, and it is not necessary to think of Thomas' rhetoric merely as self-serving in order to see that his magazine's call for the diffusion of literature implied an important role for the printing trade.

Literature, in such a context, resembles the modern notion of literacy as a ground of basic and general competence, though it does not denote literacy in the modern sense. "When I speak of a diffusion of knowledge," writes Noah Webster, "I do not mean merely a knowledge of spelling books and the New Testament [the two texts most used to teach writing and reading, respectively]. An acquaintance with ethics and with the general principles of law, commerce, money, and government is necessary for the yeomanry of a republican state." Although he means more than mere literacy, nonetheless he continues to associate the diffusion of this broad range of knowledge with the diffusion of letters, for he goes on to say: "This acquaintance they might obtain by means of books calculated for schools and read by the children during the winter months and by the circulation of public papers."[15]

If the rhetoric of diffusion rested on the implicit or explicit model of print, it also required a very specific set of assumptions about the nature of print: letters, on this model, imply generality. It was taken for granted that print, motivated and organized in a capitalist economy, extends itself dynamically to the largest possible market. Equally taken for granted was that speech in the print medium conforms to special standards of utterance, so that diffused letters could be assumed to be different in nature from, say, well-disseminated royal decrees. In turn, the rhetoric of diffusion articulated a political significance and value for the traits assumed to inhere in print: "the art of print, the invention of modern times . . . is extremely instrumental in propagating a competent, or indispensible portion, of knowledge throughout a nation."[16] At least one newspaper writer could make the link fully explicit: "It must highly gratify every lover of his country, to see in it the triumph and the perfection of the *Arts*. That of *printing,* which gives the most diffusive extent, certain perpetuity to knowledge, to all that is pleasing, interesting and important to mankind, demands the first and most liberal encouragement."[17]

Printers and observers of print constantly cited republican arguments about literature as the reason for the great proliferation of newspapers and magazines at the end of the century. It was the heyday of the small newspaper. More newspapers were founded in the 1790s than had been started in the entire century preceding. Inaugural issues of newspapers in the period typically contain paeans to print's diffusive power, condensing the rhetorical tradition I have been tracing.[18] Magazines presented themselves to readers in the same way. The *New-York Magazine,* for example, offered its subscribers the following rationale: "Those institutions are the most effectual guards to public liberty which diffuse the rudiments of literature among a people . . . A few incautious expressions in our constitution, or a few salaries of office too great for the contracted feelings of those who do not know the worth of merit and integrity, can never injure the United States, while literature is generally diffused, and the plain citizen and planter reads and judges for himself."[19] As a market strategy, such rhetoric about print articulates a republican reading of general public discourse, rather than a leisurely consumption of luxury goods. David Nord, who has analyzed the subscriber list of this magazine, shows that although it includes few of the poor (not surprisingly, since it cost money to subscribe), the journal had a strong artisan readership. The rhetoric of diffusion had broad social appeal.[20]

The same rhetoric contains a strand of anxiety about the unlettered. Samuel Knox vividly depicts a scene of general turpitude: "Ignorance, more especially literary ignorance, has ever been the parent and stupid nurse of civil slavery—and in proportion as this ignorance prevails or is dissipated, so are men in every situation more or less disposed to support the interests of civil liberty or political happiness. Hence it has happened and ever will happen that despots either in religion or in politics have uniformly sought to maintain their tyrannical systems over the minds of men, by keeping those minds in the gloom of a stupid, uninformed, state of ignorance and insensibility."[21] Though he is more eloquent than most, Knox is making what was at the time a common observation. Isaiah Thomas' *Worcester Magazine* has it thus: "While learning expands the heart, and is the sure basis of a republican government, ignorance by an opposite tendency, is the only foundation of a monarchical. Let us for a moment examine the state of those nations where monarchy presides; there we find the common people but little superiour to the untutored herd. It is the interest of this kind of government to keep them in total ignorance of their natural rights, to cramp their minds, and bend them to servitude."[22] The common, untutored herd, with their cramped and bent minds, are necessarily minds without letters. Any kind of stupor would do to characterize the illiterate. As Richard Beresford asked in his *Plea for Literature,* "Who daily sees not drunkenness the occupation of unlettered solitude?"[23]

This anxiety about "literary ignorance" reveals an assumption, or at least a desire, that the public sphere be identical with the realm of letters. And the graphic pictures of stupefaction show that the public character of print required an especially active and virtue-laden notion of reading. Just as the *generality* of literature appears in the term "diffusion," the empowering *virtue* of literature appears in accounts of the mind and education. Let us take as another example a text by a young man of Charles Brockden Brown's age named Wilkes Wood, addressing a "philological society" in Vermont in 1795:

> Do we declare, that the main object of our thus associating is the improvement of the mind? Then let each one be inspired with an incessant ardour for acquiring useful knowledge, and stimulated to pursue the paths of science; as it is that which distinguishes us from the brute creation, and as that is the ornament of civilized life.—Let us be Readers, by which we may acquire that fund of knowledge which will make us instructive companions, and useful to our country; and which, when the time comes in which we shall say, the pleasures of sense have become to us insipid, shall afford to the mind a source of enjoyment, and buoy us up through the calamities of old age. And to this end, let us be anxiously engaged in establishing a judicious and well regulated Library, as a common reservoire, from which we may extract such materials as will, while they afford a delicious entertainment, enlarge our views of human nature, and make us more acquainted with ourselves. By employing our leisure hours in these pursuits, we shall be able to view the human species

as in one group; and in our solitary moments, contemplate the terrestrial globe as one grand theatre beautifully diversified, and each scene productive of rational amusement and useful instruction.[24]

Although Wood here provides the founding language for what we would call an institution of literary culture, his rhetoric turns decisively away from literary refinement as an end. Instead, it bases its appeal on a picture of the virtuous activity of the mind. The emphasis is on "useful" knowledge and on the socializing influence of letters, which separates organized society from "brute creation." Wood consistently imagines the benefits of letters as transindividual, even actively expansive. The reading citizens will be instructive to their companions and useful to their country. So powerful is this strand in his thinking that he arrives at a virtual apotheosis of the reader, whose socially expansive mind will be able to envision the entire history of the species from a synoptic vantage, immune to vicissitude and corruption. The logic of such writers so strongly identifies the value of letters with the virtue of the reading citizen that we can see how fine writing could come to be associated with the dangers of luxury. Letters are paramount in republican rhetoric, but they are never disengaged from the active and public dimensions of personhood.

The nationalist ideology of republican literature allows the same assumptions equally to motivate legislation such as Connecticut's "Act for the Encouragement of Literature and Genius"—an early copyright law that aimed to promote indigenous authorship—and educational laws such as Jefferson's "Bill for the More General Diffusion of Knowledge" in Virginia. By such acts, republican categories of literature and diffusion were finding their way into law. The rhetoric of diffusion governed most public policy having to do with print, since lawmakers understood the circulation of newspapers as the arena of public power. Early American governments spent a great deal of time and money on the post roads, and politicians from all camps agreed to maintain the preferential postal rates for newspapers that Franklin had established as postmaster. Many, including Washington, wanted free distribution.[25] Elbridge Gerry of Massachusetts invoked the republican rhetoric of literature when he propounded the rationale for the postal policy in a congressional debate of 1791:

Mr. Gerry observed . . . [that] wherever information is freely circulated, there slavery cannot exist; or if it does, it will vanish as soon as information has been generally diffused. The light of information has enabled the French to discover their rights, which so long lay concealed from their eyes, and has put them in possession of their present Constitution. However firmly liberty may be established in any country, it cannot long subsist if the channels of information be stopped; instead, therefore, of taking any steps that might tend to prevent the diffusion of political information, the House ought to adopt measures by which the information, contained in any one paper within the United States, might immediately spread from one extremity of the continent to the other; thus the whole body of the citizens will be enabled to see and guard against any evil that may threaten them.[26]

Here Gerry is able to take for granted that the same natural features of print that make it essential to a republic also enable it to define the territorial expansiveness of the national continent. The handiness of diffusion lies in just this identification. And even those who opposed Gerry in the debate over franking and newspaper rates were forced to argue their position as a better means toward "a general diffusion of information."

Similarly, as Benjamin Rush would argue in a work whose very title called for the "Diffusion of Knowledge in Pennsylvania," "the establishment of newspapers in a few of the most populous county towns will contribute very much to diffuse knowledge of all kinds through the state. To accomplish this, the means of conveying the papers should be make easy, by the assistance of the legislature."[27] And if it is beginning to seem in my account that a great deal was promised by assertions about literature, Rush shows that there were no limits: "Henry the IVth of France used to say he hoped to live to see the time when every peasant in his kingdom would dine on a turkey every Sunday. I have not a wish for the extension of literature in the state that would not be gratified by living to see a weekly newspaper in every farmhouse in Pennsylvania. Part of the effects of this universal diffusion of knowledge would probably be to produce turkies and poultry of all kinds on the tables of our farmers, not only on Sundays, but on every day of the week."[28] Print metonymically produces poultry because of its relation to the political economy of the nation. Given the conditions of representational polity, letters can be seen as the medium not just of utterance but of regular civilization.

By now my examples may seem somewhat monolithic and repetitive. That is the point. Since I am claiming that the obsession with this rhetoric was almost universal in the 1780s and 1790s, we might well ask: Whose tradition is this? Since it supports a value for the printing trade, we might expect it to bear the interest of those identified with print discourse as its agents. Certainly the rhetoric of diffusion appears most often in official or semiofficial contexts, and probably not just because these are the contexts in which print was most used. The men who developed this rhetorical tradition identified themselves with both print and public affairs. Some, such as Thomas, were printers; others, such as Jefferson, belonged to the class of men who were at once the political leaders and the largest consumers of print. As I have already argued, the dispositions entailed by print were an important political and cultural resource for them. Historical scholarship has shown convincingly, however, that the republican political paradigm saturated popular culture to a high degree. Some evidence—such as subscription lists for republican magazines—suggests that even the print ideology of political literacy was embraced by groups in society that were scarcely distinguished by letters. Nevertheless, the ideology of diffusion poses a problem in that it simultaneously entails a special, interested construction of the print medium *and* the construction of the political world.

The very idea of the diffusion of literature presupposes a recalcitrant social difference. Its implicit center-periphery metaphorics registers the centralization of literacy that the thematic content of the discourse disavows. The problem of the self-erasing center can be somewhat astoundingly exemplified by Benjamin Rush, who says: "From the observations that have been made it is plain that I consider it as possible to convert men into republican machines. This must be done if we expect them to perform their parts properly in the great machine of the government of the state. That republic is sophisticated with monarchy or aristocracy that does not revolve upon the wills of the people, and these must be fitted to each other by means of education before they can be made to produce regularity and unison in government."[29] Here the same rhetoric that claims to base government on "the wills of the people" is the rhetoric that conceives itself as mechanically fitting those wills together. The people appear active with respect to the public sphere, but passive with respect to the institutions of letters. In another setting that disjunction might look like the hegemonic problem of theory in a democratic movement, where the difficulty might be to distribute the skills and materials of literacy for the purpose of collective self-clarification. Rush's perspective, however, is that of the state, and it is his regulative social agenda that here finds expression in an ideal of distribution.

At least one writer, a former Minuteman named William Manning, took a different perspective on republican literature. Where Rush was a prolific publisher, a professor, statesman, and man of letters, Manning was a barely literate farmer. His one text, a republican essay written in 1797 called "The Key of Libberty," was not published until this century. And though he claims to be a "Constant Reader of publick Newspapers," any reader of his text can see that no false modesty underlies his confession, in the essay's moving introduction, that he was unpracticed in letters:

> I am not a Man of Larning my selfe for I neaver had the advantage of six months schooling in my life. I am no travelor for I neaver was 50 Miles from whare I was born in no direction, & I am no grate reader of antiant history for I always followed hard labour for a living. But I always thought it My duty to search into & see for my selfe in all maters that consansed me as a member of society, & when the war began betwen Brittan & Amarica I was in the prime of Life & highly taken up with Liberty & a free Government. I See almost the first blood that was shed in Concord fite & scores of men dead, dying & wounded in the Cause of Libberty, which caused serious sencations in my mind.[30]

Having accounted for his entry into the public sphere through its metonymic realization in corpses rather than letters, Manning can identify the distribution of letters as the obstacle to republican government. He presents society as divided into two orders: those who earn their living by bodily labor and those who do not. The latter, among whom he includes "all in the literary walkes of Life," he calls the few; they embody the principle of corruption in a republic. Manning writes eloquently of the antidemocratic forces in a society so organized, rallying with passion the opposition of laborers. The main burden of his long essay is that because of the division of labor, the means of literature lie not in the hands of the republic's virtuous citizens, but rather in those of its enemies. Newspapers, he recognizes, are organized essentially around the market-dependent interests of their producers, and for that reason cannot be the purely public institutions they claimed to be. "Newspaper knowledg is ruened by the few" (248). (This was an argument easily made in Manning's Massachusetts, where all but a couple of the fifteen newspapers were Federalist.)

Manning might seem to be the lone dissenter from the ideology of diffusion in early national America. To the extent that this is true, however, he is the exception that proves the rule, since the standard for his critique of the social organization of letters is none other than the norm of republican literature. The heading over the introduction reads, "Learning & Knowledg is assential to the preservation of Libberty & unless we

have more of it amongue us we Cannot Seporte our Libertyes Long."
Like the other writers I have cited, Manning believes that the principle of
despots is "to train up their subjects as much in ignorance as they can."
For each of the economic and policy evils he catalogs with paranoid vigor,
"the ondly Remidi is knowledge" (247). He operates within the republican ideology of literature, even to the extent of assuming that the "knowledge" of virtuous citizens must come in the form of diffused print. "The
prinsaple knowledge nesecary for a free man to have is obtained by the
Libberty of the press or publick newspapers" (232).

It is because of this republican norm of literature that Manning writes
so bitterly of the private appropriation of letters. And it is because his
critique has this shape that his grand proposal, delivered after an exhaustive description of the nation, is in effect a collectivization of print. Manning proposes a society to be organized by and for workers, appropriately
to be called the "Labouring Society." He does not propose that this society act as a political party, that it organize as a trade union, that it form
a platform, or that it agitate for resistance. He proposes only that it fund
and organize its own printing system. The "Munthly Magazein" produced
by this system, he argues, could be cheap, since he envisions a vast network
of local cell groups, each with its own librarian, to share the cost; "one
will do for a hole Neighbourhood" (248). He also suggests that the towns
should begin to provide "six weeks of wrighting school in the winter &
twelve weeks of a woman school in the summer"; these two versions of
literature constitute the entire social program of his proposal.

Manning's social utopia of literature matches the republican ideology
of print in its identification of letters with the public sphere, of literacy
with virtue, and of reading with supervision. His critical insight into the
ideology of diffusion—unique, as far as I have been able to tell—was that
the claims of that ideology were at odds with the social organization of
letters and print. Whereas Benjamin Rush depicted a dissemination of
print that would yield turkeys and leisure, Manning's program works in
the other direction, envisioning a republic in which "Labour & Larning
would be conected together & lesen the number of those that live without
work" (231). I want to emphasize, despite this contrast, that the ideal of
a society without a division of labor in letters is predicated in some form
by all who write within the republican ideology of literature. Manning's
essay, representing as it does the radical extreme of laborer opposition,
testifies to the encompassing power of the discourse. His ability to articulate the critical potential in the norm of generality dramatizes what was
true across the board in the early national period: the values of literature

were defined in opposition to private appropriation and distinction. For this reason the republican paradigm of literature had an antiaesthetic tendency, where aesthetics was increasingly being formed around private appropriation and distinction.[31]

Politeness

Literature's tension with early liberal aesthetic categories for the appreciation of luxury goods can be seen in the ideological complexity of politeness. Consider the double appeal of *The Hapless Orphan* in the language of its advertisement for "lovers of virtue and polite literature." The link with virtue depended on the assumptions about the public sphere that I have been tracing. Politeness, like virtue, was a character value that could confer value on the consumption of books. Yet it established a value for the private appropriation of letters by the consumer. It is the self-interested individual, not the polity, that profits from the cultivation of politeness through the consumption of books. Republican writers consequently betrayed anxiety about use of the term for appreciating printed goods. The roots of their anxiety were deep, for they understood the very nature of print to express the values of diffusion.

The category of politeness had a long tradition in England and the continent, where the discourse of politeness developed in the late seventeenth and early eighteenth centuries as an adaptation of courtesy literature.[32] As the term lost its courtly associations and became the subject of a widely disseminated literature, it came to define a normative value for commerce, where "commerce" had the dual sense of social interaction and trade. In the words of an early-eighteenth-century writer, "*Politenesse*, may be defined a dextrous management of our Words and Actions, whereby we make other People have better Opinion [*sic*] of us and themselves."[33] The power of the term—especially for Americans, for whom it legitimated trade rather than nobility—came in part from its ability to establish two things at once: a norm of subjectivity, since it implies a special kind of experience and a set of prescribed behaviors to go with it; and a way of thinking about commerce, such that the normal interactions of trade will be seen to have a meliorative, civilizing outcome.

Politeness had been an especially important term from the early eighteenth century for the small pockets of belletristic culture in colonial society, such as the Maryland literati known as the Tuesday Club. This rather genteel circle, which included Doctor Alexander Hamilton, revolved around a printer and bookseller named Jonas Green. Members exchanged poetry and essays but also engaged in criticism of each others' works.[34] In consuming print, they thought of themselves as being polite gentlemen in a cosmopolitan world of civility. When Hamilton traveled through the colonies in the early 1740s, he carefully noted in his journal the signs of politeness he saw in different regions. In Philadelphia, for example, he found "polite conversation," as he puts it, "among the better sort." He decided that Philadelphia "is a degree politer than New York tho in its fabrick not so urban, but Boston excells both for politeness and urbanity tho only a town."[35] This anglicizing discourse of politeness and civility was not uncommon among the wealthier colonists of the eastern seaboard. Even a product of Puritan society such as Mather Byles, prominent Boston minister and a nephew of Cotton Mather, aspired in his youth to the world of polite letters. Before publishing a slim volume of poetry in 1744, he wrote his M.A. thesis in divinity at Harvard on the proposition that "polite literature is an ornament to a theologian."[36]

Most modern readers of these eighteenth-century American belletrists complain that theirs is but a belated Augustan writing. Byles was a particularly enthusiastic admirer of Pope, to whom he wrote a fan letter; when the great man returned a letter of acknowledgment, Byles put it in his coat pocket next to his heart and wore it there for years, until it frayed and crumbled. It is important to remember, however, that this imitative commerce with the imperial capital is something that we can only describe as an unfortunate belatedness given a modern set of assumptions about literature. In the pursuit of politeness, originality is not a goal, and provincial deference is not an evil. Byles's flattering letter from Pope was material testimony to his politeness, and polite letters required no further evidence of worth.

Strikingly, but perhaps not coincidentally, a vastly disproportionate number of colonial belletrists, from Byles to the Tuesday Club to William Smith's Philadelphia circle, showed loyalist sympathies during the imperial crisis. The connection seemed logical to the more radically republican Americans at the time, since until the last quarter of the century the republican paradigm classed politeness with the corrupt insubstantiality of persons in aristocratic society. American skepticism derived from the fact that the category of politeness exemplified the "dextrous management" of status through esteem. It could easily seem to be the radical opposite of virtue, having more in common with other categories of fictitious and artificial selfhood such as opinion, credit, fame, and honor.

In the contemporary language of social description, the defining principle of aristocratic polity—honor—was just such a theatrical form of self-constitution. In Montesquieu the controlling principles of monarchy, republics, and despotisms were honor, virtue, and fear, respectively. Honor, which Montesquieu associates with politeness, is not a simple passion like fear, but a regulative and reflective passion. "Politeness, generally speaking, does not derive its original from so pure a source: it rises from a desire of distinguishing ourselves. It is pride that renders us polite, we are flattered with being taken notice of for a behaviour that shews we are not of a mean condition."[37] Louis Althusser has pointed out that two important consequences follow for Montesquieu from this understanding. First, honor is not a virtue but a regulative principle; it makes people want the *appearance* of the virtues, in accordance with self-interest. Althusser makes the point in a telling sentence: "Honour is the economy of virtue."[38] Second, any society structured by honor and politeness must necessarily presuppose an inequitable distribution of what Montesquieu calls "preeminences and ranks"—otherwise it would make no sense to strive competitively for esteem. The scarcity of honor is the premise of its economy. That is why it is the constitutive principle of aristocracy. As Althusser remarks, "Honour is *the passion of a social class*."[39] Because this was generally taken to be true in eighteenth-century America, any reflective management of esteem could be held accountable to the charge of aristocratic pretension.[40] Luxury goods, genteel manners, polite letters, and above all theater were suspect because they constructed personhood in a way that seemed neither ethically secured nor potentially republican.

As Lawrence Klein has shown in his studies of politeness in English discourse, the problem was that, as a description of personhood and social interaction, the "dextrous management" of politeness was dangerously theatrical, "the creation of an image, not the manifestation of the soul." "'Politeness' was the art of sociability, the art of pleasing in company, an art involving self-presentation, inter-subjectivity, and self-love. Social status was not something granted, but rather something up for grabs."[41] Because the discourse of politeness pioneered the transformation of the social self into a manipulator of roles, it could serve as "a program for modernity." But because the role-playing subject of politeness was constituted by the interactive management of image and status, it seemed to have come unmoored from moral categories. As an account of the social self, therefore, politeness appeared in competition with virtue. Klein writes: "Virtue involved others, but being virtuous involved no dependence on others. One did not become by being beheld." The ethical instability of the polite mode of subjectivity, moreover, was a problem *within* the category of politeness; "the art of pleasing in company was insufficient to establish the normative claim of 'politeness,' because such a definition meant making the other the reference of one's own being."[42]

As Klein shows, the establishment of the normative claim of "politeness"—its integration with the ethical categories of social description such as "virtue"—was a major task of eighteenth-century English social reflection, especially in Shaftesbury, Addison, and Steele. The term otherwise tended to be associated with luxury and corruption because it designated an artificiality of personhood, while virtue tended to be associated with the unaffected simplicity of the self-present individual. As we have seen in the case of Franklin, the reconciliation of these models of personhood was an important task for Americans as well. Franklin's oxymoronic *"art of virtue"* attempts to mediate the same disparity between role-playing and ethical accountability that is addressed by Shaftesbury's "polite philosophy." By the later stages of his career Franklin had developed an extremely subtle understanding of the issue. In his 1783 pamphlet *Remarks Concerning the Savages of North-America,* written during his mission at the French court, he went so far as to argue that the most simple societies were themselves organized by "Rules of Politeness." The very traits of simplicity and virtue that republican thought had long opposed to the artificial management of esteem were, he argued, its products.[43]

Mediating between politeness and virtue doubtless had a somewhat different meaning in America since the joining of the two was not the task of a nobility. Politeness appeared relevant not only to the imitative class aspirations of colonial tradesmen but also to relations between America and the commercial center in London. It could express the values of trade, but it could also focus the anxieties of dependence in a market structured by credit and largely controlled by London. The tension between politeness and virtue as models of personhood was overdetermined both by class politics at home and by the struggle for autonomy in a commercialized imperial network.[44] Here it is important to remember that virtue and politeness, simplicity and luxury, were not just theoretical accounts of polity but self-understandings, criteria of accountability, and relations to goods. Franklin's early essay on simplicity, for example, uses republican ethical categories to argue for homespun over fine cloth, just as Jefferson's Query 19 uses the same assumptions to promote an agricultural model of society.[45] Yet American society with its republican market was rapidly developing a commercialized economy of luxury consumption, and Franklin later showed himself to be competitive in the purchase of fine cloth. So although a rhetoric of simplicity could mobilize anxieties about dependence on an imperial economy, republican categories were continually undergoing adjustment as the market—largely defined by those very republican categories—made reflective luxury consumers of its subjects.

It was within the context of this problematic that politeness was extended first to a value for printed goods and later to a normative subcategory of writing. For most of the century, in England as in America, phrases such as "polite letters," "polite learning," or "polite arts" designated reflective discourses in general. In the book catalogues printed in New York by Hugh Gaine in 1755 and 1759, for example, "Polite letters" is not a separate category but a comprehensive description of the entire inventory. As late as 1792 a bookseller named Ebenezer Larkin could advertize his wares as "Books in every branch of Polite Literature." His catalogue includes only one volume of poetry and is dominated by books of travel, medicine, and religion.[46] Despite the breadth of the term, it bestowed a very particular feature on letters, since it valued printed goods insofar as their use enabled the self-managed individual of commercial relations. The same principle would lead, in the late decades of the century, to a notion of the "fine arts" as a normative subcategory. Thomas Jefferson, for example, used "fine arts" to group poetry, criticism, and novels in a reading list that he drew up for young gentlemen in 1771.[47] It is emphatically a list for gentlemen, and its value depends on the function of self-managing reflection in the establishment of status.

In the context of late-eighteenth-century America, in short, status-forming categories were emerging within the republican vocabulary. The history of these categories, and the corresponding dispositions toward goods and social relations, remains unwritten. Clearly their emergence was an important development in the history of the book trade and in the history of writing. But I pause over politeness here mainly to observe that, along with related terms, it could shape perceptions of print in a deep way. Insofar as print was understood as a medium of commerce—again, in the dual sense of trade and interaction—politeness could describe the social nature of the technology. It was an accepted truism that, as one newspaper declared in 1790, "The inventions of language, of arms, of writing, printing, and engraving, have been the principal means of extending the influence of man, and of his acquiring the dominion of the earth. By these acts the dispositions of men are softened, their manners become more and more civilized, humanity is gradually extended and refined, and the grosser animosities yield to external politeness and decorum, at least[,] if the feelings themselves be not blunted."[48] Books were in their very nature instruments of manners, the environment of the reflective subject of commerce. Within a certain symbolic context, print could be a sign of refinement, and that connection could be explained through a theory of the effects of printing in society. On one hand, a gentleman who bought a book, by understanding himself as showing politeness, had a way of valuing the book precisely in its private appropriation, as a ground of distinction. On the other hand, he also had a way of thinking about the book as putting him in the general discourse of managed esteem, a credit market of which printed objects were tangible evidence.

Still, few were willing to advocate politeness without important qualifiers. And in the context of the rhetoric of republican literature, politeness could be decidedly hazardous. In a 1778 Fourth of July oration David Ramsay (soon to become the war's first great historian) argued for independence by appealing to the theme of republican literature: "No wonder, that so little attention has been paid to learning; for ignorance was better than knowledge, while our abject and humiliating condition so effectually tended to crush the exertions of the human mind, and to extinguish a generous ardor for literary pre-eminence."[49] For Ramsey, republican "exertions of the human mind" might be expected to lead to "literary pre-eminence." It would seem to be easy to read the sermon as an expectation of a new American literature. Yet the same logic that produces the value of literature leads Ramsey to devalue politeness:

> Our free governments are the proper nurseries of rhetoric, criticism, and the arts which are founded on the philosophy of the human mind. In monarchies, an extreme degree of politeness disguises the simplicity of nature, and "sets the looks at variance with the thoughts"; in republics, mankind appear as they really are, without any false colouring: In these governments therefore, attentive observers have an opportunity of knowing all the avenues to the heart, and of thoroughly understanding human nature. The great inferiority of the moderns to the ancients in fine writing, is to be referred to this veil cast over mankind, by the artificial refinements of modern monarchies. (53)

Ramsey's argument implies that republican writing will be valued by public standards of truth and usefulness, while polite literature becomes a symptom of corruption. The "extreme degree of politeness" and "artificial refinements" that he ascribes to monarchical polity are separate but related charges against the British. They refer to the cluster of evils surrounding dependence, which forces false behavior and the projection of a pleasing surface by the dependent. This is the rhetoric in which attacks were launched against the corruption of ministers and "placemen." It also refers to the degradation of luxury, that stage in the growth of empires in which indulgence of sensual pleasures brings the passions back to the prominence they enjoyed in the state of savagery, and in which the passivity of luxurious consumption renders manners "effeminate," extinguishing virtue. According to Samuel Williams' *The Natural and Civil History of Vermont* (1794), under the influence of luxury the mind, "subdued by indolence and inactivity, scarcely retains its rational powers; and becomes weak, languid, and incapable of manly exertions, or attainments. To a state thus degraded, effeminate, and unmanly, luxury frequently reduces those, who bear the remains of the human form."[50] The English, then, could be expected to be luxuriously passive in character and corruptively false in their relations to each other. The same paranoid logic would cause the threat (and lure) of the unmanly to surface repeatedly when republican writers attempted to measure themselves by reflective standards of appreciation such as politeness.

If, as I am suggesting, politeness and virtue remained unreconciled as descriptions of social value, that fact was seldom remarked upon. In all likelihood, people who produced and bought print thought of themselves as being polite and virtuous at once. (It is worth remembering, however, that the *owning* of print remained irrelevant to the self-image of virtue.) Yet there was a tension between the civic humanist paradigm of print as a public and general sphere of action and a proto-liberal paradigm of print as an arena for managed esteem and distinction. That tension became most clearly visible whenever anyone attempted a programmatic account of what writing and publishing should do.

Problems of Republican Literature: Brackenridge

In 1778 Hugh Henry Brackenridge began a publication called *The United States Magazine*. It opened with an introduction by the editor, and, like so many other publishers, printers, and editors of the period, Brackenridge bases the magazine's appeal on a supposed relation between print and politics:

> We regard it as our great happiness in these United States, that the path to office and preferment, lies open to every individual. The mechanic of the city, or the husbandman who ploughs his farm by the river's bank, has it in his power to become, one day, the first magistrate of his respective commonwealth, or to fill a seat in the Continental Congress. This happy circumstance lays an obligation

upon every individual to exert a double industry to qualify himself for the great trust which may, one day, be disposed in him. It becomes him to obtain some knowledge of the history and principles of government, or at least to understand the policy and commerce of his own country. Now it may not be the lot of every individual to be able to obtain this knowledge from the first source, that is from the best writers, or the conversation of men of reading and experience. In the one case it would require a larger library than most of us are able to procure, and in the other a greater opportunity of travelling than is consistent with our dayly occupations.

The want of these advantages must therefore be supplied by some publication that will in itself contain a library, and be the literary coffee-house of public conversation. A work of this nature is *The United States Magazine.*[51]

The logic of this introduction should by now seem familiar, as Brackenridge is making the same kinds of claims for the dissemination of writing as the ground of a general virtue that we have seen in other writers of the time. He holds it as self-evident that the best men are "men of reading" and that the yeoman who will fit himself for civic duty must do so through the discourse of letters.

At the same time, Brackenridge's version of the rhetoric of diffusion does not turn simply on a general participation in politics; he emphasizes political *preferment* and public *distinction*. Literature at once erases the differences of political status, making it open to all who read, and yet reinscribes those differences by enabling the private reader to attain distinction. Dwelling a little longer on the contradiction, Brackenridge arrives at the subject of *literary* distinction:

It has been said that Magazines are oftentimes preventive of the acquirement of more solid literature, because that while they make the path to knowledge easy, it is more swiftly travelled over, and cannot be so accurately examined, as when the student is reduced to plod upon it through a tract of long and heavy reading of the authors, that are found in libraries. But suppose it may be true that we are likely to become more deep and systematic writers, and *diving deeply* to the fountain head of classic information, yet this is not to be obtained by every one, and is it not more eligible that the greater part be moderatly instructed, than that a few should be unrivalled in the commonwealth of letters, and all the world besides a groupe of ignorant and brainless persons?   (*USM*, 1:10)

Brackenridge addresses the possibility of distinction in literature only to disavow it. The line of argument here says a great deal about the literate practice of the late eighteenth century because it shows how much certain aims for writing were privileged over others, and how much those preferences limited and conditioned discourse. Although Brackenridge does not disparage scholarly endeavor, the nature of the political claim being made for writing—that there is a "commonwealth of letters"—ensures that such things as magazines will be seen as truer to the nature of writing than less general productions, and thus as more "eligible."

But distinction must also be an essential feature of the commonwealth: "The honest husbandman who reads this publication will rapidly improve in every kind of knowledge. He will be shortly capable to arbitrate the differences that may arise amongst his neighbours. He will be qualified to be a Magistrate. He will appear a proper person to be appointed Sheriff of his county. He will be equal to the task of legislation. He will be capable of any office to which the gale of popularity amongst his countrymen may raise him" (*USM*, 1:10). What is most striking about this passage is the "gale of popularity" that comes breezing onto the scene of argument seemingly without warning. The arbitrariness of this gale allies it with fortune and accident. And just as the cyclone of popularity is an arbitrary event in the life of a husbandman, a husbandman is an arbitrary focus for popularity; the whole elective process stands high risk of going wrong. Literature is posed as a solution to both problems. It will render the husbandman impervious to fortune (a form of transcendence closely allied to his ability to arbitrate the differences of his neighbors). And it will make him a meet object of popularity; that is, it will properly ground reputation.

Having imagined that literature will make a man truly fit for his arbitrary popularity, Brackenridge goes on finally to imagine a specifically literary reputation:

> Many men of great abilities have been prevented from venturing into literary life and reputation, from a want of some such means of making their first appearance to the public. In these respects a Magazine may be compared to the sun; for as that luminary exhales the water of the ocean, and pours it on the hills and vallies, so this miscellany, draws forth the drops of human genius that lie amongst society, and as it were condensing them to showers, carries pleasure and refreshment to the plains and mountain tops, and form the rivers that flow down again to mingle with the ocean. (*USM*, 1:11)

Literature, the medium of generality, must also be the medium of distinction. And though it is the heart of his argument, Brackenridge can only suggest it through an extended metaphor of condensation and rain—a metaphor designed to blur the difference between concentration and diffusion. Equally remarkable is the appearance—at precisely the moment in his argument where the general and the eminent have to be fudged—of the phrase, "literary life and reputation." For although Brackenridge predicates generality on a submergence of self into public discourse, the nature of the "literary life," the role of the person in the "commonwealth of letters," must inevitably be a matter of "reputation." Reputation is both participation in the public and distinction. It is both submission to the terms of generality and distinction from generality. Does literature erase social difference or mark it?

When Americans did manage to discuss distinction more clearly than Brackenridge finally does, they commonly described it as a principle of dynamism. Thus Samuel Smith can say, a little uncertainly: "Emulation and competition too come in with all their forces and, perhaps, produce more virtue in the world than they found in it." Or Richard Beresford can argue that publicly sponsored literary societies would help promote "the general principle of literary emulation, which would animate the wisdom of the nation." This way of describing fame avoids the problem of distinction by treating it as a necessary evil on the road to generality. As Beresford puts it, "a complete transmutation of the nature of man being impracticable, and the love of wealth and fame being predominant passions therein, he must be acted upon as he is; wherefore, literature should be made to lead to these objects, that virtue may flourish under its influence. By means of literature and virtue, will the blessings of order and good government, among others, be best understood, valued, and preserved." [52]

In 1806 Yale College began publishing *The Literary Cabinet* "for the purpose of encouraging the youth of this college in the art of writing." Yale took that task very seriously. The first issue explained that writing is "an invention, which if it is not derived from God, is the most important that man can claim to be the author of." But the college recognized a general danger: young men would be tempted to think of their own productions as a means of distinction. The institution of the magazine would avert this danger, as the students' writing may "adorn our pages, and procure for their talents that esteem they deserve, and which persons of their disposition will not value the less, because the encomiums are paid to the representatives of their minds rather than to themselves *in propria persona*." Yale, in other words, wanted a way to promote writing without distinguishing persons, and thought, like Brackenridge, that it had found the solution in the magazine, with its diffuse composition and circulation.

Men would compete for esteem, but the virtuous would transcend their personal interests. The negativity of print discourse—its natural difference from presence *in propria persona*—would guarantee that esteem be assigned on general grounds.

Problems of Republican Literature: Ames

Fisher Ames seeks a more thorough solution to the problem of distinction in literature in his much-cited essay, "American Literature." I wish to discuss it at some length, partly because it is so much more complex than my other examples and partly because it shows more interestingly the deep contradiction of republican literature. The essay, along with some remarks by Noah Webster, is often regarded as a watershed in its expression of a nationalist hope for a distinctively indigenous body of writing. That reading of Ames's essay can assimilate his use of the word "literature" to the modern sense—all the more easily in that Ames begins by asking whether the muses, "like the nightingales, are too delicate to cross the salt water, or sicken and mope without song if they do."[53] The image of nightingales introduces the subject of poetry, as the essay's main subject—the tension between literary distinction and the general virtue of literature—will turn out to lead to the subject of poetry. But this anticipates Ames's argument; the muses he refers to are all of the muses, and "literature" is still being used in Noah Webster's sense.

For that reason the first argument in praise of American literature that has to be dealt with is the claim that Americans are better schooled than Europeans. "It may be true," Ames says, "that neither France nor England can boast of so large a portion of their population who can read or write . . . Nobody will pretend that the Americans are a stupid race" (430). He turns the subject from diffusion, in which he grants America preeminence, to distinction. And on this new ground he makes no concessions: "our country has certainly hitherto no pretensions to literary fame" (431).

He soon finds it necessary to say why literary fame is such an engrossing subject for him, and he has a strong claim: the desire for fame is, of all the human passions, that "which acts with the greatest force" (433):

There are very few men who are greatly deceived with respect to their own measure of sense and abilities, or who are much dissatisfied on that account; but we scarcely see any who are quite at ease about the estimate that other people make of them. Hence it is, that the great business of mankind is to fortify or create claims to general regard.

The man who, like Midas, turns all he touches into gold, who is oppressed and almost buried in its superfluity, who lives to get, instead of getting to live, and at length belongs to his own estate and is its greatest encumbrance, still toils and contrives to accumulate wealth, not because he is deceived in regard to his wants, but because he knows and feels, that one of his wants, which is insatiable, is that respect which follows its possession. After engrossing all that the seas and mountains conceal, he would be still unsatisfied, and with some good reason, for of the treasures of esteem who can ever have enough? Who would mar or renounce one half his reputation in the world? (433–434)

This is a brilliant passage, not only for its insight into the motivations of wealth but for the rhetorical analysis of personality that it enables, allowing the passion for wealth to be seen as itself a symptom of the rhetorical needs shaping personhood. The subject of wealth is thus by no means marginal to the discussion of fame, for the operations of esteem that Ames here describes are, as he understands, the principles of a credit economy, and the discourse of fame, esteem, reputation, and opinion governs questions of literature and money alike.

The effect is to make personal distinction the principle of a general economy; "the great business of mankind is to fortify or create claims to general regard." The paradox here is that with respect to literary fame, claims to general regard can only be fortified or created within the discourse that is itself the general regard. There is no exterior standard for the adjudication of literary fame. One's reputation belongs—by definition—neither to oneself nor to another, but to the public exchanges in which it is negotiated. Ames's move to locate personhood in that negotiation makes it inaccessible; no wonder "we scarcely see any who are quite at ease about the estimate that other people make of them."

Just as there is no exterior standard of reputation, neither is there an inner essence to stabilize the judgment of value. Men are sure in their sense of their own value, Ames asserts at the beginning of the passage; but that does them no good, for the currency they compete for is not the hard specie of inner worth but the paper money of opinion. The tyranny of opinion, moreover, derives from the nature of desire, since desire is satisfied not by possession, as we always suppose, but by the reputation that follows possession. The least satiable and greatest of possible desires is the passion of fame—greatest because it purely displays the need of self-representation that governs other desires which appear to have possessible objects; least satiable because the goal of public credit is definitionally unpossessible. The passion of fame is the exemplary case of desire because it is the exemplary case of the insatiable.

The argument that the passion of fame is the general condition of the social leads Ames to the one acknowledged standard for the height of literary fame, the one place where fame and literature were most evidently passionate: ancient Greece. Yet what he depicts in Greek society, curiously, is a "universal state of turbulence and danger," in which "violence and injustice prevailed." In these most unrepublican conditions, fame is possible because relations among men are manifestly relations of domination and subjection, making distinction the necessary principle of political organization. Literary fame can be enrolled in the work of distinction and political activity. But it could only work to reinforce social division by means of the passions—it being more important, in such a primitive social state, to rouse the feelings than to diffuse knowledge. The two are incompatible, since in the republican vocabulary what Ames calls "the accurate social sciences" oppose the passions. The literary fame of ancient Greece turns out to be absolutely inimical to republican literature properly conceived.

If the conditions of near barbarism do not further the diffusion of knowledge, they do further poetry. "Views of refined policy, and calculations of remote consequences were not adapted to the taste or capacity of rude warriors, who did not reason at all, or only reasoned from their passions. The business was not to convince, but to animate; and this was accomplished by poetry" (435). At the beginning of the essay Ames found it necessary to disavow the standard of diffusion as an appropriate basis for distinction in literature. But that general standard, set aside at the beginning, now serves as the implicit counterpoint to Ames's fascinated but slightly horrific account of literary fame as it operates in ancient society. There men are the subject of barbaric passions, and kings vaunt themselves by means of poets. In such a world only the poets remain to be the vehicles of the warriors' traditions, "to diffuse and perpetuate the knowledge of memorable events and illustrious men."

Because the argument opposes a modern diffuse market of reputation with an intensely passionate scene of fame in a semicivilized state, it is not surprising to see Ames invoke explicitly the difference between writing and speech—a subject already implicit in the narrative that leads from Greek passions to modern manners. "Books are now easy of access," he reminds his readers, "and literary curiosity suffers oftener from repletion than from hunger." In this modern, lettered world, reputation and tradition are negotiated in writing rather than in song. Because Greek poetry is identified with the need to rouse feelings and animate the passions, letters are seen as neutralizing such effects, though the acknowledgment first appears in the essay as a lament: "National events slip from the memory to our records; they miss the heart, though they are sure to reach posterity."

Though the Greek poets were servants of the passions, the advantage they drew from the fact was that their fame was immediate and impassioned. For Ames their fame was different chiefly because it was orally transmitted:

> Though the art of alphabetic writing was known in the east in the time of the Trojan war, it is nowhere mentioned by Homer, who is so exact and full in describing all the arts he knew. If his poems were in writing, the copies were few; and the knowledge of them was diffused, not by reading, but by the rhapsodists, who made it a profession to recite his verses.
>
> Poetry, of consequence, enjoyed in that age, in respect to the vivacity of its impressions, and the significance of the applauses it received, as great advantages as have ever since belonged to the theatre. Instead of a cold perusal in a closet, or a still colder confinement unread, in a bookseller's shop, the poet saw with delight his work become the instructor of the wise, the companion of the brave and the great . . . That reward, which writers are now little excited to merit, because it is doubtful and distant, "the estate which wits inherit after death," was in Greece a present possession. That public so terrible by its censure, so much more terrible by its neglect, was then assembled in person, and the happy genius who was crowned victor was ready to expire with the transports of his joy.
>
> (436–437)

Given the conceptual tradition for literature and its public that I have been describing, it might be surprising that Ames should speak so nostalgically of ancient poetry, describing it as a passionate oral immediacy from which written records effect a decline in feeling. For this moment in the essay nostalgia is indulged with a vengeance. Fame, which had earlier been the insatiable passion that makes men the greatest encumbrance to their own estates, Ames now depicts as a "present possession." It forms a bond of contact with auditors "assembled in person," who cannot "neglect" the person of the author. The tone of the passage betrays a bitter despair over the dereliction of books that languish in booksellers' shops.

But we should guard against taking the passage at face value, for elsewhere in the essay he subjects himself to criticism for indulging in unrepublican nostalgia.

Having presented this portrait of full personal presence and fatal transports of poetic joy, Ames distances himself from the scene. He reminds us not only that such times are past (an essential element of the nostalgia) but also that rhapsodic poetry was the product of "peculiar circumstances." He is markedly ambivalent about those peculiar circumstances, for although they allowed the works of Homer and Virgil to reach and animate the multitudes rather than being "confined to the closets of scholars," that was only the case because the multitude were governed by "military passion" and "fanaticism." The people who listened so avidly to Homer's poems were the same "rude warriors" whom Ames has already characterized as uninterested in knowledge. "Societies are no longer under the power of single passions, that once flashed enthusiasm through them all at once like electricity. Now the propensities of mankind balance and neutralize each other, and, of course, narrow the range in which poetry used to move. Its coruscations are confined, like the northern light, to the polar circle of trade and politics, or like a transitory meteor blaze in a pamphlet or magazine."

Here a republican perspective returns to modify the thrill of poetry's oral immediacy. Specifically, the republican narrative of the history of society appears in a way that associates the "single passions" of the Homeric age of heroism with the state of unlettered barbarism—a fragile condition for society and one in which men had no protection from the whims of fortune. In language that recalls Federalist #10, Ames describes the modern world, in which "the propensities of mankind balance and neutralize each other," as a world where commerce has civilized the passions and driven out war. He clearly prefers the latter world, despite his nostalgia, and thinks that its most laudable characteristics are what have caused the rhapsodists to give way to pamphlets and magazines. (Pamphlets and magazines, by the way, are the more suggestive examples because of their close association with the public sphere of diffusion.)

In this respect it is interesting that Ames does not imagine anything between rhapsody and magazines. The possibility of a marginal poetic culture, possessing a recognizable identity but in a subordinate or ornamental position regarding the nation at large, is one he does not entertain. The reason why he does not is the requirement of general virtue: whatever literature is, it must be the principle by which citizens participate in the political. The question is of the best mode of diffusion, and Ames offers only two kinds: the first, for a rude and passionate society of warriors, is poetic and oral; the second, for the civilized republic, is prosaic and literate. As an indication of how strongly bound these associations are, he tellingly informs us that the heroic age produced *nothing but* poetry, and has left us next to nothing in the way of history and political science (438–439).

If the republic is a place of balance and diffusion, it is also fragile. This is after all the late Ames, who thought, as did most of the republic's founders, that the republican order was decaying from a loss of virtue. The republic had grown out of the ages of despotism, but it was decaying into democracy from which despotism would arise again. Whereas despotism allowed for a lively sense of distinction but an imperfect degree of diffusion, democracy brings the reverse, preventing distinction of any kind. Between these disastrous poles the republic is situated on the premise that diffusion and distinction can coexist. The difficulty of that premise can be felt in Ames's image of the northern lights in the polar regions, of poetry flashing like a meteor in the pages of a pamphlet.

What is unfortunate about the image, for the purposes of Ames's argument, is that it suggests the possibility of an ornamental poetry in a republic otherwise devoted to the diffusion of letters. And an ornamental poetry, for Ames, is a discourse without virtue. Here I should amend my earlier remark that Ames does not envision anything like a marginal poetic culture between rude rhapsody and republican literature, because in the context of the decay of the republic he now begins to entertain the possibility of a literature founded on distinction. Far from being valued as the birth of an indigenous national culture, it is a vision of the apocalypse, bitter and ironic:

> But the condition of the United States is changing. Luxury is sure to introduce want; and the great inequalities between the very rich and the very poor will be more conspicuous, and comprehend a more formidable host of the latter. The rabble of great cities is the standing army of ambition. Money will become its instrument, and vice its agent. Every step, (and we have taken many,) towards a more complete, unmixed democracy is an advance towards destruction; it is treading where the ground is treacherous and excavated for an explosion. Liberty has never yet lasted long in a democracy; nor has it ever ended in any thing better than despotism. With the change of our government, our manners and sentiments will change. As soon as our emperor has destroyed his rivals, and established order in his army,

he will desire to see splendor in his court, and to occupy his subjects with the cultivation of the sciences.

If this catastrophe of our public liberty should be miraculously delayed or prevented, still we shall change. With the augmentation of wealth, there will be an increase of the numbers who may choose a literary leisure. Literary curiosity will become one of the new appetites of the nation; and as luxury advances, no appetite will be denied. After some ages we shall have many poor and a few rich, many grossly ignorant, a considerable number learned, and a few eminently learned. Nature, never prodigal of her gifts, will produce some men of genius, who will be admired and imitated.

Thus ends Ames's essay. Critics have never known how to read this ending. Is it really an example of nationalist aspiration for literary culture?

The standard summary of Ames's argument is Van Wyck Brooks's: "American genius was foredoomed to fail."[54] That summary is wrong, and it is worth saying why it is wrong because the critical misreading of this essay is emblematic of a pattern of misreading early national writing in general. It might be possible to read the remarkable final paragraph straight, as hopeful anticipation, if one carefully avoided the references to "many poor and a few rich, many grossly ignorant"; or if one were unaware of the ideological weight borne by such terms as "luxury" and "appetite"; or if the paragraph did not appear in the context of the preceding argument. It would also be necessary to ignore parallel arguments such as Brackenridge's: "is it not more eligible that the greater part be moderatly instructed, than that a few should be unrivalled in the commonwealth of letters, and all the world besides a groupe of ignorant and brainless persons?" In these contexts, the conclusion carries the heavy and caustic irony characteristic of Ames's late writings. The American republic, like all republics, will be short-lived. Ames's argument about literature, then, is not that American genius is foredoomed to fail. Rather, it is that genius, where defined by distinction and private appreciation, will find its appropriate environment in luxury and corruption. The absence of such cultural distinction in the fine arts can be taken as a sign that the republic, though imperiled by luxury, yet lives. Ames does not call for a national culture. He dreads the social conditions of its possibility.

I suspect that most modern readers will find it astonishing that an idea of "men of genius, who will be admired and imitated" should carry a tone of foreboding. The clearest image of a literary culture that anyone articulated in early national America appears as the butt of a critique. More astonishing yet, that critique rests precisely on a faith in the letters of the republic. Of course Ames's last bitter paragraph is a fair description of the actual course of nineteenth-century literary history. Subtracting only the Napoleonic despot that Ames fears, his expectations were by and large fulfilled: the civic orientation of virtue waned; luxury consumption rose; the arts became more organized by concentrated distinction and by private appropriation; men of genius appeared and were admired and imitated; and they understood their activities as having less and less to do with the public sphere. Ames's narrative of anxiety describes the very paradigm of literary history with which early national writing has always been invidiously compared. No wonder the essay has been so often misread, since modern readers find it difficult to see what Ames fears as anything other than a standard of value.

It is equally easy to misread Ames's nationalism. Just as his civic orientation leads to a republican model of literature rather than a liberal one, so also it leads him to think of the Americanness of that literature in republican rather than nationalist terms. Whatever literature the American republic might have, its value will be public and therefore universalist. Ames imagines nothing specially indigenous about the literature of the republic. It will be American in the sense that it will support virtue in the American public sphere, just as a more advanced republican literature in France or Lithuania would promote a more republican state of civil society there, erasing rather than creating differences between these societies.

The same republican rhetoric that had brought the nation-state of the United States into being now blocked the development of a national imaginary by its rigorous construction of citizenship in the public sphere. Modern nationalism is more at home. It constructs "Americanness" as a distinctive but privately possessed trait. It allows you to be American in the way you tailor your coat, or the way you sing, or the way you read a book. It does not insist that you regard such activities as public, virtuous actions. I speak of a modern nationalist *imaginary* to emphasize that it *requires* your public self-imagery to develop in the private sphere. As a nationalist subject, you have a repertoire of self-perceptions that, though national, can be detached from any context of action understood as political. Any rigorous insistence that all publications belong to the public sphere, that all literature is a dimension of civic virtue, that the actions of literacy are political actions—any such insistence remained as much at odds with a nationalist imaginary as it did with a liberal ideology of culture.

As I read the writings of Americans in the 1780s and 1790s, that insistence is everywhere. Typical in this regard is Philip Freneau's poem "Literary Importation." The title refers not to imitation of British poetic models, but to the dangers of a foreign-trained episcopacy. Even in the novel, American writers consistently regard their writing as belonging to the civic arena. They write novels that are answerable to the standards of virtue. And they imagine the readers of their publications as participants in public discourse rather than as private consumers of luxury goods. At the same time, however, the novel generated extraordinary tensions for the republican paradigm. Its generic conditions required that any public identification found there be an imaginary one. The reader of a novel might have a virtuous orientation, but his or her virtue would be experienced privately rather than in the context of civic action. So the novel, despite the most rigorous intentions of its authors, developed a nationalist imaginary of the modern type.

· VI ·

The Novel:
Fantasies of Publicity

IN THE PRECEDING chapter I traced some tensions between two ways of conceptualizing print in the late eighteenth century: a republican paradigm of public virtue; and categories for private appropriation such as politeness, fame, and luxury. Eventually these latter categories would allow some kinds of printed discourse to be definitively separated from the arena of public decisionmaking. My contention, however, has been that Americans to a surprising degree, and even in aesthetic discourse, understood their engagements with print as activities in the republican public sphere subject to its norms. The republican paradigm had such widespread influence in official discourses of and about print that early national American society developed no coherent alternative model for letters analogous to the liberal discourse of the literary or the mass-cultural discourse of the police gazette.

At least one kind of printed good, other than those made for the strongly residual religious culture, might seem to be an obvious exception: the novel. We commonly consider the novel to be by nature divorced from the public sphere, designed as an occasion for a specially private kind of subjectivity. There are good reasons for such a view, but it is not the full story, at least with American writing. It is precisely to explicate the peculiar character of early American novels that I have bothered to document the political-cultural context that, as printed goods, they share. For American novels before Cooper are all anomalous from the perspective of literary criticism. Often didactic, seldom unified in plot, even more seldom interested in distinctive characterizations, and almost never given to ambiguous resonances of meaning, they are universally regarded as several decades' worth of failures. I do not intend to redeem these novels as

triumphs of artistic intention. But I do think that their character and
desirability can be better accounted for by treating them as features of a
republican public sphere rather than a liberal aesthetic.

A better account of the early American novel might, for its own sake,
interest only professionals in a rather obscure subspecialty. And who cares?
In another frame of reference, however, there are motives for rethinking
the relation of cultural goods to the public sphere. Recent social movements have made the consecration of art, including the literary, appear as
a mystification of the cultural public sphere. Those movements, whether
feminist, Afro-American, gay, or Chicano, have looked to cultural goods
to redefine a public. At the same time, the undoing of the consecration
of art, with its bracketing of public discourse, has become the task of an
impressive number of artists: Barbara Kruger, Jenny Holzer, Hans
Haacke, Victor Burgin, and others. Even the semiofficial public discourse
of video capitalism rests on its ability to saturate all goods with the affect
of publicity, if only the more completely to relegate political activity to a
specialized social subsystem. At the intersection of these contexts, a look
at the crises of publicity in a proto-literary field need not be mere antiquarianism.

I shall concentrate on the example of *Arthur Mervyn,* by Charles
Brockden Brown, which exhibits a republican paradigm for its own
medium in both thematic and unthematic ways. The plot of *Arthur Mervyn* cannot be summarized intelligibly. Its underlying principle, however,
can be stated very simply. Brown did just that in a fictitious review essay
called "Walstein's School of History." There he summarizes a number of
books (none actual), including one that is essentially his own novel. He
calls it "Olivo Ronsica" and describes its premise as follows:

> He [Olivo or Arthur] is destitute of property, of friends, and of
> knowledge of the world. These are to be acquired by his own exer-
> tions, and virtue and sagacity are to guide him in the choice and use
> of suitable means.
>
> Ignorance subjects us to temptation, and poverty shackles our be-
> neficence. Olivo's conduct shews us how temptation may be baffled,
> in spite of ignorance, and benefits be conferred in spite of poverty.[1]

Given the wild and bewildering complexity of events in *Arthur Mervyn,*
Brown's summary is strikingly simple. Can it be trusted?

Many critics take the main character's virtue ironically. They see his
protestations of disinterested benevolence as stretched and improbable.
Warner Berthoff finds "moral irony in the contrasts between the hero's

priggish reflections on events and the melodrama of his actual career."[2] Michael Bell discovers a "full, deliberate, and devastating irony" in the book because Brown portrays Mervyn as too rational, too confident in sincerity.[3] The reader, in this view, is asked to attain a higher and more skeptical understanding of the world than Arthur's naive republicanism allows.

Interpreting the novel ironically has two related functions, both desirable for modern critics but both, in my view, mistaken. First, it brackets the explicit republicanism of the book, allowing us to see republican explanations as the main characters' views rather than author-sanctioned didacticism. Second, it assimilates the novel to a liberal aesthetic of authorial craft. What is desirable in that aesthetic is a disjunction between the expressive particularity of craft (the way the text is *distinctively* formed) and generally ratifiable assertions (propositions *any* citizen could make). The sense of such a disjunction produces the effect of a specially private subjectivity which is the basis for literary appreciation. Brown rises in artistic stature as his aims are seen to be more indirect, artful, and privately anchored. And the text gains aesthetic status as it is fitted to modern standards of appreciation.

Because of the nature of the value judgments made here, our reading of Brown's relation to Mervyn will determine how we see the novel's relation to the public sphere. A reading based on the aesthetic of the literary presupposes, and thus discovers, a fundamental gap between the novel and public discourse. In particular, the ironically distanced judgment valued by Berthoff and Bell helps make the novel a communication between authors and readers who jointly distinguish their exchange from publicly certifiable descriptions of the world, and who by that negation make the reading of the novel an experience of interiority and privacy. The two critical operations performed by an ironic reading thus turn out to be related. The modern reading produces the interiority of art on both the level of style (irony) and the level of theme (critique). It does so by making the novel's depiction of a republican public sphere problematic—an important thing to do, since the literary negation of public discourse could only be treated *within* the republican paradigm as a loss of virtue.

Against such a reading I contend, with Norman Grabo, that "Arthur's virtue itself is the strange but true element Brown expected to dominate his readers' attention."[4] All of the novel's events can be seen as illustrating the central premise given in Brown's summary of "Olivo Ronsica." Mervyn begins his career in the confinement of rustic ignorance, and ends possessed of virtue and liberty. What makes the transformation possible is the sheer energy of his mind, coupled with a perfect sincerity. Mervyn's naivete is depicted in detail, but the effect is all the more to display the energy of his virtuous mind in overcoming his initial ignorance. Brown cues us to read the tale in this way when he has Dr. Stevens, the auditor of Mervyn's narrative, summarize Mervyn's career: "He stept forth upon the stage, unfurnished, by anticipation or experience, with the means of security against fraud; and yet, by the aid of pure intentions, had frustrated the wiles of an accomplished and veteran deceiver."[5] In accepting this summary at face value, I could also cite evidence outside the novel. For example, the intellection that Berthoff and Bell regard as excessive is endlessly praised in republican rhetoric, and much contextual evidence suggests that the degree of sincerity they see as absurd was embraced by Brown.[6] Rather than add to the argument against an ironized reading, however, I will discuss what it would mean to take the novel's republican presentation seriously. For it is not as simple as it looks.

When Brown says that Olivo Ronsica "shews us how temptation may be baffled, in spite of ignorance, and benefits be conferred in spite of poverty," he can be read as making both a thematic description and a practical claim. Thematically the novel would be making the theoretical point that virtue is possible. But the stronger reading, consistent with Brown's other claims for his work, is the practical claim that by showing *how* ignorance may be overcome and benevolence actualized, the novel itself helps to effect those goals. If *Arthur Mervyn* is the kind of object that Brown describes, then its value is that of an exemplary public instrument. The standards for its appreciation would be nearly the same as those for historical accounts, execution narratives, sermons, or ethical treatises. The most salient difference would be that fiction's inventedness allows one to make an even closer fit between theoretical problem-solving and practical knowledge. The challenges of republican society can be examined in the mode of history. Brown's claim for the book rests on the public ratifiability of its practical and theoretical assertions rather than on any subjectively expressive dimension. He implicitly devalues the personalizing indicators of craft, since to read his assertions as expressions of subjective nature would be to set aside the civic standard of proof. For that reason, the organizing standards of the book are not standards by which literary criticism is prepared to adjudicate, and any strictly literary-critical account of the novel will falsify it accordingly.

Taking Brown's civic claims seriously does, however, have an important implication for a literary-critical account. It discloses a fit between the efficacy desired for *Arthur Mervyn,* the printed artifact, and the efficacy desired for Arthur Mervyn, the exemplary citizen. Both are loosely imagined as overcoming ignorance and effecting benevolent intentions. Perhaps nothing in that fact alone is remarkable. But if we read Arthur Mervyn's behavior in the context of the rhetoric of republican literature, we can see the novel as figuring, in theme and in fantasy, culturally dominant assumptions and desires about the value of printed goods. Doing so will clarify the standards of value implicit in republican publication; all the more because their extension to the novel was uneasy.

As Brown's plot summary notes, Mervyn's initial ignorance is his political hazard. Through "his own exertions," guided by "virtue and sagacity," he is to overcome temptations and translate beneficence into action. Accordingly, his character is defined by beneficent intentions and rational exertions. The latter are especially striking. What Mervyn narrates about himself is not so much events as the virtuous working of his mind during those events. To the modern reader the effect is occasionally ludicrous, as when he accounts for the decision to get a drink of water: "Thirst was the evil which chiefly oppressed me. The means of relief were pointed out by nature and habit" (214). This exhaustive narration of thought makes sense less as a Lockean study of psychology for its own sake than as posing the problem of how virtue can come out of ignorance. There is a direct—often fantasmatically direct—connection between the acquisition of knowledge and virtue. We need not attribute a thematic intention to Brown for that to be so, since the republican discourse of letters rests primarily on that paradigmatic connection between public virtue and the acquisition of knowledge.

Yet the novel contains many indicators that the context I have traced is not far from Brown's mind. In the first place, Mervyn's only marketable skill is the use of the pen. His dependence on the corrupt Welbeck begins when Welbeck hires him as a scrivener. In contrast, the family that Mervyn leaves behind at the beginning of the novel are "totally illiterate": "The father was a Scotch peasant, whose ignorance was so great that he could not sign his name" (234). This original but foreign illiteracy remains a powerful negative example in the novel, for Mervyn's father abuses authority, succumbs to seduction, is swindled out of his property, and ends in ignominy and degradation. Such allegorical fates are possible only because, for Brown, literacy correlates with personality structures. Mervyn, who has exhausted his library and who never spots a book or paper without taking it up to read, defines himself by the inquisitive activity and rational transcendence associated with letters. His father, on the other hand, remains sunk in dependence, vulnerable to accident, a sport of his passions, and the dupe of corrupt designs.

Mervyn himself draws the conclusion, commenting on the dangers of the rural life in which he began as an ignorant and unsocialized being. Rustic manners, he says, have a "tendency to quench the spirit of liberal curiosity; to habituate the person to bodily, rather than intellectual, exertions; to supersede, and create indifference or aversion to the only instruments of rational improvement, the pen and the book" (311). Although it may be an overassertion, even for Brown, to say that the pen and the book are the *only* instruments of rational improvement, he certainly thinks that letters promote the kind of vigilant thinking exemplified by Mervyn. That is why Mervyn requires literature in his beloved and prescribes a course of letters to render Eliza's mind worthy of his: "Her pen might be called into action, and her mind be awakened by books, and every hour be made to add to her stores of knowledge and enlarge the bounds of her capacity" (312).

Nowhere does the peculiar character of Mervyn's virtuous and literate mind appear more vividly than in chapter 13 of part 1. Mervyn finds himself in retreat from the city at Hadwin's farm. His passions have been aroused by Eliza, Hadwin's nymphlike daughter. "To foster my passion," he tells us, "was to foster a disease destructive either of my integrity or my existence." In order to avoid the savage condition of dependence on passions (his father's fate) Mervyn turns, naturally enough, to literature. Doing so, he says, will help to "discover some means of controlling and beguiling [his] thoughts." Luckily, in leaving the city he has brought with him a bound manuscript in Italian that had been in Welbeck's house. The curious part is that Mervyn does not know Italian, but he resolves to translate the manuscript anyway. He has such confidence in the propulsive power of his mind that he resolves to go about the translation unaided: "My project was perhaps singular. The ancient language of Italy [Latin] possessed a strong affinity with the modern. My knowledge of the former, was my only means of gaining the latter. I had no grammar or vocabulary to explain how far the meanings and inflections of Tuscan words varied from the Roman dialect. I was to ponder on each sentence and phrase; to select among different conjectures the most plausible, and to ascertain the true, by patient and repeated scrutiny" (126).

Improbably, Mervyn succeeds in this task, which shows "how the mind, unassisted, may draw forth the principles of inflection and arrangement." In this fantasy of language, letters wait only to unfold themselves before an active mind. Mervyn's impossible success reveals a certain optimism for literature as a field of virtuous exertion. Furthermore, the fantasy has tangible rewards, since in the process of translating the book Mervyn uncovers a fortune in banknotes cemented between the pages. Because his rational transcendence is shown to be a product of his exemplary literacy, the episode can be read as thematizing the necessity of literature. The banknote fantasy also indicates the depth of Brown's (unthematic) desire that literature have its own rewards.

Illiterate ignorance and virtuous letters do not exhaust the novel's thematic alternatives. Whereas Mervyn embodies the disposition of republican literature and implicitly allegorizes its necessity through his adventures, the villain Welbeck embodies the disposition of polite letters and becomes equally a figure of allegory, though a negative one. It will later turn out that Welbeck wanted to translate the same Italian manuscript. He too possesses, he has told Mervyn, a "thirst of knowledge" that he calls "ardent" (85), and his luxurious library is a key setting for much of the novel's action. Yet his wish to translate the manuscript grows out of his desire for "the *reputation* of literature and opulence" (100; my emphasis). He discloses that his intention was to add some episodes to the manuscript's narrative and pass off the whole as his own invention. The difference between Mervyn and Welbeck is that Mervyn engages the dynamism of his mind in opposition to the passions and in hope of virtuous literature, while Welbeck possesses what Fisher Ames analyzes as a passion of fame. Mervyn actually translates the book, while Welbeck wishes primarily to be known for having translated it. Mervyn's literature is thus allied with the substantial values of the novel; Welbeck's with their corruption. Mervyn discovers money in books; Welbeck counterfeits money and plagiarizes. These are only extreme versions of the paradigmatic difference: Mervyn's standard of value in letters is primarily civic, while Welbeck's is one of private appropriation.

Brown leaves no doubt that Welbeck's evil stems from the personality structures of civility and credit economies. Early in the novel the virtuously rude Mervyn is shocked to witness Welbeck's polite self-management in action. He notes that at a social gathering Welbeck deceptively transforms himself from sullen and reserved to vivacious. Welbeck thereby achieves "the utmost deference" from his companions; but as soon as he leaves them, he lapses into his true severity (73). Just before, Mervyn has made the contrast with himself explicit: "I saw the emptiness of fame and luxury when put in the balance against the recompence of virtue" (71).

The two personality structures, one defined by managed esteem, the other by civic action, orient the ethical-political order of the novel. The

conflict between them governs every event in the narrative. These two personality structures are also capable of being thematized through the characters' different relations to letters. That is because republican culture contained
an understanding of letters designed to fit and elaborate its understanding
of political personhood. So the thematic of letters can be read less as artistic
self-reference than as an index to the vexed politics of late republican–early
liberal culture. Welbeck's crimes—fraud, plagiarism, forgery, seduction,
and the like—are symptoms of the economy of esteem. So, however, is
his love of literature. "The esteem of mankind," he says, "was the spring
of all my activity, the parent of all my virtue and all my vice" (89). The
allegorized struggle between Mervyn and Welbeck thus implicitly devalues
standards of appreciation for letters that were culturally current but in
tension with the republican paradigm—in this case, those of polite letters.

Because dispositions toward letters are at stake in the most basic premises of the novel's ethical-political order, the book figures a relation to its
own medium in unthematized elements of its form and narrative structure.
The first indication that the issue of literature might exert an influence
deeper than thematic issues again has to do with Mervyn's character.
One of Brown's most intimate friends, William Dunlap, wrote in a biography of Brown that Arthur Mervyn's busy intellection is an exact description of Brown's own "modes of thinking."[7] Whether biographically
accurate or not, Dunlap's remark is a direct index of the rhetoric of the
novel, and it is tempting on the basis of such a statement to see Mervyn
as embodying elements of Brown's own self-image.

Curiously, almost nothing of Brown is recorded but his literature. In
narrating his final illness, Dunlap announces his death in this fashion:
"Thus at the age of thirty nine, died Charles Brockden Brown, taken from
the world at a time when the mass of knowledge which he had acquired
by unwearied but desultory reading, and by acute and accurate observation, being preserved by a strong memory and marshalled by an uncom-
monly vigorous understanding, was fitted with the aid of his perseverance
and zeal in the cause of virtue, to have conferred the most important
benefits upon his fellow men."[8] One would hardly know that the man
who had died was Dunlap's bosom friend. All he describes is a mass of
knowledge, a great deal of reading, and a vigorous understanding exerting
itself in the service of virtue and public benefit. Compare the passage with
what Mervyn says upon turning down a temptation to easy riches: "The
accumulation of knowledge, and the diffusion of happiness, in which
riches may be rendered eminently instrumental, were the only precepts of
duty, and the only avenues to genuine felicity" (128).

Dunlap's language, however strange it now may seem, was anything but peculiar to him. The *American Daily Advertiser's* brief obituary pauses only to say that Brown died a Christian before detailing the traits that made his knowledge "extensive": "the unwearied inquisitiveness of a rich and active mind, . . . that never failing propensity to scrutiny and investigation, . . . the most facile capacity for the acquirement of knowledge, and . . . at the same time a laudable but modest ambition for the acquirement of literary fame."[9] Even the manuscript obituary probably composed in part by Brown's widow is mostly devoted to the "ardor" of Brown's "love of letters." "Ever on the alert in quest of information," the manuscript tells us, "he patiently inquired, he read, reflected, examined," and so on. "It is difficult to conceive what acquisition a mind thus constituted possesses above ordinary men. Those hours devoted by the generality of the world to colloquial amusement, and which the memory afterward retains no vestige of, were to him all subordinate to the grand purpose of his life, the acquisition of knowledge."[10] All parties involved in praising Brown as a man of literature found it necessary to emphasize the very disposition of mind that dictates Mervyn's character and actions. Here, Brown's ardor for letters displaces all other details of his behavior. I conclude from such evidence that in *Arthur Mervyn* Brown is exploring, in ways that are only partly thematized, the political self-understanding made available to him in the republican discourse of and about print. Mervyn is, among other things, a fantastic self-image.

Yet Mervyn possesses neither the greatest virtue nor the greatest literature in the novel: those honors belong to Dr. Stevens. It is not accidental that the two go together in his case. The physician's task is a higher form of the hero's: to acquire knowledge of the world and confer benefits at the same time. In the eighteenth century medical practitioners were markedly distinguished from the general population by book learning rather than by institutional accreditation. And for Brown, whose closest friend (Elihu Hubbard Smith) had been one of Benjamin Rush's students in medicine, medical learning was a powerful example of virtuous literature. These assumptions can be seen at work when Stevens decides that Mervyn can perfect his "career of virtue" by becoming a physician. Medicine, in his account, is a branch of literature capable of converting Mervyn's "strenuous" mind to public benefit. It might be noted in this connection that one function of the yellow fever epidemic in the novel is to define a specifically *public* need for virtuous physicians. Stevens does not exert his literature on behalf of private persons for profit; he labors for the benefit of an entire civic population.

As with the case of the Italian manuscript, this vision of the lettered mind furthering the welfare of mankind is a displaced but strong image for Brown's own work as a writer. It is Stevens, after all, who writes down Mervyn's tale (Mervyn commends his "nimble pen" [354]), thus serving as Brown's double; and the importance of his literature to the public is something that Brown no doubt would like to claim for himself. In other words, Brown regards medicine as an ideal image of the reciprocal relation between letters and virtue toward which his own career aims.[11]

It may strike us as a magical wish to think that writing could produce effects on the public comparable to the benefits of medicine. But it did not seem so in the republic, where the political virtue of the active mind was attributed to the agency of letters. What makes *Arthur Mervyn* of interest beyond its reproduction of that rhetoric is the logic by which Brown gives such connections dramatic form. Mervyn's drive to acquire knowledge is a principle of dynamism. The effect is to make the outline of the novel's plot implicit in the properties of the hero's mind. The bookish cogitation described by Berthoff as a "priggish reflection on events" is exactly the force that directs the course of events. Arthur himself points to this fact in order to explain why, when ordered to leave Mrs. Villars' house, he instead went searching through the upper stories: "I pretend not to the wisdom of experience and age; to the praise of forethought or subtlety. I chuse the obvious path, and pursue it with headlong expedition. Good intentions, unaided by knowledge, will, perhaps, produce more injury than benefit, and therefore, knowledge must be gained, but the acquisition is not momentary; is not bestowed unasked and untoil'd for: meanwhile, we must not be unactive because we are ignorant. Our good purposes must hurry to performance, whether our knowledge be greater or less" (323).

Mervyn's exploratory behavior, in his view, naturally follows from the need for knowledge. When first denied entry to the house, he "reflected on the rectitude of [his] intentions"—and if the subsequent reflection seems priggish to the modern eye, Mervyn employs Brown's own republican vocabulary: "I thought, with scornful emotions, on the bars and hindrances which pride and caprice, and delusive maxims of decorum, raise in the way of human intercourse. I spurned at these semblances and substitutes of honesty, and delighted to shake such fetters into air, and trample such impediments to dust. I wanted to see an human being, in order to promote her happiness. It was doubtful whether she was within twenty paces of the spot where I stood. The doubt was to be solved. How? By examining the space. I forthwith proceeded to examine it" (317).

Mervyn's imperative of knowledge translates directly into action: solving a doubt, crossing a spatial boundary, and defying unrepublican social restrictions exactly coincide with each other. The novel is a showcase for the dynamism of Mervyn's mind. If there is a door, Mervyn will walk through it. If there is a book, Mervyn will open it. Because of this trait he avoids the traps of ignorance and attains a secure liberty. He ascribes his improbable behavior to "an inquisitive temper." "I was eager after knowledge," he says (64); elsewhere he reflects that "the source of all energy, and even of life, is seated in thought" (169). The result may resemble headlong idiocy, but since Mervyn's adventurous behavior is the unmediated result of his need for knowledge, Brown is able to regard that direct translation of knowledge into virtue as evidence that learning—conceived now as a necessary and continuing acquisition of knowledge, the expanding impulse of the mind—is inherently virtuous. Because it produces good republican self-assertion, Mervyn's "curiosity" (73) is more than an unpleasant quirk of his personality; it defines his political agency. The plot's premises, which allow the pursuit of knowledge to appear identical with virtuous action, are Brown's ingenious narrative solution to the cultural problem of integrating a diffuse public sphere.

By this means Brown's novel exploits an ambiguity in the idea of learning; for republican literature requires both a dynamism of the mind—its expansion through time—and an imperturbable virtue that mirrors letters in its transcendent fixity. Literature is both an activity performed in the world and a state transcending the fortunes of that world. Mervyn embodies its activity perfectly, but only at the expense of its transcendence. Although Brown goes to great lengths to represent Mervyn's inquisitiveness as producing benefit by propelling virtuous action, Mervyn's ignorance is a painful and restrictive condition. The effort of acquiring knowledge socializes Mervyn and establishes his virtue, but his ignorance entails a state of vicious dependence. He is always aspiring to a state of knowledge in which that effort will no longer be entailed upon him.

Late in his adventures he shows signs of having attained the liberty he desires, especially in the following passage (the same one Dunlap cites when saying that Mervyn resembles Brown): "If men be chiefly distinguished from each other by the modes in which attention is employed, either on external and sensible objects, or merely on abstract ideas and the creatures of reflection, I may justly claim to be enrolled in the second class. My existence is a series of thoughts rather than of motions. Ratiocination and deduction leave my senses unemployed. The fulness of my fancy renders my eye vacant and inactive. Sensations do not precede and suggest, but follow and are secondary to the acts of my mind" (265). The immunity from "vicissitude" that Mervyn claims in this and similar descriptions of his mind is an ideal—clearly an ideal that does not entirely exist in practice for most of the novel's duration. Dr. Stevens possesses lettered tranquillity from the beginning; Mervyn only gradually attains it as his acquisition of knowledge gradually secures his virtue from the threats of dependence on fortune and the senses. In the meantime he remains ignorant, and his ignorance subjects him to perils in which he cannot afford the tranquillity of pure thought.

This ambiguity necessarily follows from the premises of Brown's plot construction. The beneficial ability of Mervyn's mind to frustrate Welbeck's wiles only appears from within his ignorant condition. Only the dramatic circumstances of his dependence allow for his virtuous actions. At one point he exclaims: "Why, said I, as I hasted forward, is my fortune so abundant in unforeseen occurrences? Is every man, who leaves his cottage and the impressions of his infancy behind him, ushered into such a world of revolutions and perils as have trammelled my steps? or, is my scene indebted for variety and change to my propensity to look into other people's concerns, and to make their sorrows and their joys mine?" (332).

It is at moments such as this one that some critics detect irony, for they read Brown as implicitly answering "Yes" to the last question. Mervyn, in their view, pokes his nose where it does not belong. But it is also possible to read such passages as expressing a tension within the novel's values rather than a disparity between Brown's judgment and Mervyn's. Mervyn's propensity to look into other people's concerns is the source of his virtue, allowing him to confer benefits. That propensity, however, is defined as an inquisitiveness seeking to escape the state of ignorance, and therefore it produces its virtuous effects only within an essentially vulnerable and dependent condition. In *Arthur Mervyn* Brown has devised a plot in which the acquisition of knowledge has the dramatic function of virtuous action, but the same plot must keep its hero in a condition of ignorant dependence which is the antithesis of virtue.

Because of this contradiction, the relation between thematic content and narrative condition entails a thematic and formal problem. The temporal duration of Mervyn's adventures takes on the connotations of fortune and dependence, and the untrammeled knowledge to which he aspires is defined against the temporal medium of the novel's action. "To act under the guidance of another," he explains, "and to wander in the dark, ignorant whither my path tended, and what effects might flow from my agency was a new and irksome situation" (63). Not knowing what effects might flow from one's agency is exactly to be embedded in a narrative. By describing it in this way, Brown implicitly opposes the republican standards of virtue and liberty—which are defined by the assertion of agency—to the "irksome situation" that defines Mervyn's narrative, since the events of that narrative coincide with the ignorant and restrictive "path" that Mervyn here resists. In a later chapter Mervyn says, "I had acted long enough a servile and mechanical part, and been guided by blind and foreign impulses. It was time to lay aside my fetters, and demand to know whither the path tended in which I was importuned to walk" (114). His will to knowledge—opposed in characteristic fashion to "fetters"— sustains him throughout his narrative, promising a possibility of full, surveying enlightenment at the end of his dark, adventurous path. But Mervyn's demand to know, his desire to assume virtuous agency, must be partially suspended or frustrated for the duration of his adventures; if he knew "whither the path tended," there would be no story to tell. Brown's plot is ingenious for making Mervyn's learning function as virtuous action, but in so doing it defines its ideal standards of knowledge and virtue in opposition to its own narrative form.

Brown almost acknowledges that tension in the following passage, in which Mervyn says: "The condition of my mind was considerably remote from happiness. I was placed in a scene that furnished fuel to my curiosity. This passion is a source of pleasure, provided its gratification be practicable. I had no reason, in my present circumstances, to despair of knowledge; yet suspicion and anxiety beset me. I thought upon the delay and toil which the removal of my ignorance would cost and reaped only pain and fear from the reflection" (73). The delay that causes Mervyn to shudder is the duration of his narrative. Beyond it, after the "removal" of his ignorance, he imagines happiness and the gratification of his curiosity. In what might be called the meantime of his narrative, however, he sees at once fuel to his curiosity and the toil of its frustration. (Again, a contrast with Poe might be helpful. Writing in the context of liberal society and the bureaucratic nation, Poe can treat the temporal duration of narrative as expressing the fateful nature of experience in general. *Pym*, properly speaking, has no ending; and it is typical of novels in that later period to resolve themselves without a moment of enlightenment interpreted as transcending or escaping the narrative condition.)

If the narrative duration appears as restrictive and threatening, the novel's writing—its existence in the public medium of print—is implicitly associated with the liberty of knowledge toward which Mervyn aspires. This is the case partly because of the analogy noted earlier between

Brown's writing and the literature of Stevens and Mervyn. It is also because Brown associates Mervyn's virtuous curiosity with the reader's own,
as he intimates in the scene in which Mervyn translates the Italian manuscript with impulsive and suspenseful curiosity. Because of the novel's
writtenness, moreover, there is an important difference between the
reader's curiosity and Mervyn's: for the reader, curiosity's gratification is
already in hand.

The point would be trivial, except that the difference between Mervyn's
restrictive condition and the more liberating context of the novel's writing
is explicitly rendered within the novel. For here it will be remembered
that Brown goes to considerable lengths in drawing attention to the
novel's mise-en-scène. Most of the novel is Dr. Stevens' written record of
Mervyn's oral narration as delivered on several separate occasions, and the
difference between the oral and written contexts sensibly reproduces the
difference between Mervyn's painful dependence and Stevens' secure literature. At several points Brown tells us in detail about an interruption in
Mervyn's narration; in each case, the interruption associates the delay and
toil of his oral telling with the delay and toil of his perilous condition.
Chapter 14 of part 2, for example, begins:

> Mervyn's auditors allowed no pause in their attention to this story.
> Having ended, a deep silence took place. The clock which stood
> upon the mantel, had sounded twice the customary *larum,* but had
> not been heard by us. It was now struck a third time. It was *one.* Our
> guest appeared somewhat startled at this signal, and looked, with a
> mournful sort of earnestness, at the clock. There was an air of in-
> quietude about him, which I had never observed in an equal degree
> before.
>
> I was not without much curiosity respecting other incidents than
> those which had just been related by him; but after so much fatigue
> as he had undergone, I thought it improper to prolong the con-
> versation.
>
> Come, said I, my friend, let us to bed . . . Much has happened in
> your absence, which is proper to be known to you, but our discourse
> will be best deferred till to-morrow. I will come into your chamber
> by day-dawn, and unfold to you my particular.
>
> Nay, said he, withdraw not on my account. If I go to my chamber,
> it will not be to sleep, but to meditate, especially after your assurance
> that something of moment has occurred in my absence. My thoughts,
> independently of any cause of sorrow or fear, have received an im-
> pulse which solitude and darkness will not stop. It is impossible to

know too much for our safety and integrity, or to know it too soon.
What has happened? (339–340)

Unlike Mervyn, Dr. Stevens shows himself willing to set narrative aside
as though it were written; this security reflects his role as recorder and
implies the liberty of his lettered virtue. Mervyn lacks that liberty, but
Brown is very clear in pointing out that Mervyn's impatience with the
narrative is not emotional ("sorrow or fear") but intellectual: his
"thoughts" have been propelled forward again by the discovery that he is
still in the condition of ignorance. The difference in their behavior reproduces that between Brown's ideal of knowledge—which is immune to
fortune and lies beyond narrative—and the dramatic knowledge of Mervyn, which is made to coincide with virtuous action only by being partial.
If Stevens' ideal literature is associated with the written context, the
dramatic limitations of Mervyn's knowledge are associated with the
marked temporality of the oral narration. Hence the aural clarity of the
chapter's beginning: what "Mervyn's auditors" hear is first the tale, then
silence, and then the tolling of the mantel clock. And Stevens' detailed
calendar of times for deferring and resuming the tale further demonstrates
the association between Mervyn's dependence and the temporality of spoken narrative, since the deferral of the telling both keeps Mervyn ignorant
and maintains the narrative suspense.

In contrast, when Mervyn says, "It is impossible to know too much for
our safety and integrity, or to know it too soon," he invokes an ideal of
untrammeled knowledge exemplified in scenes of writing such as that of
the translation. And if the oral conditions of his narrative suggest the
frustration of his desire for such expansive and atemporal knowledge, he
will find what he seeks in the fixed publicity of writing. Late in the novel
the mise-en-scène suddenly changes, as Arthur takes over Stevens' nimble
pen and begins to write his own story. His doing so indicates the moment
at which he knows the full of his own story, and equally indicates the end
of his dependent condition, for it is immediately after Welbeck's death
that he takes up the pen.

It can only be a problem for a novel to associate its own narrative
organization of knowledge with dependence and fortune, while associat-
ing its medium with the transcendence of publicity. Yet that is the case
in *Arthur Mervyn*. It is both a narrative and a publication, though the
terms of its ethical-political order encourage us to think of these as opposites, in exactly the same way that dependence and liberty are opposites.
Brown has a way of mediating this tension in his premises through a
fantasy of publication. Virtually every episode in the novel occasions not

just the acquisition of knowledge and the conferring of benefits, but more precisely a strategy of disclosure. In each instance a dramatic act of publication appears as the escape from the perils entailed upon Mervyn by his duration in ignorance and fortune. Mervyn's narrative is itself such an act of disclosure, called forth with much prodding by Stevens in order to allay the accusations raised against Mervyn. "Arthur," Stevens says, "something is the matter with you. Will you not disclose it to us? Perhaps you have brought yourself into some dilemma out of which we may help you to escape" (12). From this moment Arthur's escape from difficulty is brought about by the labor of disclosure recorded—and disclosed—by the novel. And within the adventures disclosed by the novel occur an astonishing number of episodes that turn on an act of disclosure. When a chance expression of Thetford's reveals a plot to Mervyn, for example, he says, "This little word, half whispered in a thoughtless mood, was a key to unlock an extensive cabinet of secrets . . . To detect and to counterwork this plot was obviously my duty" (77–78).

For Mervyn, being the novel's hero entails the adoption of disclosure as a principle of conduct: he determines to be in the right by publishing information. The trouble he gets into stems from his not having done so from the beginning. One of the peculiarities of the novel's plot is that Welbeck has extracted from Mervyn several pledges of secrecy that vitally endanger Mervyn and interfere with the narration. "I was far from expecting," Mervyn says, "that any exigence would occur, making disclosure my duty" (62). He soon ceases to reason in this fashion and adopts the duty of disclosure not just as a contingent tactic, but as an abstract principle. He is, he later explains, so far from eluding curiosity, "so far from studying concealment," that he is "anxious to publish the truth" (388). On another occasion, when he is wondering whether to "disclose the truth" to Welbeck about having purloined the volume from the study, he says: "The first impulse was to hide this truth: but my understanding had been taught, by recent occurrences, to question the justice, and deny the usefulness of secrecy in any case" (199).

Disclosing information, making things public, is understood as ensuring a civic source of validity. For that reason the strategy of disclosure in this novel can be taken as a fantasy-equivalent of the act of publication, even when no thematic connection with writing occurs. The strategy of disclosure is more than an interest in publication as such, because there is an added twist. Disclosure bears a punitive character. When Mervyn decides to disclose his knowledge of Wallace and Villars he speaks of "charges" and "vindication," and in general there are dire consequences for those about whom information is disclosed: Wallace, Villars, Thetford, and especially Welbeck. In the last scene between Welbeck and Mervyn, Welbeck cries out in the pain of Mervyn's publicizing gaze:

> Thou has done me harm enough, but canst do, if thou wilt, still more. Thou canst betray the secrets that are lodged in thy bosom, and rob me of the comfort of reflecting that my guilt is known but to one among the living.
>
> This suggestion made me pause, and look back upon the past. I had confided this man's tale to you. The secrecy, on which he so fondly leaned, was at an end. Had I acted culpably or not?
>
> (338)

The answer to the last question is no. Mervyn's disclosure in this case—identical with the novel's narration—operates in lieu of the law. Welbeck on his deathbed cringes in fear: "terror of more ample disclosures, which the simplicity and rectitude of Mervyn might prompt him to make, chained up his tongue, and covered him with dismay" (258). Although Welbeck's crimes are such that at least one character would "exult to see him suffer all the rigors of the law" (228), the only trial he ever faces is that of publicity—a trial in which evidence and punishment are the same.

If such is Welbeck's fate, it had been determined considerably earlier, when Mervyn first pledged himself to publish: "Welbeck had ceased to be dreaded or revered. That awe which was once created by his superiority of age, refinement of manners and dignity of garb, had vanished. I was a boy in years, an indigent and uneducated rustic, but I was able to discern the illusions of power and riches, and abjured every claim to esteem that was not founded on integrity. There was no tribunal before which I should faulter in asserting the truth, and no species of martyrdom which I would not cheerfully embrace in its cause" (200). The possibility not considered by the novel is that the assertion of truth is itself a tribunal, that in representational polity no one is martyred for having made a public assertion, because the standard of publicity defines the legitimate. When Welbeck complains under the discipline of that publicity, he can only be seen as "fondly" leaning on illicit secrecy.

The strategy of disclosure confers the power of the law upon the publicity exemplified in writing. It can do so because of the close identification of the public and the legitimate in representational polity, for the consequence of that identification is that the secret and the hidden automatically appear as illegitimate. The connection is vividly imaged in the scene in which Stevens realizes that some banknotes have been buried on the corpse of one of Welbeck's victims:

> It was just to restore these bills to their true owner; but how could this be done without hazardous processes and tedious disclosures? To whom ought these disclosures to be made? By what authority or agency could these half-decayed limbs be dug up, and the lost treasure be taken from amidst the horrible corruption in which it was immersed?
>
> This ought not to be the act of a single individual. This act would entangle him in a maze of perils and suspicions, of concealments and evasions, from which he could not hope to escape with his reputation inviolate. The proper method was through the agency of the law. It is to this that Mervyn must submit his conduct. The story which he told to me he must tell to the world. Suspicions have fixed themselves upon him, which allow him not the privilege of silence and obscurity.
>
> (252)

In this luridly thrilling passage Stevens' language—with such terms as "entanglements," "evasions," "escape," and "submit"—displays the violence with which the law defines Mervyn's person: suspicions "have fixed themselves upon him." Under this boundless inspection Mervyn's fixed position resembles nothing so much as that of the corpse, since both await the unearthing agency of the public eye. To resist inspection, as Welbeck does, is to be illegitimate; hence Stevens' dread of "concealments" and his notion that they would violate one's reputation. Suffering the rigors of the law, Mervyn's only defense is to adopt the very same agency of disclosure that subjects him, and thereby to render himself a function of that agency. Thus, if Mervyn resembles the corpse as the object of the law's exhuming vision, by adopting the strategy of disclosure he also becomes the law's agent.

Stevens' logic in this passage has grand implications for the written context of the novel. Telling the story orally, Stevens implies, did not satisfactorily justify Mervyn because that narration was not sufficiently public. "The story which he told to me," Stevens says, "he must tell to the world." Again, Brown calls attention here to the relation between the narrative mise-en-scène and its publication as a printed artifact. Because he identifies the public with the legitimate, submitting Mervyn's conduct to "the agency of the law" is seen as naturally coincident with telling his tale "to the world." Despite Stevens' decision that Mervyn must submit his conduct to the agency of the law, however, there is no trial scene in *Arthur Mervyn*. Only the existence of the novel itself answers the imperative expressed here by Stevens: in telling Mervyn's story to the world, it performs the agency of the law. The change of the novel's mise-en-scène is again revealing, for Mervyn's justification becomes final only after Welbeck's death, when he takes up the pen. At the moment of his writing no perils of dependence remain for him and his identification with the novel's vantage is complete. The strategy of disclosure reaches completion in the publicity of the novel's written context. Through it, Brown implicitly identifies his writing with the validity of the public sphere. It is not an allegory of publication as such that interests him, but a fantasy of publication that carries the full authority of law. (Note here the extensive similarities with *Wieland,* where the same conflict of personality structures finds resolution in a fantasy of disclosure. There a key role in the narrative is played by the transcript of a courtroom trial, and again the villain shows himself addicted to forms of secrecy.)

What does this analysis of *Arthur Mervyn* prove? I have tried to indicate that republican print discourse creates both the imperatives and the problems of the text. On thematic and unthematic levels, it produces narratives of virtuous literacy. Formally it creates a problem in the relation between the narrative organization and the mise-en-scène, because of their conflicting symbolic political valences. And last, republican categories allow a fantasy of disclosure as the solution to the contradiction of a republican narrative. I believe that, although the details of these patterns are specific to this rather ingenious if chaotic novel, the underlying cultural imperatives are givens for the novel as a genre in the republican national context. As a publication, the early American novel strives for the performative virtue of republican textuality.

I have by no means accounted for all of this novel, let alone all of early American novels in general. In some ways I have omitted the most interesting parts of *Arthur Mervyn.* The most obvious omission is the latter part of the book, which becomes increasingly devoted to the psychodrama of Mervyn's romance with a character named Achsa Fielding. As more and more of the narrative becomes devoted to the then-emergent ideology of love, Mervyn becomes more and more a site of imaginary erotics. The elaborate otherness of Achsa Fielding—maternal, foreign, and Jewish—allows the appearance of an eroticized self/other problematic, in a way reminiscent of Goethe's *Werther:* "You say she loves; loves *me!* me, a boy in age; bred in clownish ignorance, scarcely ushered into the world; . . . I shall be anxious, vacant and unhappy in her presence. I shall dread to look at her, or to open my lips lest my mad and unhallowed ambition should betray itself" (434–435).

Insensibly the premises of the novel have changed. Thematically, civic virtue is no longer an issue. Narrative tension is no longer a struggle between ignorant dependence and lettered transcendence. Fantasies of disclosure no longer address the structuring problem. Instead, problems of intersubjective recognition and mutual esteem have brought Mervyn's ego into focus ("She loves; loves *me!* me . . ."). One consequence is that the novel's exorbitant but repressed erotics—masochistic, narcissistic, anal-paranoid, necrophiliac, aggressive, and homoerotically utopian—get charged with a sudden relevance. They return to trouble the ideal of the citizen's literate transcendence of his unacknowledged male body. And it is on the site of that supercharged contradiction that the novel struggles for closure. In the novel's concluding paragraph, Mervyn forsakes his pen ("Lie there, snug in thy leathern case"), not for enlightenment but for an unpictured reintegration that he can obtain only in the intimate recognition of romantic love.

Because of cross-currents such as these, I do not claim that *Arthur Mervyn* is a text unified by the context of republican discourse. What seems most interesting is the way its internal shifts reproduce the contradictions between republican print discourse and a liberal-national imaginary. These contradictions are just what make Brown's novel illustrative of its contemporaries. The novel as a genre articulated a troubled divide in the culture. Simultaneously a *publication* subject to the diffusion of literature *and* a site of private imaginary identifications, the early American novel produces endless variations on the contradictory symbolic determinations of its own form. In Brown's novel that means a contradiction between the narrative of Mervyn's performative virtue and the narrative of his self/other ego-erotics. That these are deeply contradictory can be seen in how they represent the problem of esteem. Mervyn's ego-anxieties (*"me!"*) find their solution in the valued esteem of Achsa Fielding ("she loves"). Her esteem is a sentimental model for the reader's relation to the text. In the republican narrative, however, the need for esteem is the problem to be transcended. And it can be transcended only through the fundamentally performative virtue of literature.

Arthur Mervyn must narrate rhetorically before an often skeptical audience, because he inhabits a credit economy and a social order of managed esteem. And the environment of credit and esteem, which accounts for the profusion of fictional analogues in the novel, exhaustively constitutes the novel's stock of evils. Fictiveness finds its chief analogue in the personality structure embodied by Welbeck. Against Welbeck's polite self-presentation, his forgery, his fraud, his seduction, his plagiarism, his "dependence on the world's erroneous estimation," his "devotion to imposture" (199), even his mobile wealth—against all these Mervyn commits himself to acts of publication. "I was unhabituated to ideas of floating or transferable wealth," he says, explaining the impression made on him by Welbeck's opulent appearance (56).

As Mervyn narrates his tale before Dr. and Mrs. Stevens, he is repeatedly interrupted. And in the intervals between narrations, other characters appear with rival narratives. The result is a central scene of audition, analogous to the reader's position, which the novel constructs as a perilous tribunal of credit. "I can keep hold of your good opinion," Mervyn acknowledges to Stevens, "only by a candid deportment" (15). But a rival narrator, one Wortley, tells Stevens: "If, after this proof, you can give credit to his story, I shall think you made of very perverse and credulous materials" (226). Wortley goes so far as to invoke legal proceedings, making the narrative fully juridical: "The suspicions to which he is exposed will not easily be obviated; but if he has any thing to say in his defence, his judicial examination will afford him the suitable opportunity. Why are you so much afraid to subject his innocence to this test? It was not till you heard his tale, that your own suspicions were removed. Allow me the same privilege of unbelief" (248).

It would be forcing the issue to read this drama of credit as a conscious thematization of novelistic fictionality. But it *can* be read that way for the simple reason that it derives from the same anxieties about personality structure and social order that made fiction so suspect in republican America. Those anxieties go to the heart of the nature of economic and political personhood, and Wortley himself makes the connection with capital explicit. He suspects Mervyn of abetting a fraud. But he sees fraud as merely an extension of commercial speculation, citing with scorn a merchant "who employed money, not as the medium of traffic, but as in itself a commodity." Wortley here identifies the capitalist economy as the threat to virtue, and it is against that danger that the narrative raises its tribunal of credit. Wortley wants to try Mervyn's personal credit because he believes himself to be Mervyn's victim in the domain of economic credit. "Happily," he reminds Stevens, "you are a stranger to mercantile anxieties and revolutions. Your fortune does not rest on a basis which an untoward blast may sweep away, or four strokes of a pen may demolish" (227). Remember that Arthur's adventures begin with his departure from his yeoman-father's farm, toward the urban world of the capitalist market. And it is a significant index of the novel's republican anxieties about capital that nothing survives of the original Jeffersonian setting: Arthur eventually returns to find that his father has sold the farm in a disastrous land speculation.

Brown fills the novel with analogues to fiction: forgeries, look-alikes, bank notes, seductions, credit schemes, and the like. But he interprets them in the republican mode, as a corrupt environment. Only in retrospect do they appear as figuring the emergent liberal-capitalist model of personality and social relations. The thematic and narrative device of disclosure is directed against that model. The wish at the core of *Arthur Mervyn,* at least in its republican mode, is that the book might have the value of a publication as opposed to the value of a fiction or of a narration. It (vainly) strives for the same performativity as the Constitution.

What are we to make of this book? Although it would seem that the dense figuration of republican literature within the narrative testifies to the power held by the republican paradigm over Brown's imagination rather than to an allegorical intention on his part, it must also be remarked that this reading—which apparently depreciates the novel's merit—is entirely compatible with Brown's criteria of value. Republican literature, in the extreme formulation represented by Brown's career, establishes the criteria of public benefit and law for all questions of value. It therefore defines as irrelevant those criteria which pertain to the author's control, or voice, or expression. If it is thus difficult to see how republican writing could be judged inferior on its own terms (unless it were to promote luxury and vice), Brown's rhetorical purpose in writing—to bolster the republic through the diffusion of literature—also subordinates to the point of insignificance any appreciation of his role as author. Criticism typically commends authors rather than the public discourse privileged in *Arthur Mervyn,* and the available terms of critical praise—that Brown presents a message about virtue in the novel or that the novel is social criticism or an allegory of writing—are inappropriate to the novel because they ultimately valorize the author's utterance rather than the generality.[12] Republican literature, in short, defines itself by means of political standards for which criticism currently possesses no vocabulary of commendation. And although I read *Arthur Mervyn* as a dense and fascinating text, to do so is to be struck by the final incommensurability between our own standards of appreciation and those of Brown's republican literature.

In another sense, the tensions I have traced in *Arthur Mervyn* show that the paradigm of republican literature was already undergoing transformation. The novel was already turning a civic ideology of publication into the kind of private imaginary appropriate to nationalism. Though Brown's ambition was undoubtedly that of "embodying virtue in a novel," as a contemporary observer put it, a novel cannot embody virtue.[13] That is why Brown goes to such great lengths to fill *Arthur Mervyn* with what I have called fantasies of publicity. His republican cognitive vocabulary for print values a book as publication; but its public value can only be imagined through the mediation of private virtues. In the best of cases the reader's imaginary identifications become the means for the reader's reflective self-management. Those imaginary identifications also produce a pleasure in the same suspension of knowledge, the same narrative duration of ignorant temporality, that is the source of Brown's deepest republican anxieties. Where the disclosure of knowledge is linked to the public authority of publication, and where the temporal and dependent condition of ignorance is construed as the obstacle to civic participation, the pleasure of narrative identification must be private in a strong sense. It becomes cognitively possible and enjoyable only through the reader's negative relation to the public. So although Brown finds ways to identify the reader's calm surveyance with publicity, the reader simultaneously identifies with the character's ignorant dependence, *precisely in opposition to the full knowledge of the public sphere.* And because novel-reading, given this symbolic order, produces that experience of privacy as such, the reader can claim Arthur's public success through a private appropriation that is tangibly imaginary.

This imaginary participation in the public order is, as I have suggested, a precondition for modern nationalism, though it is anathema to pure republicanism. The modern nation does not have citizens in the same way that the republic does. You can be a member of the nation, attributing its agency to yourself in imaginary identification, without being a freeholder or exercising any agency in the public sphere. Nationalism makes no distinction between such imaginary participation and the active participation of citizens. In republicanism that distinction counted for everything. So the early phase of post-Revolutionary nationalism is marked by a gradual extension of a national imaginary to exactly those social groups that were excluded from citizenship—notably women. Women were more and more thought of as symbolic members of the nation, especially in their capacities as mothers.[14] But this symbolic reclassification changed the nature of the nation and the imaginary of its extension more than it changed the access of women to the public sphere. For the public of which women were now said to be members was no longer a public in the rigorous sense of republicanism, and membership in it no longer connoted civic action. Politics was developing into a specialized social system, entrusted to career experts and mediating institutions, while the nation was developing an imaginary and a discourse divorced from the self-contained institutions of politics.[15]

The emergent vocabulary of sentiment was designed to attribute public value to reader identification. And the triumph of sentiment in the novel marks a crisis for the paradigm of republican literature in which Brown writes. The connections between sentimental discourse and women, or between sentimental discourse and the private liberal subject, are now well known.[16] The turn toward sentiment can be seen as a key element both in the extension of the national imaginary to the female readership of novels and in the emergence of a liberal paradigm for appreciating printed texts. If the privatizing discourse of sentiment marks a break with the republican paradigm of diffused literature, nevertheless in the 1780s and 1790s the two lead a tense coexistence in the American novel.

American novels of the period typically revolve dramatically around an ethical-political conflict between the personality structures of virtue and politeness. This is true of adventure narratives, such as *Fortune's Foot-ball,* as well as seduction narratives, such as *Amelia; or the Faithless Briton.* In Hannah Foster's *The Coquette,* both of the main characters, seducer and seduced, represent the ethical order—or unethical order—of politeness. Foster stresses to no end that Sanford, the gallant rake, is the epitome of politeness. He equally epitomizes the credit economy. We learn from the beginning that he lives on credit alone, and his ruin comes about through the enlightenment of his creditors. But Eliza Wharton, the heroine, also represents the reflective management of esteem, here called by its female name: "coquetting artifice."[17] Predictably it ruins her as well, and the reader is called to identify with a chorus of minor characters who admonish her to a more republican comportment. One of the ideological functions of the seduction novel in such a case was to integrate the authority of public opinion with self-present virtue rather than reflective management of esteem, an integration that could come about most easily with the charged subject of a woman's reputation. As one female character tells Eliza: "Slight not the opinion of the world. We are dependent beings; and while the smallest traces of virtuous sensibility remain, we must feel the force of that dependence, in a greater or less degree. No female, whose mind is uncorrupted, can be indifferent to reputation."[18] But neither can any female, whose mind is uncorrupted, *manage* her reputation. The seduction plot focuses the ideological ambivalences surrounding the personality type of modernity. It dramatizes the order of politeness in order to supply, against it, fantasies of virtue and authoritative publicity.

Moreover, early American novels sustain a relatively continuous thematic content that links them to the public discourse. They deliberate explicitly the issues of the republic. Part of the reason for this prevalence of public themes is that, as publications, the novels were taken to be part of the public discourse. But more pointedly, the public themes taken up in novels tend to be those with the most potential for valuing publications as civic activity. Cathy Davidson has remarked the rather extraordinary fact that all early national novels, without exception, contain a discussion of the theory of education, a topic that always implicitly contained a specially political value for the diffusion of letters.[19] The obsessive discussions of education in the novels both align the characters with the personality structure of virtue in a diffuse public sphere and express the fantasy that novels themselves carry the political valence of publication.

The most striking example of a thematic continuity with the public sphere is Brackenridge's *Modern Chivalry,* a comic epic about the tribulations of a virtuous freeholder whose activities consist largely of trying to sustain the identity between letters and the public sphere. Farrago, the main character, finds himself faced repeatedly with the challenge of his servant, Teague. For Teague, though illiterate, manages to have himself elected to office. The illiterate Teague even manages, in a fantasy that says much about the paradigm of republican literature, to write a book. Such episodes continually provide a staging ground on which Brackenridge can deliberate the nature of the republic, always keeping in view the value of letters for the republic. But even where republican literature recedes from the thematic focus, its value remains implicit simply in the fact that the novel regards itself as an exercise in republican theory for a freeholder public. All of its extended considerations of policy and constitution imply the integration of the text with other publications in the political discourse.

Finally, the antifictional prejudice itself testifies to the power of Americans' desire to maintain an identity between publication and public discourse. Americans endlessly avowed a fear that fiction would detach readers' sentiments from the social world of the polity, substituting a private drama of fancy. They wrote of such fears in virtually every magazine and newspaper in the country; no figure of the period seems to have been exempt from the anxiety (or at least from the discourse of anxiety)—including the novelists themselves. William Hill Brown's *The Power of Sympathy,* generally called the first American novel, declares in its full title that it is "Founded in Truth" and thus not a fiction at all. *The Coquette,* according to its title page and popular knowledge, was "Founded on Fact." Most eloquent in the attack on novel-reading, however, was Tabitha Tenney's

Female Quixotism, a novel devoted entirely to the plight of a reader no longer able to distinguish private imaginary from general virtue. Novels of the period in this way typically argue against their own generic conditions, paradoxically claiming exemptions for themselves on the grounds that they teach the authority of publicity as against the private fancy of the reader. Even *Arthur Mervyn* bears the subtitle *Memoirs of the Year 1793;* its preface explicitly classes the novel among "the medical and political discussions" of the plague of that year. Brown, as I have noted, considers his novel as different from public treatises only insofar as the convenience of narrative allows him to "methodize his own reflections." Defenses of novel-writing thus exhibit the same logic as attacks on novel-reading. Both uphold an ideal of republican literature in which publication and the public sphere remain identical; both worry that the environment of fictitious identification might no longer entail public knowledge or civic activity.

In the American culture of the late eighteenth century there was no independent language of value for novels. And on my reading, the peculiar American combination of outright hostility and uneasy defensiveness toward novels was, given the nature of the republican public sphere, no small ideological prejudice. Until the joint triumphs of literary publishing and of nationalism in the liberal society of the nineteenth century, when the political system and publication became specialized in a mutual separation, novels could only narrate their anxieties about the hazard to the republic that they themselves posed.

NOTES
INDEX

NOTES

I. The Cultural Mediation of the Print Medium

1. John Adams, "A Dissertation on the Canon and the Feudal Law," in *Papers of John Adams,* ed. Robert J. Taylor et al. (Cambridge, Mass.: Harvard University Press, 1977–), 1:103–128. Further references to this text will be made parenthetically. The now-familiar title was assigned by the Englishman Thomas Hollis, who reprinted Adams' essay in London in 1768.

2. John Foxe, *Acts and Monuments,* quoted in Stephen Greenblatt, *Renaissance Self-Fashioning* (Chicago: University of Chicago Press, 1980), 98–99.

3. Ibid., 97.

4. The argument that emancipation is structural to reason as self-reflection can be found in Jürgen Habermas, *Knowledge and Human Interests,* trans. Jeremy Shapiro (Boston: Beacon Press, 1971). Without necessarily sharing the confidence of that argument, we can see in Habermas that the two Enlightenment doctrines of emancipation and reflection for its own sake are mutually determined in the structure of rationality. See especially pp. 205–213.

5. The relation between letters and the Revolution has been frequently noted. See Daniel Boorstin, *The Americans: The Colonial Experience* (New York: Random House, 1958); Arthur M. Schlesinger, *Prelude to Independence* (New York: Knopf, 1958); Philip Davidson, *Propaganda and the American Revolution, 1763–1783* (1941; repr. New York: Norton, 1973); Bernard Bailyn, *The Ideological Origins of the American Revolution* (Cambridge, Mass.: Harvard University Press, 1967); and Bernard Bailyn and John Hench, eds., *The Press and the American Revolution* (Worcester, Mass.: American Antiquarian Society, 1980).

6. The problem here is virtually the same as that announced in the opening of Max Weber's *The Protestant Ethic and the Spirit of Capitalism* (New York: Counterpoint, 1958). Weber argues that although the development of capitalism involves universalizing values, narratives of technological advance, even the notion of "development," yet it remains culturally specific and local. His book still presents a challenge to theorize the relation between an international phenomenon like capitalism and the local cultural history in which it is constituted. The same

challenge arises with the subject of modernity. "Modernity" is most usefully—if controversially—defined by Jürgen Habermas in the first chapter of *The Philosophical Discourse of Modernity*, trans. Thomas McCarthy (Cambridge: MIT Press, 1987).

7. Elizabeth Eisenstein, *The Printing Press as an Agent of Change* (Cambridge, Mass.: Harvard University Press, 1979); Walter J. Ong, *Interfaces of the Word* (Ithaca, N. Y.: Cornell University Press, 1977), and *Orality and Literacy* (London: Methuen, 1982); Jack Goody, *The Domestication of the Savage Mind* (Cambridge: Cambridge University Press, 1977). The most recent example of this school in literary studies, and one that carries its premises to ridiculous extremes, is Alvin Kernan, *Printing Technology, Letters, and Samuel Johnson* (Princeton: Princeton University Press, 1987). For an early and incisive critique of the McLuhanite assumptions adopted by this school, see Kenneth Burke, "Medium as 'Message,'" in *Language as Symbolic Action* (Berkeley: University of California Press, 1966), 410–418.

8. Alvin Gouldner, *The Dialectic of Ideology and Technology* (1976; repr. New York: Oxford University Press, 1982), 40–41.

9. Eisenstein, 703–704.

10. Another tradition, for which this criticism will not hold, is exemplified by Raymond Williams, *The Long Revolution* (1961; repr. Westport, Conn.: Greenwood Press, 1975). See also Michael Gurevitch et al., eds., *Culture, Society, and the Media* (London: Methuen, 1982); especially the essays by Stuart Hall ("The Rediscovery of 'Ideology': Return of the Repressed in Media Studies," 56–90), James Curran ("Communications, Power, and Social Order," 202–235), and Tony Bennett ("Media, 'Reality,' Signification," 287–308). Also of use are the essays in James Curran, et al., eds., *Mass Communication and Society* (Beverly Hills, Calif.: Sage, 1979). For an example that deals, albeit briefly, with the history of print in America, see Daniel C. Hallin, "The American News Media: A Critical Theory Perspective," in John Forester, ed., *Critical Theory and Public Life* (Cambridge, Mass.: MIT Press, 1985), 121–146.

11. Kernan, *Printing Technology,* 49.

12. Jonathan Goldberg has written a splendid book on this subject. See *Writing Matter* (Stanford: Stanford University Press, 1990), especially the last chapter.

13. Lucien Febvre and Henri Martin, *The Coming of the Book,* trans. David Gerard (London: Verso, 1976), 28.

14. See Walter Benjamin, "The Work of Art in the Age of Mechanical Reproduction," in *Illuminations* (New York: Harcourt Brace and World, 1969), 217–252.

15. Weber, *Protestant Ethic;* see especially the Introduction, where printing is discussed.

16. See, for example, Phyllis Wheatley's poem "On Being Brought from Africa to America."

17. Olaudah Equiano, *The Interesting Narrative of the Life of Olaudah Equiano* (1789; quoted from the first American edition; New York, 1791, 1:75). There are similar stories about the perspective of North American Indians. See James Axtell, "The Power of Print in the Eastern Woodlands," *William and Mary Quarterly* 44 (1987): 300–309.

18. The strong version of this position is that taken by Jürgen Habermas in

The Theory of Communicative Action, trans. Thomas McCarthy (Boston: Beacon Press, 1984). The point I am making, however, need not be understood as a grounding of validity—only as an operative condition of practice.

19. This view has been developed in a wide range of sociolinguistic studies. The general understanding of literacy implicit in such studies has been argued for in Brian Street's excellent book, *Literacy in Theory and Practice* (Cambridge: Cambridge University Press, 1984).

20. Implicitly I am arguing against the notion of a predictable social meaning or outcome of literacy, just as I am arguing against a predictable social meaning or outcome of print. An antiessentialist model of sociology is required by this argument, so my foregrounding of dispositions of character and collectivity in this account can be taken as a shorthand reference to Pierre Bourdieu's emphasis on what he calls habitus. See, for example, his *Distinction,* trans. Richard Nice (Cambridge, Mass.: Harvard University Press, 1984), and "The Economics of Linguistic Exchange," *Social Science Information* 6 (1977): 645–668. There is also a growing body of research in the anthropology of literacy challenging the standard view, set by Jack Goody, that literacy has a regular crosscultural social meaning. For a brief summary, see Sylvia Scribner, "Literacy in Three Metaphors," in Eugene Kintgen, et al., eds., *Perspectives on Literacy* (Carbondale, Ill.: Southern Illinois University Press, 1988), 71–81.

21. Alexander Hamilton, *Itinerarium,* ed. by Carl Bridenbaugh as *Gentleman's Progress* (Chapel Hill: University of North Carolina Press, 1948), 40–41.

22. Kenneth Lockridge, *Literacy in Colonial New England* (New York: Norton, 1974). See also William Gilmore, "Elementary Literacy on the Eve of the Industrial Revolution: Trends in Rural New England, 1760–1830," *Proceedings of the American Antiquarian Society* 92 (1982): 87–178; and Lawrence Cremin, *American Education: The Colonial Experience, 1607–1786* (New York: Harper & Row, 1970).

23. David Hall, "The Uses of Literacy in New England, 1600–1850," in William Joyce et al., eds., *Printing and Society in Early America* (Worcester: American Antiquarian Society, 1983), 1–47. Hall has contributed more than any other contemporary historian to the history of the book in America, and in this chapter I have relied heavily on his many essays. See especially "The World of Print and Collective Mentality in Seventeenth-Century New England," in John Higham and Paul Conkin, eds., *New Directions in American Intellectual History* (Baltimore: Johns Hopkins University Press, 1979), 166–180; and "On Native Ground: From the History of Printing to the History of the Book," *Proceedings of the American Antiquarian Society* 93 (1983): 313–336.

24. Sandra Gilbert and Susan Gubar, *The Madwoman in the Attic* (New Haven: Yale University Press, 1979), 3–44.

25. Sarah Kemble Knight, *Journal* (Boston: Godine, 1972), 22.

26. *Pennsylvania Gazette,* July 3, 1732.

27. *South Carolina Gazette,* January 8 and 15, 1732.

28. On Nuthead, see Lawrence C. Wroth, "The St. Mary's City Press: A New Chronology of American Printing," *Colophon* n.s. 1 (1936): 333–357, which reproduces samples of her printing. On women's education, see E. Jennifer Monaghan, "Literacy Instruction and Gender in Colonial New England," *American Quarterly* 40 (1988): 18–41.

29. "The Autobiography of Increase Mather," quoted in Hall, "Uses of Literacy," 25.

30. Kenneth Lockridge, noting the correlation between literacy and wealth or occupation, offers the obvious reason that the wealthier-and more leisured had better access to schooling. He also argues that literacy promoted upward mobility, so that a poor farmer's son who learned to write was less likely to remain a poor farmer than his brother who did not learn to write; see Lockridge, *Literacy in Colonial New England*. Robert Gross, observing in an unpublished paper that Lockridge's figures indicate writing skills rather than reading, extends the argument to suggest that literacy statistics correlate not simply to wealth as such, but to commercialization. Writing and the commercial economy, he argues, are nearly coextensive: most highly developed in New England and in the seaports, less so in the South and in rural areas.

31. *South Carolina Gazette,* April 22, 1732.

32. Lockridge, *Literacy in Colonial New England*. Lockridge is opposed on this point to the more Whiggish narrative of literacy in Cremin, *American Education*. For a similar debunking of the correlation to modernization, but in a nineteenth-century urban setting, see Harvey Graff, *The Literacy Myth: Literacy and Social Structure in the Nineteenth-Century City* (New York: Academic Press, 1979).

33. Hall, "Uses of Literacy," 26.

34. Cotton Mather, *Diary of Cotton Mather,* 2 vols. (New York: Ungar, 1957), 2:193 (March 18, 1713).

35. Mather, *Diary,* 2:538 (June 1718).

36. Preface, *The Book of the General Lawes and Libertyes* (Cambridge, Mass., 1660).

37. Samuel Whiting, *Abraham's Humble Intercession for Sodom* (Cambridge, Mass., 1666), v.

38. Mather, *Diary,* 1:65 (June 11, 1683).

39. Julius Tuttle, "The Libraries of the Mathers," *Proceedings of the American Antiquarian Society* 20 (1910): 269–356.

40. The extreme form of this claim is to be found in Harry S. Stout's "Religion, Communications, and the Ideological Origins of the American Revolution," *William and Mary Quarterly* 34 (1977): 519–541. The essay displays an unabashed and uncritical sentimentality, assuming that print was "elitist and hierarchical" (540) and that any form of speech, such as evangelical oratory, must be an egalitarian "opposition to the established social order" (527–528).

41. I refer to the critique of Levi-Strauss in Jacques Derrida, *Of Grammatology,* trans. Gayatri Spivak (Baltimore: The Johns Hopkins University Press, 1976). Although the subsequent American history of literary deconstruction has obscured the connection, Derrida's deconstructive project arose in the context of an inquiry into the political history in determinations of writing. Indeed, it was to this inquiry that "grammatology" referred.

42. Anon., *Some Few Remarks Upon a Scandalous Book* (Boston, 1701), 11.

43. Cotton Mather, *Utilia* (Boston, 1716), iv.

44. Quoted in Kenneth Silverman, *Life and Times of Cotton Mather* (New York: Columbia University Press, 1985), 198.

45. See Perry Miller, *The New England Mind* (Cambridge, Mass.: Harvard

University Press, 1953), 2:245–246. See also Bartholomew Green's *The Printer's Advertisement* (Boston, 1700–1701), on Brattle's accusations.

46. Anon., *Some Few Remarks,* 9.

47. Thomas Symmes, *A Discourse Concerning Prejudice in Matters of Religion* (Boston, 1722), i.

48. The point could also be illustrated by the bookplates that Thomas Prince had printed for his library: "This *Book* belongs to *The* New-England-*Library,* Begun to be collected by Thomas Prince, upon his entring *Harvard-College,* July 6, 1703; and was given by said *Prince,* to remain therein forever"; reproduced in Carl Cannon, *American Book Collectors and Collecting* (New York: H. W. Wilson, 1941), 2–3. The durability of the book inspires Prince with the thrill of that closing "forever"; it also contributes to the meaning of his effort to write a history of New England.

49. Symmes, *Discourse Concerning Prejudice,* ii.

50. Hall, "Uses of Literacy," 27–28.

51. Mather, *Diary,* 2:242 (September 27, 1713).

52. Anon., "Father Abbey's Will" (Cambridge, Mass., 1713).

53. Cynthia Stiverson and Gregory Stiverson, "The Colonial Retail Book Trade: Availability and Affordability of Reading Material in Mid-Eighteenth-Century Virginia," in Joyce, *Printing and Society,* 132–173.

54. Richard Beale Davis, *Intellectual Life in the Colonial South,* 3 vols. (Knoxville: University of Tennessee Press, 1983) 2:526–579.

55. Rhys Isaac, *The Transformation of Virginia: 1740–1790* (University of North Carolina Press, 1982). Two portions of the book relevant to this study were published in longer form as articles: "Books and the Social Authority of Learning: The Case of Mid-Eighteenth-Century Virginia," in Joyce, *Printing and Society,* 228–249; and "Dramatizing the Ideology of Revolution: Popular Mobilization in Virginia, 1774 to 1776," *William and Mary Quarterly* 33 (1976): 357–385.

56. Charles Sydnor, *Gentlemen Freeholders* (University of North Carolina Press, 1952), 116.

57. Ibid., 114–115.

58. Ibid., 18–22.

59. Isaac, *Transformation,* 131–132.

60. The republican tradition is discussed masterfully by J. G. A. Pocock in *The Machiavellian Moment* (Princeton: Princeton University Press, 1975). See also his *Politics, Language, and Time* (New York: Atheneum, 1973), and *Virtue, Commerce, and History* (Cambridge: Cambridge University Press, 1985).

61. The quotation comes from the oration known as *Pro Archia Poeta,* and can be found in the Loeb edition at 11:22. The translation is my own.

62. The phrase "light of letters" was often used in eighteenth-century America with this meaning. For an exploration of the context and meaning of such usage, see Chapter 5.

63. Most of the information in this paragraph can be found in Lawrence C. Wroth, *The Colonial Printer,* 2d ed., rev. (New York, 1938). See also Helmut Lehmann-Haupt et al., eds., *The Book in America* (New York, 1951). For the comparative perspective on the spread of printing in the West, see the classic study by Febvre and Martin, *Coming of the Book.*

64. The most famous discouragement of printing is that by Governor William Berkeley of Virginia in 1671: "I thank God, there are no free schools nor *printing,* and I hope we shall not have these hundred years; for *learning* has brought disobedience, and heresy, and sects into the world, and *print* has divulged them, and libels against the best government. God keep us from both." Fourteen years later a printer named Buckner published the laws of the state and was forced to post bond under the promise never to print again. The Pennsylvania Council, with Penn in attendance, ordered in 1683 that the colony's laws not be printed. See Leonard Levy, *Emergence of a Free Press* (New York: Oxford University Press, 1985), esp. 16–22.

65. Quoted in Anna DeArmond, *Andrew Bradford, Colonial Journalist* (Newark: University of Delaware Press, 1949), 21.

II. The Res Publica *of Letters*

1. The taxonomy of law invoked here derives from Roberto Mangabeira Unger's *Law in Modern Society* (New York: Free Press, 1976), 48–66. It is also by means of Unger's book, as well as the classic studies of law by Weber and Durkheim, that we can see the relation between forms of law, broadly defined, and social organization. On changes in colonial law, see Bruce Mann, *Neighbors and Strangers* (Chapel Hill: University of North Carolina Press, 1987). Mann, however, still speaks rather naively of "law and society" as positive and distinct entities, in a way that remains blind to the social theory of law exemplified in the tradition from Weber to Unger.

2. Samuel Whittelsey, *A Public Spirit Described & Recommended* (New London, Conn., 1731), 7. Further references to this text will be made parenthetically. See also similar sermons by Timothy Cutler, *The Firm Union of a People Represented* (New London, 1717), and William Balch, *A Public Spirit* (Boston, 1749).

3. The metaphor of the fountain is closely associated with this model of society, as Louis Althusser shows in a brilliant passage: *Montesquieu, Rousseau, Marx: Politics and History,* trans. Ben Brewster (London: Verso, 1982), 68.

4. Mather, *Diary,* 2:17 (September 14, 1709).

5. Anon., *An Appeal to the Men of New England* (Boston, 1689).

6. Wroth, "The St. Mary's City Press" (see n. 28 in Chapter 1).

7. "An Epistolar Preface to the Maryland Readers," in *The Charter of Maryland,* with *The Proceedings and Debates of the Upper and Lower Houses of Assembly in Maryland* (Philadelphia, 1725), iii–iv.

8. On Parks, see J. A. Leo Lemay, *Men of Letters in Colonial Maryland* (Knoxville: University of Tennessee Press, 1972), and Lawrence C. Wroth, *A History of Printing in Colonial Maryland, 1686–1776* (Baltimore, 1922).

9. Anon., *A Letter from a Freeholder, to a Member of the Lower House of Assembly* (Annapolis, 1727). Further references will be made parenthetically.

10. Habermas, *The Structural Transformation of the Public Sphere,* trans. Thomas Burger (Cambridge, Mass.: MIT Press, 1989), esp. 1–26.

11. Jürgen Habermas, "The Public Sphere: An Encyclopedia Article," trans. Sarah Lennox and Frank Lennox, *New German Critique* 3 (1974): 49–55. "To the

principle of the existing power, the bourgeois public opposed the principle of supervision—that very principle which demands that proceedings be made public. The principle of supervision is thus a means of transforming the nature of power, not merely one basis of legitimation exchanged for another."

12. This principle may be described as a special form of the negativity of democratic politics in general, as explained by Ernesto Laclau and Chantal Mouffe in *Hegemony and Socialist Strategy* (London: Verso, 1985). The argument of my book presupposes the arguments of Laclau and Mouffe.

13. *Maryland Gazette,* April 29, 1729.

14. *Maryland Gazette,* May 6, 1729.

15. *New England Courant,* March 12, 1722.

16. *Boston News-Letter,* August 23, 1714.

17. [Paul Dudley], *Objections to the Bank of Credit* (Boston, 1714), 3.

18. Anon., *A Letter, from One in Boston, to his Friend in the Country* (Boston, 1714), 6.

19. Anon., *The Postscript* (Boston, 1720).

20. Anon., *Reflections upon Reflections: Or, More News from Robinson Cruso's Island, in a Dialogue Between a Country Representative and a Boston Gentleman* (Boston, 1720).

21. Ibid., 5.

22. Anon., *A Letter, from One in Boston,* 1.

23. Anon., *Some Proposals to Benefit the Province* (Boston, 1720).

24. [John Colman], *The Distressed State of the Town of Boston, &c. Considered in a Letter from a Gentleman in the Town, to his Friend in the Countrey* (Boston, 1720), 9.

25. Anon., *A Letter from One in the Country to his Friend in Boston* (Boston, 1720), 22.

26. *Boston News-Letter,* August 18, 1720.

27. *A Letter From a Gentleman* (Boston, 1720), 13.

28. *Reflections on the Present State of the Province of Massachuset-Bay in General* (Boston, 1720), 3–4.

29. Quoted in Andrew MacFarland Davis, ed., *Colonial Currency Reprints, 1682–1751,* 4 vols. (Boston: The Prince Society, 1910–1911), 2:122. Davis handily reprints all of the pamphlets from the Boston crisis.

30. Gary Nash, *The Urban Crucible* (Cambridge, Mass.: Harvard University Press, 1979), 86.

31. The main treatment of the case is Stanley Katz's introduction to James Alexander, *A Brief Narrative of the Case and Trial of John Peter Zenger* (Cambridge, Mass.: Harvard University Press, 1963). See also Livingston Rutherfurd, *John Peter Zenger: His Press, His Trial and a Bibliography of Zenger Imprints* (1904; repr. Gloucester, Mass.: Peter Smith, 1963); Paul Finkelman, "The Zenger Case: Prototype of a Political Trial," in Michal R. Belknap, *American Political Trials* (Westport, Conn.: Greenwood Press, 1981), 21–42; Leonard W. Levy, *Emergence of a Free Press* (New York: Oxford University Press, 1985); and Stephen Botein's Introduction to *Mr. Zenger's Malice and Falshood: Six Issues of the New-York Weekly Journal, 1733–34* (Worcester, Mass.: American Antiquarian Society, 1985).

32. On the background generally, see Nash, *Urban Crucible,* and Patricia U. Bonomi, *A Factious People: Politics and Society in Colonial New York* (New York: Columbia University Press, 1971).

33. *New-York Weekly Journal,* December 17, 1733.

34. Quoted in Bonomi, *Factious People,* 129.

35. *New-York Weekly Journal,* November 12, 1733.

36. Quoted in Botein, *Mr. Zenger's Malice,* 7.

37. *Barbados Gazette,* July 1737, reprinted in Katz, ed., *Brief Narrative,* 154.

38. *New-York Weekly Journal,* November 12, 1733.

39. Ibid.

40. *New-York Weekly Journal,* February 18, 1734.

41. *New York Gazette,* February 4, 1734.

42. This is recorded in James Alexander's preparatory brief, which can be found in Katz, ed., *Brief Narrative,* 139.

43. Ibid., *Brief Narrative,* 77.

44. Ibid., 78.

45. Ibid., 75.

46. *New York Journal,* March 15, 1770.

47. Timothy Breen, "War, Taxes, and Political Brokers: The Ordeal of Massachusetts Bay, 1675–1690," in *Puritans and Adventurers* (New York: Oxford University Press, 1980), 81–105.

48. Patricia U. Bonomi, *Under the Cope of Heaven: Religion, Society, and Politics in Colonial America* (New York: Oxford University Press, 1986), 153, 158.

49. Quoted in ibid., 159.

50. The most egregious case of this moralistic libertarian projection is Levy, *Emergence of a Free Press.*

51. The relation between this constitutional shift in England and the related shift in the colonies is discussed by Jack Greene in *Peripheries and Center: Constitutional Development in the Extended Polities of the British Empire and the United States, 1607–1788* (Athens: University of Georgia Press, 1986), esp. 55–58.

52. On this subject, see William E. Nelson, *Americanization of the Common Law* (Cambridge, Mass.: Harvard University Press, 1975), and Jack Greene, "From the Perspective of Law: Context and Legitimacy in the Origins of the American Revolution," *South Atlantic Quarterly* 85 (1986): 56–77.

53. Quoted in J. R. Pole, *Political Representation in England and the Origins of the American Revolution* (London: Macmillan, 1966), 120.

54. Nash, *Urban Crucible,* 140.

55. *A Collection of the Proceedings of the Great & General Court or Assembly of His Majesty's Province of the Massachusetts-Bay* (Boston, 1729).

56. Pole, *Political Representation,* 61, 70.

57. The *Boston Gazette* of January 4, 1720, for example, asserts that the paper's purpose is "to endeavour to advance, but not prejudice Trade." Shortly thereafter the Philadelphia *American Mercury* declared that "The Design of this Paper" was "to Promote Trade"; quoted in Anna DeArmond, *Andrew Bradford, Colonial Journalist* (Newark: University of Delaware Press, 1949), 41.

58. *Some Considerations upon the Several Sorts of Banks* (Boston, 1716), 7.

59. Benedict Anderson, *Imagined Communities* (London: Verso, 1983).

60. Pocock, *Machiavellian Moment,* passim. For an account of the differences

between Pocock's approach and the model of historiography it has been replacing, see Joyce Appleby, "Republicanism and Ideology," *American Quarterly* 37 (1985): 461–473. To say that the language of republicanism was to be found on such a fundamental ideological level is not to deny that there were variations and conflicts within republicanism, nor to deny that other conceptual vocabularies were lingering or emerging in the cultures of the American colonies. No reader of Pocock's work can fail to notice the ceaseless transformations of even the most central terms he studies. It is to say what is now relatively uncontroversial among historians: that for the colonists, the intelligibility of the political world and the possibility of action in it were constituted by the categories of a broad republican tradition.

61. Katz, ed., *Brief Narrative,* 101–105, 155.

62. Timothy Breen, *Character of the Good Ruler: A Study of Puritan Political Ideas in New England, 1630–1730* (New Haven: Yale University Press, 1970); Bailyn, *Ideological Origins.* Both historians have also registered, at least indirectly, the close relation between republicanism and print discourse. Breen, for example, writes that the Country party's "most important contribution to the political life of New England may well have been the way it used the printing press to educate the public" (247). See also Caroline Robbins, *The Eighteenth-Century Commonwealthman* (Cambridge, Mass.: Harvard University Press, 1959).

63. Thus, in 1702 Governor Dudley of Massachusetts could complain of the "Commonwealthmen" in the Assembly who "so absolutely Depend for their Station upon the People, that they dare not offend them"; Breen, *Character of the Good Ruler,* 321.

64. This point is amplified by Bernard Bailyn in *The Origins of American Politics* (1967; repr. New York: Vintage, 1970).

65. Gary Huxford, "The English Libertarian Tradition in the Colonial Newspaper," *Journalism Quarterly* 45 (1968): 677–686.

66. *Spectator* #1, quoted from Angus Ross, ed., *Selections from the Tatler and the Spectator* (Harmondsworth: Penguin, 1982), 197. The remarks made here about the Spectator repeat a theme of an unpublished paper by Jerome Christensen on Byron.

67. Bailyn, *Ideological Origins,* 1–2.

68. Benjamin Franklin, quoted in Philip Davidson, *Propaganda and the American Revolution, 1763–1783* (Chapel Hill: University of North Carolina Press, 1941; repr. Norton, 1973), 15.

69. Febvre and Martin, *Coming of the Book,* 211.

70. Arthur M. Schlesinger, *Prelude to Independence: The Newspaper War on Britain, 1764–1776* (New York: Knopf, 1953), 58. See also Michael Kraus, *Intercolonial Aspects of American Culture on the Eve of the Revolution* (New York: Columbia University Press, 1928), esp. 91–105.

71. David Ramsay, *History of the American Revolution* (Philadelphia, 1789), 1:61–62. Ramsay was not off the mark when he wrote, later in the same history, that in "establishing American independence, the pen and the press had a merit equal to that of the sword" (2:319).

72. On the Stamp Act and the press, see Schlesinger, *Prelude;* Edmund Morgan and Helen Morgan, *The Stamp Act Crisis: Prologue to Revolution* (1953; rev. New York: Collier, 1963), and Edmund Morgan, ed., *Prologue to Revolution:*

Sources and Documents on the Stamp Act Crisis, 1764–1766 (Chapel Hill: University of North Carolina Press, 1959).

73. Quoted in Arthur M. Schlesinger, "The Colonial Newspapers and the Stamp Act," *New England Quarterly* 8 (1935): 68n.

74. Schlesinger, *Prelude*, 73.

75. "A DREAM upon a Subject which engages Men's Minds very much, when they are awake, as well as when they are asleep," in *A New Collection of VERSES Applied to the First of November, A.D.* 1765 (New Haven, 1765), 19–24.

76. Richard Merritt, *Symbols of American Community, 1735–1775* (New Haven: Yale University Press, 1966). Despite the naive positivism of Merritt's book, it has the virtue of chronicling the rapid rise of this term in the mid-1760s.

77. John Adams, "Dissertation," in *Papers*, 1:121.

78. Habermas, *Structural Transformation*, esp. 31–51, 141–159.

III. Franklin: The Representational Politics of the Man of Letters

1. François Furet, *Interpreting the French Revolution* (Cambridge: Cambridge University Press, 1981), 48, 51; my emphasis.

2. Benjamin Franklin, "Epitaph," in Leonard W. Labaree et al., eds., *The Papers of Benjamin Franklin* (New Haven: Yale University Press, 1959–), 1:111. Further references to Franklin's works will refer to this edition, except where otherwise noted, and will be made parenthetically.

3. On the textual history of the epitaph, see Lyman H. Butterfield, "B. Franklin's Epitaph," *New Colophon* 3 (1950): 9–30.

4. Dating of the epitaph rests only on Franklin's later recollection. We do not know exactly when it first appeared, but the description of himself as "B. Franklin, Printer" suggests that he must already have been contemplating the establishment of his own printing house, even if he had not yet brought it about. On the events of Franklin's career, the best single source is still Carl Van Doren, *Benjamin Franklin* (New York: Viking, 1938).

5. *Autobiography,* in the Franklin volume of the Library of America, ed. J. A. Leo Lemay (New York, 1987), 1307. Further references to the *Autobiography* will be to this edition and will be made parenthetically.

6. *Cato's Letters* No. 15 appeared in the *London Journal* on February 4, 1720, and was largely reprinted as Silence Dogood No. 8 in the *New-England Courant* for July 9, 1722. Selections from *Cato's Letters,* including the reprinted essay, have been published as *The English Libertarian Heritage,* ed. David Jacobson (Indianapolis: Bobbs-Merrill, 1965).

7. The novelty of Franklin's career is acknowledged by the period's other great man of letters, David Hume, who wrote to Franklin: "America has sent us many good things, gold, silver, sugar, tobacco, indigo, etc.; but you are the first philosopher, and indeed the first great man of letters, for whom we are beholden to her"; quoted in Van Doren, *Benjamin Franklin,* 290. On this subject generally, see Lewis Simpson, "The Printer as Man of Letters: Franklin and the Symbolism of the Third Realm," in J. A. Leo Lemay, ed., *The Oldest Revolutionary: Essays on Benjamin Franklin* (Philadelphia: University of Pennsylvania Press, 1976), 3–20.

8. "Musing near a Cool Spring," in *Papers,* 7:73.

9. My general understanding of the career of the man of letters relies on

Jerome Christensen, *Practicing Enlightenment: Hume's Career as Man of Letters* (Madison: University of Wisconsin Press, 1986), though Franklin's case requires that more centrality be accorded to republicanism. See especially Christensen's discussions of the career and generality in chaps. 1 and 5.

10. Franklin's remarks on writing and print typically employ a contrast with spoken oratory in order to emphasize the republican advantages of print. In the 1749 *Proposals Relating to the Education of Youth in Pennsylvania,* for example, he writes: "History will show the wonderful Effects of ORATORY, in governing, turning, and leading great Bodies of Mankind, Armies, Cities, Nations . . . Modern Political Oratory being chiefly performed by the Pen and Press, its Advantages over the Antient in some Respects are to be shown; as that its Effects are more extensive, more lasting, &c." (3:412–413). Similarly, in 1782 Franklin would write to Richard Price, urging him to follow Franklin's own practice of press agitation: "The ancient Roman and Greek orators could only speak to the number of citizens capable of being assembled within the reach of their voice. Their *writings* had little effect, because the bulk of the people could not read. Now by the press we can speak to nations; and good books and well written pamphlets have great and general influence. The facility, with which the same truths may be repeatedly enforced by placing them daily in different lights in *newspapers,* which are everywhere read, gives a great chance of establishing them"; Franklin to Richard Price, June 13, 1782; in Albert H. Smyth, ed., *The Writings of Benjamin Franklin,* 10 vols. (New York: Macmillan, 1906), 8:457. This contrast between the general politics of print and the localized person of the orator often appears with great animus, as in the 1735 *Poor Richard's Almanac:* "Here comes the Orator! with his Flood of Words, and his Drop of Reason" (2:9). See also 3:448–449, 4:104, 6:276. On Franklin's extraordinary covert press campaigns, see Verner Crane, *Benjamin Franklin's Letters to the Press, 1758–1775* (Chapel Hill: University of North Carolina Press, 1950).

11. I am indebted here to Jonathan Goldberg's *Writing Matter,* a provocative study of the investitures of the hand and writing in an earlier period. In particular, my earlier use of the phrase "being-in-print" responds to his discussion of Heidegger's "being-in-the-hand," and its relation to Western understandings of technology. That discussion shows by contrast the extent to which Franklin's fantasy of writing without (or inviolation of) the hand endangers the constitutively human in the Western tradition.

12. The image of castration implied in Franklin's struggle not to father offspring will reappear below in the Dogood papers; it also bears a strong resemblance to Hume's depiction of himself as incapacitated or castrated, which, as Jerome Christensen has argued, is for Hume a powerfully enabling strategy in shaping a career in letters (Christensen, *Practicing Enlightenment,* chaps. 1 and 2).

13. The relation of reason to the self is a common theme in Franklin criticism. See, for example, Robert F. Sayre, *The Examined Self* (Princeton: Princeton University Press, 1964). The best study of the subject, however, is Mitchell Robert Breitweiser's *Cotton Mather and Benjamin Franklin* (Cambridge: Cambridge University Press, 1984). I entirely endorse Breitweiser's emphasis on what he calls the "abstract blankness" of Franklin's character, which results in "a corollary reduction of the world to calculability" (258). Or rather, the relation between blankness and rationality must work both ways; as Breitweiser elsewhere says, Franklin's con-

struction of reason is such that "behind the masks is the universal capacity to take on masks" (233). The main point of difference between this book and Breitweiser's lies not in any detail of interpretation, but in the general source of interest. Where Breitweiser regards the self as a subject in its own right, traceable from Mather directly to Franklin, I am trying to direct attention to the social practices and political structures of which self and reason are only related manifestations.

14. *The American Weekly Mercury,* April 25, 1734. Bradford, the printer, is drawing heavily on Trenchard and Gordon, and the ideas discussed here would have been a familiar way of relating republicanism and print for any reader of *Cato's Letters.*

15. See, for example, "Self-Denial Not the Essence of Virtue" (1735), in which Franklin argues that "Self-denial is neither good nor bad, but as 'tis apply'd"—an argument that exhibits Franklin's habit of subdividing the self out of existence. The self that not only denies itself but further applies that denial is scarcely recognizable *as* a self.

16. *Busy-Body* No. 3, from the *American Weekly Mercury,* February 18, 1729, in *Writings,* 97.

17. "Plan of Conduct," in Franklin, *Papers* 1:99–100.

18. It is because Franklin locates himself in generality that he is so difficult to locate. Hence Carl Becker's well-known remark in the *Dictionary of American Biography* that Franklin was never fully immersed in anything he did. (See the discussion of Becker's remark in Breitweiser, *Mather and Franklin,* 233, 258.) The same relation to self helps to account for Franklin's addiction to pseudonyms and fictional personae—exceptional even in his time. Crane counts forty-two different pseudonyms just in the period covered by his study. No one has counted the fictional personae, such as Alice Addertongue or the King of Prussia, but they abound. That perfection is associated with print for Franklin takes a less serious form in the 1738 *Poor Richard's Almanac,* where Bridget Saunders exclaims, "What a peasecods! cannot I have a little Fault or two, but all the Country must see it in print!" (2:191).

19. *A Fragment of the Chronicles of Nathan Ben Saddi* (Constantinople [Philadelphia], 5707 [1758]). I have been unable to determine whom "Jacobs" designates in the Philadelphia scene; the available information on the pamphlet and its key seems to be limited to the notes in the Evans *Bibliography.* One would like to know, if for no other reason than the oddly homoerotic language of the satire against Franklin.

20. *An Answer to the Plot* (Philadelphia, 1764). The poem was a reply to a satire called *The* PLOT *by way of a* BURLESK, *To turn F——n out of the Assembly* (Philadelphia, 1764), and in at least some copies was printed on the verso of the latter. Both are election polemics in a year in which the election turned decisively on the interpretation of a printed text. Seeking to turn the German population against Franklin, his opponents uncovered an old publication in which he had referred to Germans as *"Palatine Boors."* They then publicized the remark among the German population. Franklin's allies leapt to his defense, in part by writing *The Plot,* which, addressing those who were using the remark to attack Franklin, says: "Your *Wisdoms* have mistook a Letter. / *Boar* may be Hogs but *Boor* is Peasant . . . *Go* home ye *Dunces* learn to spell."

21. The latter was a common theme in the election of 1764, when Franklin

led the move to end proprietary government in Pennsylvania by appealing for a royal charter. At least one pamphlet accused him of wanting to be royal governor himself: *To the Freeholders and Electors of . . . Philadelphia* (Philadelphia, 1764). At the same time another pamphlet accused him of leveling, of trying to destroy "Every *necessary Subordination*"; *What Is Sauce for a Goose Is Also Sauce for a Gander* (Philadelphia, 1764). The theme of Franklin's lower-class origins appears both in the latter and in William Smith's *An Answer to Franklin's Remarks on a Late Protest* (Philadelphia, 1764). For background on the election, its polemics, and the extremes of Franklin's reputation, see J. Philip Gleason, "A Scurrilous Colonial Election and Franklin's Reputation," *William and Mary Quarterly* 18 (1961): 68–84.

22. The Hutchinson correspondence can be found in the Franklin *Papers*, 20:539–80. A good account of the whole affair is Bernard Bailyn's *The Ordeal of Thomas Hutchinson* (Cambridge, Mass.: Harvard University Press, 1974), esp. chap. 7.

23. Wedderburn's role is described in Ronald Clark, *Benjamin Franklin* (New York: Random House, 1983).

24. The joke is from Plautus, *Aulularia:* "Tun, trium litterarum homo me vituperas? fur" ["You running me down, you? You five letter man, you! You T-H-I-E-F!"]; Loeb ed., trans. Paul Nixon (London: Heinemann, 1928), 268.

25. Compare another remark of Wedderburn: "This property [correspondence] is as sacred and precious to Gentlemen of integrity, as their family plate or jewels are" (21:51). The examples of plate and jewels are telling because of their contiguity with the body. Wedderburn has to insist on a metonymy between letters and the body, a metonymy contained by the juridical force of property relations. Franklin, while denying the force of the metonymy, exploited it, for it is the *same* metonymic bond of letters to the body that had been parodically foregrounded in the 1728 epitaph, or the 1740 preface to Poor Richard.

26. At the same time, a Chancery suit brought against Franklin by Whately over the affair charges with a sneer that in disseminating the letters Franklin was merely "carrying on the Trade of a Printer" (21:432). This theme of the silent manipulator of letters became something of a tradition among Franklin's enemies. Thomas Hutchinson reports with horror seeing Franklin "staring with his spectacles" during an embarrassing speech in Parliament on behalf of the Ministry. "The relation of this speech," Hutchinson wails, "is on its way to America" (letter to Israel Williams, Sept. 29, 1774, quoted in Bailyn, *Ordeal*, 322).

27. A. Francis Steuart, ed., *The Last Journals of Horace Walpole* (London: Bodley Head, 1908), 1:333.

28. Edward Bancroft, quoted in William Temple Franklin, ed., *Memoirs of the Life and Writings of Benjamin Franklin* (London, 1818), 1:358n.

29. Franklin to Jan Ingenhousz, March 18, 1774 (21:148), and to Thomas Cushing, February 15, 1774 (21:93).

30. Anon., recorded in Horace Walpole, *Last Journals*, 2:77.

IV. Textuality and Legitimacy in the Printed Constitution

1. Since 1987, when this chapter was first presented as a talk, countless volumes have been published on the Constitution. I make no systematic attempt to review this literature. The best source on American constitutionalism remains

Gordon Wood's *The Creation of the American Republic* (Chapel Hill: University of North Carolina Press, 1969; repr. New York: Norton, 1972). The best treatment of the history of popular sovereignty is Edmund S. Morgan, *Inventing the People: The Rise of Popular Sovereignty in England and America* (New York: Norton, 1988). For a comparative history of the state constitutions, see Willi Paul Adams, *The First American Constitutions* (Chapel Hill: University of North Carolina Press, 1980). Among recent publications not cited, the most noteworthy is Terence Ball and J. G. A. Pocock, eds., *Conceptual Change and the Constitution* (Lawrence: University Press of Kansas, 1988).

2. James Otis, *Rights of the British Colonies Asserted and Proved* (Boston, 1764).

3. The tension between revolutionary rhetoric and forms of continuity such as the doctrine of state succession is explored in Peter Onuf's *The Origins of the Federal Republic* (Philadelphia: University of Pennsylvania Press, 1983). Onuf is particularly useful on the problem of the sovereignty of the states as political agents, a subject that I have had to slight in this book.

4. The distinction between customary and bureaucratic law follows Unger, *Law and Modern Society*. One of the main differences between bureaucratic and customary law, in Unger's view (and here he follows Weber), is the separation of state and society. The common-law tradition did not observe that separation, as has been amply shown by Nelson, *Americanization of the Common Law*. The emergence of a paradigm of sovereignty in constitutionalism, along with the consequent replacement of the customary legitimacy of common law, is therefore part of the emergence of the modern state.

5. Quoted in Wood, *Creation*, 289.

6. Thomas Dawes, *Oration Delivered March 5th 1781* (Boston, 1781), 20–21.

7. H. L. A. Hart, *The Concept of Law* (Oxford: Oxford University Press, 1961), 75.

8. Quoted in Wood, *Creation*, 379.

9. Philip Foner, ed., *The Complete Writings of Thomas Paine* (New York, 1945), 1:28.

10. The term "interpellation" comes from Louis Althusser's "Ideology and Ideological State Apparatuses" in *Lenin and Philosophy* (New York: Monthly Review Press, 1971), 127–186. It designates the hailing of the individual that always renders the individual as a subject within an ideology. See also note 22 below.

11. Jean-Jacques Rousseau, *The First and Second Discourses and Essay on the Origin of Languages,* trans. Victor Gourevitch (New York: Harper & Row), 294–295.

12. Jacques Derrida, *Of Grammatology,* trans. Gayatri Spivak (Baltimore: Johns Hopkins University Press, 1976), 296.

13. Quoted in Wood, *Creation*, 369.

14. Jacques Derrida, *Otobiographies* (Paris: Galilee, 1984), 17 (my translation).

15. Nelson, *Americanization of the Common Law*, 91.

16. Anon., *Four Letters on Interesting Subjects* (Philadelphia, 1776), repr. in Charles S. Hyneman and Donald S. Lutz, eds., *American Political Writing during the Founding Era* (Indianapolis: Liberty Press, 1983), 1:381–382.

17. *Rights of Man* in Foner, *Complete Writings of Thomas Paine*, 1:378.

18. For an excellent discussion of the interest-disinterest opposition in the constitutional period, see Gordon Wood, "Interests and Disinterestedness in the Making of the Constitution," in Richard Beeman et al., eds., *Beyond Confederation: Origins of the Constitution and American National Identity* (Chapel Hill: University of North Carolina Press, 1987), 69–109.

19. Quoted in Wood, *Creation*, 302–303.

20. Quoted in ibid., 182.

21. Jefferson to Madison, September 6, 1789; in *The Papers of Thomas Jefferson*, Julian Boyd et al., eds. (Princeton: Princeton University Press, 1950–), 15:392–397; Madison to Jefferson, February 4, 1790; in *The Papers of James Madison*, William Hutchinson et al., eds. (Chicago: University of Chicago Press, 1962–77 [vols. 1–10]; Charlottesville: University of Virginia Press, 1977–), 13:18–21; John Adams, quoted in Wood, *Creation*, 182.

22. My wording is meant to echo Althusser's explanation of interpellation (see note 10). Ideology, he writes, "transforms the individuals into subjects (it transforms them all) by that very precise operation which I have called interpellation or hailing, and which can be imagined along the lines of the most commonplace everyday police (or other) hailing: 'Hey, you there!' Assuming that the theoretical scene I have imagined takes place in the street, the hailed individual will turn round. By this mere one-hundred-and-eighty-degree physical conversion, he becomes a *subject*. Why? Because he has recognized that the hail was 'really' addressed to him, and that 'it was *really him* who was hailed' (and not someone else)" ["Ideology," 174].

23. Benedict Anderson, *Imagined Communities* (London: Verso, 1983).

24. The ratification parades that were held in some cities—notably in Boston—provide an interesting case in which these two modes for the realization of the public are sutured together. In the parades, printing presses were dragged through the streets on wagons, being operated en route by pressmen who distributed the products to the crowd. The civic populace and the abstract public of print are here called to bear witness to each other in a way that may be without parallel.

25. Jonathan Elliot, ed., *The Debates of the Several State Conventions on the Adoption of the Federal Constitution*, 2d ed. (Philadelphia, 1861), 2:101–102.

26. On the rhetorical strategies of *The Federalist*, see Albert Furtwangler, *The Authority of Publius* (Ithaca: Cornell University Press, 1984); and Garry Wills, *Explaining America* (Baltimore: Penguin, 1981).

27. In the *New-York Journal*, for example, Publius' strategy was described as "a new mode of abridging the liberty of the press" (January 1, 1788).

28. *Marbury v. Madison*, in John Marshall, *Major Opinions and Other Writings*, ed. John P. Roche (New York: Bobbs-Merrill, 1967), 87–88.

29. *The Narrative of Arthur Gordon Pym*, in *Poetry and Tales* (New York: Library of America, 1984). All citations will be to this edition.

V. Nationalism and the Problem of Republican Literature

1. *Maryland Journal*, May 5, 1788.

2. The classic study of this theme is Benjamin T. Spencer, *The Quest for Nationality* (Syracuse: Syracuse University Press, 1957). See also H. H. Clark,

"Nationalism in American Literature," *University of Toronto Quarterly* 2 (1933): 491–515; and Russel Blaine Nye, *The Cultural Life of the New Nation* (New York: Harper and Row, 1960), esp. 235–267. In Robert Spiller et al., eds., *The Literary History of the United States* (New York: Macmillan, 1963), "the formation of our national literature" (161) is the master narrative organizing all details. See especially 162–191. For a more recent exemplar of this venerable tradition, see Emory Elliott, *Revolutionary Writers: Literature and Authority in the New Republic, 1725–1810* (New York: Oxford University Press, 1982).

3. *American Apollo,* December 21, 1792.

4. See John Bidwell, "The Publication of Joel Barlow's *Columbiad,*" *Proceedings of the American Antiquarian Society* 93 (1983): 337–380.

5. Noah Webster, *A Dictionary of the English Language* (New Haven, 1829).

6. *Universal Asylum and Columbian Magazine* 1 (March 1790): 3.

7. *Columbian Phenix and Boston Review* 1 (January 1800): 6.

8. Phillips Payson, *A Sermon* (Boston, 1778; repr. in Charles Hyneman and Donald Lutz, eds., *American Political Writing during the Founding Era* [Indianapolis: Liberty Press, 1983], 1:523–538), 1:526–528.

9. Richard Beresford, *A Plea for Literature, More Especially the Literature of Free States* (Charleston, 1793), 20.

10. The first "Plain-Dealer" essay from William Parks's *Maryland Gazette,* for instance, had used the phrase in 1729 to explain the practice of reprinting essays from the *Spectator* and the *Tatler.* Doing so, the Plain Dealer says, will "diffuse a spirit of good Sense, among your Readers." (From a nonextant issue of the *Maryland Gazette,* reprinted in the *Pennsylvania Gazette,* April 19, 1730.)

11. Zabdiel Adams, *An Election Sermon* (Boston, 1782), 39–40.

12. Samuel Harrison Smith, *Remarks on Education: Illustrating the Close Connection Between Virtue and Wisdom* (Philadelphia, 1798; repr. in Frederick Rudolph, ed., *Essays on Education in the Early Republic* [Cambridge, Mass.: Harvard University Press, 1965], 167–224), 223.

13. Noah Webster, *On the Education of Youth in America* (Boston, 1790; repr. in Rudolph, *Essays on Education,* 43–77), 66.

14. *A Specimen of Isaiah Thomas's Printing Types* (Worcester, Mass., 1785).

15. Webster, *Education,* 66.

16. Beresford, *Plea,* 118.

17. *Gazette of the United States,* April 8, 1795.

18. For a typical example, see the inaugural issue of the Hanover, New Hampshire, *Eagle* (July 22, 1793).

19. "On the Means of Preserving Public Liberty," *New-York Magazine,* January 1790.

20. David Paul Nord, "A Republican Literature: A Study of Magazine Reading and Readers in Late Eighteenth-Century New York," *American Quarterly* 40 (1988): 18–41.

21. Samuel Knox, *An Essay on the Best System of Liberal Education, Adapted to the Genius of the Government of the United States* (Philadelphia, 1799; repr. in Rudolph, *Essays on Education,* 273–356), 309.

22. Anon., "Worcester Speculator," *The Worcester Magazine,* repr. in Hyneman and Lutz, *American Political Writing,* 1:699–701, 701.

23. Beresford, *Plea,* 23. To be without power, which is to say without liberty, is to be in a state of absolute peril, for one is then not only dominated by the tyrant but deprived from within of personality. This can best be seen in Simeon Doggett's description of the savage, in his *A Discourse on Education* (New Bedford, Mass., 1797; repr. in Rudolph, *Essays in Education,* 149–165): "His intellectual powers lying unexercised and undirected, his ideas, his language, and his knowledge are confined within the small compass of his chase. His passions undisciplined are ungovernable, impetuous and awful . . . And not only is the heart, which embraces the whole family of man, constrained to weep over millions of the human race who through the deficiency of education are low sunk in barbarity, but even in civilized life where the means of education and the light of religion are enjoyed, even among the highly privileged Americans, the tear of humanity is frequently started to see many of our brethren, some of whom the most excellent of nature's works, through the neglect of education and by bad example in a situation almost as pitiable as that of the roving Tartar.

How infinitely different is the character of him whom a well-conducted education and due attention and the grace of God have brought upon the stage of action! . . . Truth and knowledge illumine and expand his mind. His understanding is broad as the heavens" (154). Everything is at stake for Doggett when he speaks of "the stage of action." Because his language is organized around the need for republican virtue, the stage of action coincides exactly with the state of civilization.

24. Wilkes Wood, *An Oration, Pronounced Before the Philological Society, In Middleborough* (New Bedford, Mass., 1795), 8.

25. Richard Kielbowicz, "The Press, Post Office, and Flow of News in the Early Republic," *Journal of the Early Republic* 3 (Fall 1983): 255–280.

26. *Annals of Congress,* 2d Cong. 1st sess., 289.

27. Benjamin Rush, *A Plan for the Establishment of Public Schools and the Diffusion of Knowledge in Pennsylvania; to Which Are Added, Thoughts upon the Mode of Education, Proper in a Republic* (Philadelphia, 1786), 11.

28. Ibid., 11.

29. Ibid., 27.

30. "William Manning's *The Key of Libberty,*" ed. Samuel Eliot Morison, *William and Mary Quarterly* 13 (1956): 202–254. Further references to this text will be made parenthetically.

31. In his study of English painting John Barrell has written eloquently of the tension between civic humanism and the new privatization of the aesthetic: *The Political Theory of Painting from Reynolds to Hazlitt* (New Haven: Yale University Press, 1986). The modern economy of private appropriation, where judgments of taste necessarily function as kinds of capital, is described in *Distinction* by Pierre Bourdieu, who particularly discusses the ideological nature of Kantian aesthetics, which were emerging in the period under discussion (see 485–500).

32. The French tradition of this literature of *civilité* and *politesse* has been studied in almost unparalleled detail by Roger Chartier. See "From Texts to Manners; A Concept and Its Books: *Civilité* between Aristocratic Distinction and Popular Appropriation," in *The Cultural Uses of Print in Early Modern France,* trans. Lydia G. Cochrane (Princeton: Princeton University Press, 1987), 71–109.

33. Abel Boyer, *The English Theophrastus* (London, 1702); quoted in Lawrence Klein, "The Third Earl of Shaftesbury and the Progress of Politeness," *Eighteenth-Century Studies* 18 (1984): 186–214, at 190. See also Klein's "Berkeley, Shaftesbury, and the Meaning of Politeness," *Studies in Eighteenth-Century Culture* 16 (1986): 57–68.

34. Lemay, *Men of Letters in Colonial Maryland*, 185.

35. Hamilton, *Itinerarium*, 193.

36. On Byles, see Arthur W. H. Eaton, *The Famous Mather Byles* (Boston: Butterfield, 1914).

37. *Spirit of Laws*, book 4, chapter 2, from *The Works of Monsieur de Montesquieu*, trans. Thomas Nugent (London, 1777).

38. Althusser, *Montesquieu, Rousseau, Marx*, 73.

39. Ibid., 72.

40. Some colonists could frankly declare the relation between the norm of politeness and the differentiation of rank. Hamilton of Maryland, for instance, complains in his journal of some "aggrandized upstarts," their names "not worthy to be recorded in manuscript or printed journals . . . who never had the opportunity to see, or if they had, the capacity to observe the different ranks of men in polite nations or to know what it is that really constitutes that difference of degrees."

41. Klein, "Third Earl," 191.

42. Ibid., 194, 199.

43. Benjamin Franklin, *Remarks Concerning the Savages of North-America* (New York: Library of America, 1987), 969–974.

44. See Timothy Breen, *Tobacco Culture* (Princeton: Princeton University Press, 1985).

45. *Pennsylvania Gazette*, April 13, 1732.

46. *American Apollo*, December 21, 1792.

47. Thomas Jefferson to Robert Skipwith, August 3, 1771, in *Jefferson*, (New York: Library of America, 1984), 740–745.

48. *Gazette of the United States*, November 17, 1790. I infer the commonness of the sentiment in part from the fact that the quoted passage, headed "An Extract," is the entire article (source unlocated).

49. *The United States Magazine* 1 (1779): 22–25, 53–58, 101–106; 23.

50. Samuel Williams, *The Natural and Civil History of Vermont* (Walpole, N.H., 1794), 331.

51. *United States Magazine* 1 (1779): 9. Hereafter this issue will be referred to parenthetically as *USM*.

52. Smith, *Remarks on Education*, 183; Beresford, *Plea for Literature*, 15, 21.

53. Fisher Ames, "American Literature," in *Works*, 428–442; hereafter cited parenthetically. For an astonishing but typical instance of critical misreading, see Robert E. Spiller's headnote to Ames's essay in his anthology *The American Literary Revolution, 1783–1837* (New York: New York University Press, 1967), 73: "Ames, in this essay, is notable as one of the earliest to seek in other than superficial factors the causes for the failure of the new nation at once to produce a literature. The argument that equalitarianism and commercialism, as basic elements in the structure of American life, are in themselves destructive of the human spirit, and

that therefore America cannot hope to develop a life of the mind and the arts, will be heard again many times but perhaps not with the same passionate eloquence and gloomy despair." Spiller's summary of Ames's argument is exactly wrong, in ways that I make clear later in this chapter. He is able to read the essay as he does only by the strength of his assumption that a national "literary" culture is self-evidently desirable, and that Ames is discussing "literature" in this modern sense.

54. Van Wyck Brooks, *The Flowering of New England* (1936; repr. Boston: Houghton Mifflin, 1981), 13.

VI. The Novel: Fantasies of Publicity

1. Charles Brockden Brown, "Walstein's School of History," *Monthly Magazine and American Review* 1 (1799): 335–338, 407–411; 410.

2. Warner Berthoff, "Introduction" to *Arthur Mervyn* (New York: Holt, Rinehart, & Winston, 1962), xviii.

3. Michael Davitt Bell, *The Development of American Romance* (Chicago: Chicago University Press, 1980), 59, 56.

4. "Historical Essay," in *Arthur Mervyn* (Kent, Ohio: Kent State University Press, 1980), 473.

5. Ibid., 219. Further references to the Kent State edition will be made parenthetically.

6. In the diary of Elihu Hubbard Smith (Philadelphia: American Philosophical Society, 1973), or in the early documents reprinted in the Allen biography, it appears that Brown was inordinately eager to debate with his friends on the absolute value of sincerity. And through his mouthpiece, Stevens, Brown tells us that Mervyn embodies that absolute value (229). Bell is fully aware of both the textual and the contextual information (see pp. 44, 46–48, 50, 56–58 in his book), but his desire to read the novel as a "literary" text—exhibiting signs of the author's governing distance from the work–leads him finally to ignore the overwhelming weight of his own evidence.

7. William Dunlap, *Life of Charles Brockden Brown*, 2 vols. (Philadelphia, 1815), 2:41.

8. Ibid., 2:89.

9. *American Daily Advertiser*, February 27, 1810, quoted in David Lee Clark, *Charles Brockden Brown, Pioneer Voice of America* (Durham, N.C.: Duke University Press, 1952), 292.

10. Quoted in ibid., 293.

11. In saying this, again I am supported by "Walstein's School of History": "A man, whose activity is neither aided by political activity nor by the *press,* may yet exercise considerable influence on the condition of his neighbours, by the exercise of intellectual powers . . . His benevolence and justice may not only protect his kindred and his wife, but rescue the victims of prejudice and passion from the yoke of those domestic tyrants, and shield the powerless from the oppression of power, the poor from the injustice of the rich, and the simple from the stratagems of cunning . . . The pursuits of law and medicine, enhance our power over the liberty, property, and health of mankind. They not only qualify us for imparting benefit, by supplying us with property and leisure, but by enabling us

to obviate, by intellectual exertions, many of the evils that infest the world" (409). At the beginning of this passage, Brown cites the press, along with politics, as a self-evident example of opportunity for virtue. Because he is the editor of the magazine in which the essay appears, the analogy between his own career and the others mentioned is all but explicit. The other career models in the passage are those of the novel. Brown's characterization of Mervyn corresponds with that of the man whose benevolence, "by the exercise of intellectual powers," rescues the simple from the snares of the wily tyrant; and both Stevens and Mervyn practice the beneficially intellectual medicine that Brown describes at the end of the passage. In the essay their careers are seen as only approximating the power of the man of the press ("may yet exercise considerable influence"); in the novel, however, they represent that power by implied analogy.

12. These strategies of commendation are so deeply rooted in critical assumptions that even Jane Tompkins, in a book noted for its attacks on conventional definitions of literary value, attempts to redeem the value of Brown's novels by reading in them an authorial "message." "*Arthur Mervyn,*" she writes, "is a novel that must be read structurally—that is, as a series of abstract propositions whose permutations and combinations spell out a message to the reader, a message whose intent is to change the social reality which the narrative purports to represent" (Jane Tompkins, *Sensational Designs* [New York: Oxford University Press, 1985], 40–93; 67). To be sure, she recognizes the political intent of the novels, but the idea of literary expression governs her interpretation of that intent. Her description of Brown's political messages suggests that Brown wanted his readers to distance themselves from the novel, abstract from it his desired message, and then act accordingly. As Tompkins puts it in regard to *Wieland,* "Brown identified the value of *Wieland* with its usefulness, and therefore must have assumed that its *meaning* would be clear to his readers, since the usefulness of his book would naturally depend upon its being understood" (41). She is both right and wrong. Brown certainly predicates the value of his writing on its usefulness, but he imagines a much more direct translation of the reading of his novels into public virtue—one accomplished in the arousal of curiosity and inquiry, not in a moment of collected abstract interpretation. Given Brown's slightly magical notion of the virtue of letters—which, though magical, was underwritten by a long republican tradition—the question of the novel's *meaning* never properly arises.

13. John Davis, *Travels of Four Years and a Half in the United States of America* (New York, 1909), 163–164 and 222–223.

14. Jan Lewis, "The Republican Wife: Virtue and Seduction in the Early Republic," *William and Mary Quarterly* 44 (1987): 689–721; and Linda Kerber, *Women of the Republic* (Chapel Hill: University of North Carolina Press, 1980).

15. This part of the history and theory of nationalist society remains undeveloped. For one challenging version, see Niklas Luhmann, *Love as Passion: The Codification of Intimacy,* trans. Jeremy Gaines and Doris L. Jones (Cambridge, Mass.: Harvard University Press, 1986). Luhmann connects the differentiation of society, including the public sphere, with the emergence of the discourse of love and its special mode of subjectivity. He also sketches a connection between the subjectivity of love and that of novel-reading. In these two important respects,

though not in regard to his general system-theoretical approach, my argument relies on his.

16. On sentiment, see David Marshall, *The Figure of Theater* (New York: Columbia University Press, 1986), esp. 167–192; and *The Surprising Effects of Sympathy* (Chicago: University of Chicago Press, 1988).

17. Hannah Foster, *The Coquette,* ed. Cathy Davidson (New York: Oxford University Press, 1986), 92.

18. Ibid., 133.

19. Cathy Davidson, *The Revolution and the Word: The Rise of the Novel in America* (New York: Oxford University Press, 1986), 66.

INDEX

abstraction: of persons, 41, 62, 63, 77; of the public, 48, 62; of the people, 103–104, 112

Adams, John, 19, 23, 31, 32, 34, 111; "Dissertation," 1–6, 71, 123

Adams, Samuel, 67, 68

Adams, Zabdiel, 123

Addison, Joseph, 65, 135. See also *Spectator, The*

aesthetics, 117, 119–122, 132, 151, 153

Alarm, The, 98–99, 101, 108, 109

Alexander, James, 51–53

Alger, Horatio, 123

Alien and Sedition Acts, 49

almanacs, 23, 24

Althusser, Louis, 134

Amelia; or the Faithless Briton, 174

America, as symbol, 71

American Weekly Mercury, 76

Ames, Fisher, 142–149

Anderson, Benedict, 63, 112

Andros, Gov. Edmund, 36, 44

Annapolis, 4, 38

antifictional rhetoric, 175

aristocracy, 134

Bailyn, Bernard, 64, 67–68

Baltimore, 118, 121

Barbados, 64

Barlow, Joel, 121

Bell, Michael, 153–154

belles lettres, 133, 136

Benjamin, Walter, 9

Bentham, Jeremy, 92

Beresford, Richard, 126, 141

Berthoff, Warner, 152–154, 160

Bible, 3, 19, 116, 117, 124

Bonomi, Patricia, 57

Bordley, Thomas, 37

Boston, 22, 23, 31, 60, 63, 66, 82, 84, 85, 104, 122, 133; currency crisis, 43–49, 58, 64, 75

Boston Evening Post, 110

Boston Gazette, 1, 71, 75

Boston News-Letter, 46

Brackenridge, Hugh Henry, 138–141, 148, 175

Bradford, Andrew, 31, 76

Bradford, William, 51, 53, 76

Bradstreet, Anne, 15

Brattle, Thomas, 22

Breen, Timothy, 64

Breitweiser, Mitchell R., 189n13

broadsides, 24, 26, 59, 61, 75

Brooks, Van Wyck, 148

Brown, Charles Brockden, 126, 172; *Arthur Mervyn,* 152–173; "Walstein's School of History," 152; *Wieland,* 169; biography, 158; obituary, 159

Brown, William Hill, 175

Bunyan, John, 25

bureaucracy, 54, 99, 115

Burgin, Victor, 152

Burke, Edmund, 92

Byles, Mather, 133

Byrd, William, II, 27

Calef, Robert, 21, 22, 67

Cambridge, Mass., 31